D1228773

Builder's Guide to Decks

Leon A. Frechette

McGraw-Hill

New York San Francisco Washington, D.C. Auckland Bogotá
Caracas Lisbon London Madrid Mexico City Milan
Montreal New Delhi San Juan Singapore
Sydney Tokyo Toronto

McGraw-Hill

A Division of The McGraw·Hill Companies

©1996 by **Leon A. Frechette**.
Published by The McGraw-Hill Companies, Inc.

hc   1 2 3 4 5 6 7 8 9 DOC/DOC 9 0 0 9 8 7 6 5

Library of Congress Cataloging-in-Publication Data
Frechette, Leon A., 1954–
    Builder's guide to decks / by Leon A. Frechette.
        p.   cm.
    Includes index.
    ISBN 0-07-015749-9 (hc)
    1. Decks (Architecture, Domestic)—Design and construction.
2. Construction industry—Management. I. Title.
TH4970.F73 1995
690'.184—dc20   95-32897
                                                           CIP

McGraw-Hill books are available at special quantity discounts to use as premiums and sales promotions, or for use in corporate training programs. For more information, please write to the Director of Special Sales, McGraw-Hill, 11 West 19th Street, New York, NY 10011. Or contact your local bookstore.

Acquisitions editor: April D. Nolan
Editorial team: Susan Borthron, Book Editor
                        Lori Flaherty, Managing Editor
                        Joanne Slike, Executive Editor
                        Jodi L. Tyler, Indexer
Production team: Katherine G. Brown, Director
                        Lisa M. Mellott, Coding
                        Susan E. Hansford, Coding
                        Rose McFarland, Desktop Operator
Design team: Jaclyn J. Boone, Designer   0157499
                        Katherine Lukaszewicz, Associate Designer   GEN1

To those professionals who want a better understanding of deck construction and who would like to conquer the market!

Contents

Acknowledgments

I would like to thank the many people who took time out of their busy schedules to help me turn this book into a reality. Their hard work and dedication helped to create a worthwhile tool to benefit construction professionals.

The efforts of the following people are surely appreciated. These individuals supplied information and photos, answered questions, reviewed chapters so they stayed on track, and proofed materials:

Rick Parish, DECKS APPEAL
Harvey Carmel, CaddCon Designs
Russell C. Glickman, Glickman Design/Build
George Sagatov, George B. Sagatov, Inc.
Barry Klemons, Archadeck of Charlotte
Richard Provost, Archadeck
Mark Abbott, Deckshield, Inc.
James T. Hollihan, Doctor Deck, Inc.
Dan Howard, Carrousel Wood Products, Ltd.
Cynthia Hignight, MacCourt Products, Inc.
Clayton DeKorne and Steven Bliss, *The Journal of Light Construction*
Huck DeVenzio, Hickson Corporation
Thomas D. Searles, American Lumber Standard Committee
Kevin N. Dickie, American Wood Preservers Institute
Jeff Easterling, Southern Forest Products Association
Pamela Allsebrook, California Redwood Association
Candace Hobbs, Weyerhaeuser
Jerry Parks, Western Wood Preservers Institute
R. Sam Williams, Forest Products Laboratory
Sharon McNaughton, Western Red Cedar Lumber Association

Special thanks to Shelley Hershbenger, Western Wood Products Association, for her hard work on the information contained in Chapters 2 and 5; to Don Allemand, Swanson Tool Co., Inc., for his valuable assistance on the stair construction section included in Chapter

6; to Tom Craig, Certified Plan Examiner, City of Spokane, Washington, for the hours he spent reading the text and reviewing diagrams to make sure they agreed with the codes required for a successful deck and/or outdoor structure; to Jim Brewer, Freud, Inc., for the hours he spent testing the blades recommended in Chapter 4; and to Karen Craig for her hard and dedicated work in organizing and editing our third book together. The computers we both purchased sure moved the project along!

Thanks also to April Nolan, McGraw-Hill, for publishing this book. I look forward to completing my next book. We have only begun to scratch the surface of getting useful and needed information to the readers.

I would like to thank my wife, Kimberly, for her support throughout all my projects, including this one. She was especially tolerant as the project expanded and consumed every room in the house. This year she finally got her dining room back—after she moved me to the basement.

If I missed anyone, it wasn't intentional. There just isn't enough paper—and you know who you are! Again, many thanks to all.

Introduction

The purpose of the *Builder's Guide to Decks* is to provide the construction professional with a clear understanding of a difficult market, promotional ideas and materials to help win sales, and an awareness of new products and construction techniques. To compete in this field successfully, professionals must use all the tools at their fingertips to overcome the barrier of customers frightened by high bids—or the prospect of high bids—who decide to build a deck themselves.

For contractors new to the business, the *Builder's Guide to Decks* serves as both a reference manual and a sales tool when meeting with potential customers. It provides a commonsense approach to tasks such as:

- Evaluating and bidding jobs
- Effectively communicating with customers
- Understanding environmental issues
- Working with new tools, products, and alternative materials
- Performing the work in the proper sequence

Safety and code compliance are stressed. As a construction professional, you are encouraged to establish good working relationships with the staff of your local building department.

The information contained in this book is intended as an aid or resource to you and is not the final word on any given topic. Neither the author, the publisher, nor any contributors assume any liability for your use of these materials. You are specifically cautioned that each state and municipality has its own laws and practices and that you should consult with each entity yourself. It is your responsibility to work within the local governed guidelines. The information contained here is general in nature only as it relates to legal concepts.

All too often, customers see bid prices and declare, "We'll build it ourselves!" It is time for construction professionals to face this situation and find more effective sales approaches. With the environment of great concern today, alternative products (such as those made out of recycled materials) and new methods of building and preserving decks might be just the tools necessary to sell a deck project.

Decks today are not the "platforms" of 10 years ago. Families are expanding their living space outdoors and are installing pools and hot tubs in their decks. Gazebos often create a corner entertainment or eating area. The decks of the nineties are simply not do-it-yourself projects!

1

Marketing

Many of us go into business because we enjoy what we do. That's clearly a bonus, but the real purpose of being in business is to make money—not the amount that only takes us from one job to the next but enough that we can add to our savings or retirement accounts at the end of each job. However, to achieve this goal, it is essential to generate the greatest possible profit margin on every job sold, and the only way to do that is to understand the market thoroughly and produce the best quality job in the least amount of time.

This level of professionalism can become a reality if you perfect what you do best and don't spread yourself too thin. Specializing in only one facet of the construction industry, such as building decks, allows you to channel your energies into a specific market, and since an estimated 1 million decks are built every year, this might be a field worth considering as a full-time career. This chapter helps you understand your customers' needs and gives you some tools to reach those customers so that you can close more sales and achieve higher profits.

Understanding customers' needs

The first step in becoming a successful specialized contractor is determining what your customers want, and this can be difficult. Customers themselves don't really know what they want much of the time. Once they do decide, they are certain to want it "yesterday."

I think most customers want the following:

- A professional job at a reasonable price
- Minimal interruption of family life (i.e., prompt completion of work)
- Clean premises—no dirt tracked into the home
- A warranty backed by the contractor's assurance that any problems will be handled promptly and correctly
- A contractor with a professional attitude and approach

1

Although this list is pretty general, understanding and adhering to these basics quickly spreads your name and reputation. There is nothing like a word-of-mouth referral.

Customers today are smart shoppers. They do their homework and, in many cases, are quite capable of performing the work themselves but have neither the time nor the tools. One of the first processes customers must go through before they even contact you involves realizing they won't be able to do their own project and have to call in a professional—you. You are the person who, for a short time, must invade their privacy, and for many customers, that is hard to face.

On your initial appointment, it is up to you to determine what the customer really wants. This is your best opportunity to sell yourself. Sometimes it is best just to listen. Give customers a chance to express what is really on their minds and hear them out. Then guide them toward their ideal project, but do not try to sell them something they don't need. Customers, like most of us, don't like a pushy salesperson.

Keep an open mind and watch for opportunities to suggest options to customers. When you have been in the construction field for many years, ideas and options are neither overwhelming nor confusing. Your potential customers, however, might have been thinking about their project for perhaps six months or more, saving money toward the day they decide to proceed. They have probably talked with friends and relatives about their plans and thumbed through books and magazines. At this point, they might be overloaded and confused, so it is up to you to put them at ease. Being understanding and sympathetic to customer needs can indeed help you close a sale.

Russell C. Glickman, President of Glickman Design/Build, lives by his own code of ethics. He has even had the "Glickman Code of Ethics" printed and included in presentation packages to potential customers. The code keeps him focused on why he is in business and assures customers that their needs are important. Glickman's code of ethics is included in Fig. 1-1 so that you can better understand this concept.

If you haven't already done so, I suggest you mull over your past successes and failures and write your own code, one you can work by and live up to. Think about your past experiences with customers and how they might help you secure potential customers in the future.

▪ GLICKMAN CODE OF ETHICS ▪

*We, **Glickman Design/Build**, believe that, to be truly successful in our field, we must strive to deliver the finest product we're capable of while holding the ethics, listed below, in the highest regard.*

▪

WE AT GLICKMAN DESIGN/BUILD...

Believe...

that each customer, potential customer, employee and subcontractor should be treated with the utmost respect and dignity...

Believe...

that each project deserves the finest thought and action the firm has to offer...

Believe...

that every Representative should strive to present nothing but an honest, truthful and forthright presentation with each customer...

Believe...

that every project should be estimated at a fair and equitable price, not tolerating overinflated prices during the busy season or unrealistically low prices in an attempt to mislead customers...

Believe...

that every employee should make a consistent effort to carry themselves in a professional and courteous manner when representing the company...

Believe...

that every customer's concern should be addressed, no matter how small...

Believe...

that every effort should be made to fix any problem involving a **Glickman** project...

Believe...

that honesty and integrity must be the guiding forces in our daily interactions with customers, potential customers, suppliers and employees.

▪

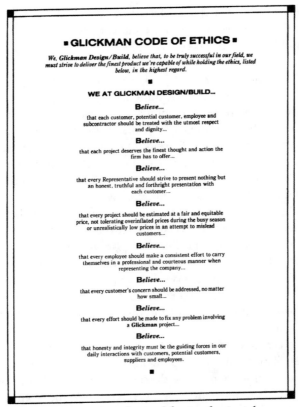

1-1 *An important sales tool for professionals.* Glickman Design/Build

Promotion

Decks can be extremely hard to sell. Some of the factors that contribute to this difficulty include the following:

- The overall price exceeds most customers' budgets.
- Once customers hear the quoted price, they decide to do it themselves to cut costs.
- Local hardware and lumber stores offer deck kits at attractive prices.
- Competing contractors bid jobs too low just so they can get the job. A realistic bid often doesn't stand a chance.

Because opposition is so formidable, it is extremely important to promote yourself. Only you can sell yourself, but you need a clear vision of both yourself and your goals. To better understand how to promote yourself, it helps to classify what you do or what your specialty is. For example, are you a contractor who:

- Builds decks occasionally
- Specializes in decks only
- Has a showroom and specializes in decks only
- Has bought into a deck franchise
- Specializes in deck maintenance—restoration and finishing

No matter how you classify yourself, the business principles you operate by are the same. Depending on the direction you choose, your overhead might be higher or you might have to hire salespeople, pay franchise fees, or purchase specialized tools and equipment, all of which I address later in the chapter.

The first step in promoting your business is your business card. The design and layout of a business card can reveal a lot about an individual or a company, and this is important because once your business card is handed out, you have no idea into whose hands it might fall. It's important to make your first impression count. Business cards should be clean, well-organized, easy to read, and quickly convey what your company does. Your company name should be clearly visible at a glance.

The business cards in Figs. 1-2 and 1-3 are appealing. The first card (Fig. 1-2) displays the type of work done by this specific company: They have a showroom, only do decks, and provide in-house design services. The second card (Fig. 1-3) indicates the company designs projects that conform to the lifestyles of their customers. Because they are a "design/build" company, they create their own house designs as well. Business cards such as these are easy for the customer to comprehend.

1-2 *Logo visually reinforces what this company does.* DECKS APPEAL

1-3 *Indicating how long a company has been in business assures potential clients of stability.* Glickman Design/Build

A portfolio or presentation package is also an important sales tool. Before you can assemble one, however, you should consider doing some or all of the following:

- Get involved with local chapters of national contractor/remodeler associations
- Support charitable organizations
- Enter contests through trade publications and associations
- Obtain testimony from satisfied customers
- Start a newsletter
- Display your business at local home and garden shows

Your professional accomplishments are of interest to your community as well as to the trade, so when you land a unique or unusual project, contact the editor of the home improvement section of your local newspaper as well as the editors of trade publications. You might have a story, and it never hurts to get your name in print. Article reprints are also a great addition to your portfolio. Take pride in your work and don't hesitate to promote yourself.

The portfolio should include the following:

- Brief history of your company
- Detailed map of your location
- Your company's code of ethics
- Articles about awards you have received
- Any magazine or newspaper articles featuring you, your company, or your projects
- Testimony from satisfied customers
- Before and after photos of unusual projects
- Company newsletter (if you have one)
- Business card

- Returnable postcard (Fig. 1-4, front and back)
- List of services offered or products sold (Fig. 1-5)
- Client home analysis questionnaire (Fig. 1-6)

Portfolios can be expensive, but the trade-off in increased sales makes them worthwhile. At your next home and garden show, you will be one step ahead of your competition with a professional package to hand to potential customers.

Specialization

Contractors who specialize in decks can be divided into various subgroups.

Showroom

If you already specialize in custom decks and the majority of your construction business is related to building decks, consider totally committing to this field. The best way to do this is to open a showroom that allows customers to view models of completed decks. Models simplify analyzing customer needs, and the visual, tactile arrangements help customers reach solid decisions. A showroom also provides an opportunity to display and sell accessory items that customers dream about once their decks are completed. Finally, a showroom gives you a meeting space so that once a month you can conduct a seminar for customers to help them learn how to maintain their decks—restoring and finishing.

As Rick Parish of DECKS APPEAL, who has run a showroom since 1989, says, "The biggest advantage is that a showroom transforms you from a small independent contractor to a legitimate credible business in the consumer's mind." He adds that anyone considering a showroom should plan on at least 2600 square feet, and 1800 square feet of that space should be devoted to deck displays. Keep regular business hours (e.g., 10:00 A.M. to 5:00 P.M., Monday through Saturday). Interestingly, Parish says he doesn't rely on the showroom for potential customers—that is the purpose of advertising. Rather, the showroom gives his company credibility and name exposure and, as he says, "a place to hang our hats" (Fig. 1-7).

During its peak season, DECKS APPEAL attracts three to eight potential customers on Saturdays. Of course, the traffic flow in your area could yield more or less, depending on location, length of season, and the volume and type of advertising you do.

Parish recommends two full-time salespeople on straight commission to keep the showroom afloat. However, during his peak sea-

1-4 *Sending postcards to certain zip code areas is an effective marketing tool.* Glickman Design/Build

son, which is February through September, two to six salespeople might be more appropriate. Assess your peak season realistically.

Because it is difficult during the off months for a sales force on straight commission, you should consider carefully the practicality of

1-5 *Brochures offering services or products whet customer appetites.* CaddCon Designs

GLICKMAN
CLIENT HOME ANALYSIS

NAME _____ OCCUPATION _____
NAME _____ OCCUPATION _____
ADDRESS _____
_____

DESIGNER _____ DATE _____

AGE OF HOUSE _____ YEARS IN HOUSE _____
NUMBER OF YEARS PLANNING TO LIVE IN HOUSE _____
NUMBER OF PEOPLE LIVING IN HOUSE: ADULTS _____ CHILDREN _____
REASON FOR GETTING STARTED ON REMODELING PLANS _____
_____
NEW AREAS SHALL BE USED FOR _____
WHEN DO YOU WISH TO GET STARTED? _____
WHAT IS YOUR BUDGET? _____
HOW DID YOU ESTABLISH YOUR BUDGET? _____
FORM OF FINANCING TO BE USED _____
UPCOMING MAJOR EVENTS _____
PRIMARY CONCERNS _____
WHAT DO YOU LOOK FOR IN SELECTING A CONTRACTOR? _____
HOW DID YOU DECIDE TO CALL GLICKMAN? _____

WHAT WE LIKE ABOUT THE HOUSE _____
_____
_____

WHAT WE DON'T LIKE ABOUT THE HOUSE _____
_____
_____

MAJOR OBJECTIVES IN REMODELING HOUSE AT THIS TIME:
(LIST BY NUMBER OF PRIORITY)

1. _____
2. _____
3. _____
4. _____
5. _____

1-6 *Good example of a client home analysis.* Glickman Design/Build

hiring people experienced in design and sales for eight months a year. Parish explains that 5 percent of their gross sales is devoted to showroom cost, and they try to maintain a 30 percent gross profit, which nets approximately 15 percent profit. A showroom can set you apart from the competition but does not guarantee success. Parish put it best when he said, "Our philosophy was and still is to design and

1-7 *This showroom has great eye appeal.* DECKS APPEAL

build the very best deck a customer could ever own and everything else would take care of itself. Our commitment to quality, service, and customer satisfaction will not be compromised. We instill this philosophy in our training and practice it daily."

Franchises

Franchise opportunities that specialize in complete deck operations give you the option to go into business for yourself even without experience in construction. Alternatively, you might want to change your occupation within the construction field and specialize in building decks. In either case, a franchise can teach you how to market and sell, how to get a project built using qualified contractors from your area, and how to manage the business.

If you choose to buy into a franchise, be sure that the corporate office provides assistance in the following areas:

Marketing You should receive guidance about advertising in the yellow pages and in the local newspaper, the creation of publicity releases, the assembly of your own portfolio or presentation package, as well as help in understanding the marketing benefits from any available national marketing programs. Find out if the franchiser's corporate office supplies all the tools necessary for a complete media campaign to generate sales leads.

Sales The franchiser should provide you with video and classroom training to sharpen your sales presentations so you can convert leads into successful sales.

Construction You need to understand standard deck building systems that have been developed within the structure of the franchise. Either you or your lead carpenter should receive field training in quick installation techniques that still maintain quality. You should have assistance when you need it in deck design for both aesthetics and engineering, and help in learning to work with local contractors as subcontractors, and with government agencies.

Administration You will need a supply of business forms for bidding, contracts, and statements, as well as software that allows you to generate the information for these forms through a computer. Make sure you have a clear understanding of how to manage cash flow, purchasing, materials, and, most important, setting a high gross profit.

Find out if you have control over plans you design for the customer or if the plans need approval from the franchiser before you apply for any building permits. You should also have a clear understanding of the type of warranty offered through the franchise, and who backs that warranty.

If you are not already aware of this, a franchise costs money. Royalties from 4 to 8 percent must be paid by the franchisee on gross sales receipts. Franchise fees run between $15,000 and $40,000, depending on the geographical area or territory you are purchasing. You are required to have working capital on hand in the neighborhood of $25,000 to $80,000, and this start-up cost might or might not include the franchise fee. Examine the financial arrangements very carefully. Also check that you do not have to pay royalties for anything else. Even if the corporation approves your application, I recommend you seek legal counsel before signing any contracts.

The franchise organization is in business to make sure its franchisees succeed in building their businesses. That is how they stay afloat. You become joined "at the hip" until you sell or close the business.

One deck construction franchise active today is Archadeck (U.S. Structures, Inc.). Their slogan is "To enhance the lives of our customers by creating unique and innovative outdoor living environments." The initial franchise fee for an Archadeck franchise is $32,500. However, there are also "mini" or "midi" franchises available. Their fees start at $16,500 and slide upward based on territory size. These types of franchises are only available in smaller "third-tier" markets that are not part of a larger metropolitan area and only in new markets where there are no other franchisees.

Archadeck provides an initial three-week training period for franchisees, which can be repeated at no charge if a franchisee so desires. Also offered at no charge are a two-week class for salespeople, in-field training seminars, and in-office training. They provide extensive technical support by phone and by FAX. To learn more about this opportunity, contact Archadeck at (800) 722-4668.

Barry Klemons of Archadeck of Charlotte, North Carolina, bought into the franchise seven years ago. He was their fifth franchisee and the first who was not in the construction field. Klemons' business occupies a 1750-square-foot office in a business complex with drive-by traffic. While he doesn't exactly have a showroom, he does have products on hand for customers to view and handle, and he features 8" × 10" and 11" × 14" photographs of previous deck projects on the walls. He says he closes two out of every ten leads.

It is his contention that customers want longevity from a professional. They want the assurance that the business/contractor will remain in business for some time and is well versed in both construction methods and products. Memberships in associations and organizations in the construction industry add to the customer's confidence. Klemons also adds that customers want value for the price. He says he enjoys putting together packages for his customers and that he made the right choice in buying into the Archadeck franchise.

Maintenance

If you have a lucrative construction company or deck-building operation already, you might consider a side operation that has a very large potential market and could be quite profitable: restoring and finishing decks. This sideline encompasses the maintenance of existing wooden decks, of which there are an estimated 25 million in the United States, according to the Hickson Corporation. With some training and practice with the equipment to acquire expertise, you could make between $60 and $100 an hour using a power washer, sprayer, and brush. Restoring two or more decks each day could be a significant addition to your income.

Consider joining a "Certified Contractor Program" presented by Wolman Wood Care Products. Professionals joining the Wolman program receive step-by-step instructions on how to restore decks professionally, a training video, and support material for getting started. The latter includes literature, advertising materials, and quarterly newsletters with stain-removal hints, business-building tips, and information on how to price jobs. To learn more, contact:

Wolman Wood Care Products
Wolman Certified Contractor Program
1824 Koppers Building
436 Seventh Avenue
Pittsburgh, PA 15219

There are all kinds of associations in the construction industry. It is important to potential customers that you belong to these organizations because such memberships help to establish your credentials as a construction professional. Of course, you should consider organizations that relate to your particular field. If you are considering the deck care business, then a great place to start is the National Deck Care Association (NDCA). The focus of the NDCA is to provide consistency and continuity to the industry through intensive and comprehensive instruction. You can reach them at 800-982-6322, or write:

National Deck Care Association
10101 Bacon Drive, Suite G
Beltsville, MD 20705

Franchising opportunities are also available in this field. Doctor Deck, Inc. is looking for success-oriented people. The franchisee in this specialty has a chance at realizing the American dream of owning a lucrative business. Initially, the lumber industry claimed that pressure-treated, or Wolmanized, lumber would last for 25 years. While that turned out to be true for protection against rot and termite infestation, the wood was not protected from water damage. Today, most treated lumber has a lifetime warranty with the recommendation that decks be protected with annual waterproofing treatments.

The deck care industry is one of the fastest growing service markets because one in four new homes is built with a deck and about 25 million decks already exist in the United States. Remodeling adds another one million decks each year. Two-income families who simply do not have the time to maintain their decks create great opportunities in the deck restoration market.

To better understand whether a franchise is right for you, Doctor Deck, Inc., has assembled and answered 19 frequently asked questions about franchise opportunities. To get your copy, write to:

Doctor Deck, Inc.
3410 Babcock Boulevard
Pittsburgh, PA 15237

Advertising

Advertising is costly and can easily devour profits, especially if potential leads do not turn into signed contracts. Therefore, it is important to make every ad count. It is always a good idea to start small and work your way up, depending on what you can afford and what your work force can handle. You might have to go through a trial-and-error process first. Take care not to oversell yourself. Of course, listing yourself in the yellow pages of the phone book does work, and it also establishes your name in the eyes of the community. In addition to the phone book, there are other forms of advertising that should be considered.

Billboards One form of advertising that works very well in my experience is the mini billboard. In a one-month period, I averaged about twenty calls a day. Unfortunately, I didn't have the sales force to keep all the appointments, so I found myself referring potential customers to other contractors in the area. In my situation, the billboard hurt me more than it helped, but I had to try it, and it was very effective in generating inquiries.

Because the person viewing your billboard is probably in a moving vehicle, it is important that your telephone number be the first thing seen. The second most visible item should be your business (e.g., building decks). The third most important item is the name of your company. Be sure to use a white background behind the telephone number to make it stand out for easy reading. I recommend using a billboard during the beginning of the season—and be sure you can handle all the calls.

Community papers You have probably noticed those small free papers full of want ads located near the exit of your local grocery store. Perhaps you even picked up a few yourself as you passed through the door. Consider advertising in one of those papers. The ads are quite inexpensive; even taking out a full-page ad is not prohibitively costly. I found that a full-page ad placed at the beginning of the season brought great results. In order to create name awareness, I ran a small ad for years before placing a full-page ad.

If you are placing a smaller ad, try one that reads across two or three columns and is at least two inches high. This makes it easier for the reader to spot. Adding color to the border (if color is an option) helps the reader identify your ad over the competition. A little trick that works when placing a border around an ad is to use a double border: a thick outer line and a thin inner line. The inside line should only be about 5 to 10 percent of the thickness of the outside border. Try rounding the corners instead of using square ones (Fig. 1-8). This layout makes your ad stand out so it almost seems to jump off the page. This is just what you want it to do—make direct eye contact with the reader.

1-8 *The jingle at the top of this ad helps readers start thinking about remodeling projects.* C.R.S., Inc.

Newspapers I have never advertised in a newspaper, but Rick Parish of DECKS APPEAL recommends placing an ad in the front page (main) section of your paper. Consider using the Saturday rather than the Sunday paper because the Sunday paper is usually so large that a small ad can become lost. It is also easier for the reader to scan a Saturday paper.

The main goal of your ad is that it be noticed by the reader. Therefore, it follows that you should place an ad as large as you can afford. The more white space in your ad, the more it stands out from all the others. Your ad can appear larger than it is if you do not use borders because the surrounding margins become part of the ad (Fig. 1-9).

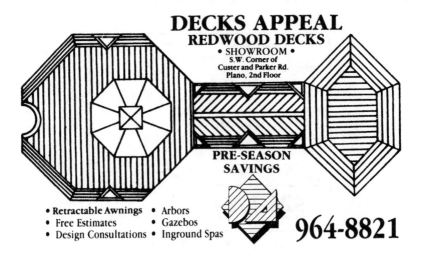

DECKS APPEAL
REDWOOD DECKS
• SHOWROOM •
S.W. Corner of
Custer and Parker Rd.
Plano, 2nd Floor

PRE-SEASON SAVINGS

• Retractable Awnings • Arbors
• Free Estimates • Gazebos
• Design Consultations • Inground Spas

964-8821

1-9 *An example of an ad without a border.* DECKS APPEAL

My recommendations about advertising in a community paper are not interchangeable with Parish's recommendations for a daily newspaper. The two types of papers are entirely different in format and content, and the recommendations included here are for those specific applications.

Associations Local chapters of national associations might be able to assist you in your advertising layout. One association that provides free ad slicks prepared for yellow pages, newspapers, and magazines is the California Redwood Association. Four different column sizes are available; all you need to do is add your company name, address, and telephone number. If you are considering a specialty in redwood decks, these ads are made for you. Figure 1-10 shows an ad that is 3 columns by 5", or 15 column-inches, which is just right for the yellow pages. The ad shown in Fig. 1-11 is 2 columns by 7", and is designed by the Archadeck franchise.

Redwood decks

- Licensed Professionals
- Deck Specialists
- Durable & Beautiful Redwood
- High Quality and Value
- Custom Designs • New Decks • Enlarge Your Old Deck
- Priced to Fit Your Budget, Your Home and Your Needs

(000) 000-0000
DEALER NAME & ADDRESS

1-10 *Combining simple illustrations with a list of your services says it all.* California Redwood Association

OUTER SPACE

1-11
This heading is a real attention-getter! Archadeck

It represents, at once, an increase in the value of your home as well as an expansion of your home's livability. It opens the door to a new lifestyle of entertainment and relaxation. Innovative and superior in craftsmanship. Affordable. Fully warranteed. Explore this unique space project. For a free design consultation, call America's leading deck builder today.

archadeck®
America's Deck Builder
000-0000

Office Name Here   ©1990 U.S. Structures, Inc.

Selling

From the moment you answer that first inquiry call, you are selling yourself. How you answer the phone and meet your appointment as well as your appearance and conduct with potential customers determines whether they hire you. Customers make up their minds about hiring a contractor within the first ten minutes of the appointment. A good first impression is essential.

Be courteous and well-informed at all times. When a customer asks you a question, be confident and answer it like a professional. Customers can detect a phony. If they ask a question and you don't know the answer, admit it, and then offer to do some research and get back to them with your findings. Of course, make sure you follow through on your promise. Be a well-rounded professional at all times: selling yourself sells the job.

I have enclosed my own list of "do's and don'ts" for meeting with potential customers. I recommend you study and practice them before going to any appointment.

Appointment Dos and Don'ts:
- Be on time. If you're going to be late, call the customer.
- Dress code:
  ~Shirt and tie are not necessary.
  ~Work clothes are OK provided they are not full of dust and don't smell. Work clothes show customers you are a hands-on individual.
  ~Work boots are OK, but make sure you do not track foreign material into the customer's home.
  ~Hair should be presentable.
- Never use profane language.
- Don't voluntarily bring up politics or religion.
- Never argue.
- Listen well: Use your ears, not your mouth.
- Handle disagreements diplomatically.
- Remember that customers are not impressed with a know-it-all.
- Don't criticize other professionals; this is not only unprofessional conduct, but customers are not interested.
- Admit it if there is something you don't know.
- Learn to say "no" for whatever the reason (ask yourself if you can realistically handle a project).
- Think twice before you attempt to force a sale.
- Most of all, treat a customer as you would like to be treated, and practice all of the above whether you are on an appointment or on the job.

You probably already know that a customer is not always right. In cases like this, it is better to listen with your ears, not with your mouth. If you have not yet read Dale Carnegie's book, *How to Win Friends and Influence People* (Pocket Books ISBN 0-671-41299-X), or Les Giblin's book, *How You Can Have Confidence & Power in Dealing With People* (Wilshire Book Company ISBN 0-87980-072-0), I recommend you do so. These two powerful books can help you understand and deal with people, and they are especially helpful in promoting effective communications.

The next time the phone rings, think like a professional. Have confidence and be well-informed. Be on your best behavior at all times. You'll be surprised how simple courtesy can influence the people around you—employees, subcontractors, customers, and yourself. Contractors don't just swing hammers any more; they're people-oriented professionals.

Sales tools

As mentioned earlier in this chapter, a portfolio or presentation package is one of the most effective sales tools you can assemble. This package can help you stand way above the competition in the customer's eyes.

Selling yourself might not be enough, especially since money (often a lot of money) is involved. There are other tools that are helpful in closing a sales lead. The ones I recommend here are offered by the California Redwood Association and are directed toward redwood decks, but they give you an idea of tools that you could design to fit your particular needs. Other associations might have similar sales tools that are directed toward the type of product you are selling.

If you are interested in getting your company name out in a selected zip code area, a door hanger might be the answer. A door hanger such as the one shown in Fig. 1-12 provides space for a business card under the line "Call for your estimate today." Hangers are available for $30 per 100.

"Redwood Landscape Architecture," a 12-page color brochure, is filled with information that might help to persuade an undecided customer. This brochure details the performance characteristics of construction woods and lumber grades and finishes, and it features many photos of decks, shelters, planters, seating, and fences. Brochures are available for $60 per 100 and contain space on the back for a company sticker or business card.

Finally, "Redwood Beauty That Lasts" is an 8-minute video that features ideas on decks, fences, and landscaping. The video is avail-

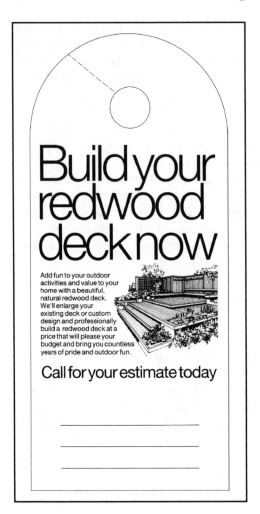

1-12
Target your market with a door hanger. California Redwood Association

able for $30 and can be viewed with potential customers in their own home. For more information on these three selling tools, contact

California Redwood Association
405 Enfrente Drive, Suite 200
Novato, CA 94949

If your customers have a hard time visualizing a finished deck project, consider acquiring the software package "3-D Deck" by Books That Work. It not only dazzles the customer but also helps close the sale. Originally designed for homeowners, it can be a great asset to professionals as a selling tool. You can quickly design a deck through 3-D computer-aided design (CAD) on a laptop computer (Fig. 1-13). Customers can watch their deck ideas grow in front of

1-13 *Programs that let the customer's ideas come to life in 3-D make good selling tools.* Books That Work

them, and they can see all the variations, including the framework, the direction of the decking boards, the type of railings, and so forth.

The animation of this program is exciting to watch and impresses customers. With its gallery of full-color photographs of actual decks, this software can help put your ideas and the ideas of your potential customers into perspective. When I evaluated this software, I discovered it was not possible to create a multilevel deck with it. This is not a problem because you can still convey the concept of a multilevel deck to the customer. Hopefully, when the software is upgraded, this capability will be added.

Closing sales

There is no "magic formula" for closing a sale. There are just too many variables from the time you first see a customer until you present the bid, and there is no guarantee, regardless of the time you have invested, that even a regular customer will choose you. Following the steps outlined in this first chapter can improve your odds. Specializing in your field and perfecting your skills helps too. Consider reading Zig Ziglar's book, *Secrets of Closing the Sale* (Fleming H. Revell Company ISBN 0-8007-1213-7) for good advice on this topic.

DECKS APPEAL, with a showroom and a sales force of two, closes four out of every ten leads. Owner Rick Parish says, "If you're not selling 35 to 40 percent of your leads, you're cheating yourself." It would be nice to close every lead you bid, but in reality you wouldn't have enough manpower to handle all those jobs comfortably, especially if you want to maintain high quality.

Decks can be a hard sell. Educate yourself, learn new techniques, experiment with alternative products, and be creative with your advertising and sales approaches. The *Builder's Guide to Decks* helps you learn and use the necessary tools to close more sales enjoyably. It is up to you to make those tools work for you.

2

Materials

Whether you are just entering the deck building business or you are an experienced deck builder, you need to be aware of both existing products and new products as they enter the market. It also helps to have a good understanding of the three most commonly used deck-building materials: redwood, cedar, and pressure-treated wood (Southern pine). Professionals continually need to adjust their approach to match both the changing lifestyles of customers and the challenge of protecting the environment. New information about products and their environmental impact should be brought to the attention of potential customers; it could make the difference between selling a deck package or not.

So rapidly is the deck market changing that by the time you read this book additional products will have emerged. Seek out those products—it's important to stay on top of the latest developments and be a step ahead of your competition.

Commonly used materials

Because of your geographical area or the costs of materials that dictate product choices, you might not have had the opportunity to work with all three of the commonly used materials—redwood, cedar, and pressure-treated wood. It is nevertheless in your best interests to fully know and understand these products. You never know what a customer will ask for and it never hurts to be prepared.

Redwood

Of the three commonly used materials, redwood is the ultimate wood of choice for decking boards, railing systems, outdoor furniture, and other exterior uses. A redwood deck can last well over 20 years if the proper grade of redwood is selected and the deck is constructed properly; that is, if effective frame construction and correct board spacing are used, and the deck receives periodic preventive mainte- nance with commercial products. In the worst case, i.e., no preven- tive maintenance, poor construction, and severe climate, redwood's life expectancy is still 15 to 20 years. This doesn't mean that the deck- ing boards will all deteriorate, but a few may have to be replaced af- ter this time. With no maintenance, the surface will fade and turn gray.

Architectural grades

Long life is a certainty only if the deck is constructed of "heartwood" because this grade of lumber has the highest level of resistance to in- sects and decay. It is cut from the inner part of the tree, the oldest part, and is cinnamon colored. Sapwood, lighter in color and cut from the outer portion of the tree, offers very little natural resistance. Use heartwood for decking surfaces and where decay hazards exist; for example, in close proximity to the ground. Sapwood grades are ap- propriate for above-ground applications in low decay-hazard envi- ronments.

It is important to choose the correct grade of redwood (see Fig. 2-1) for your customers' projects. The grade of wood used makes a great deal of difference in determining the type of warranty package you offer your customers.

When possible, select architectural grades of redwood if they are available in your area. They cost more, but they are worth the extra expense when you and your customer see the finished prod- uct. These grades are highly recommended for visible areas such as handrails, benches, and the decking surface. Architectural grades consist of:

Clear All Heart	All heartwood, free of knots
Clear	Similar in quality to Clear All Heart but containing sapwood
B Heart	Contains limited knots and characteristics not permitted in Clear grades
B Grade	Similar in characteristics as B Heart but containing sapwood

Garden grades

The economical grades of redwood are the garden grades, tailored for pricing and exterior applications. However, these grades contain knots and other natural characteristics. The most commonly used of the garden grades are Construction Heart/Deck Heart and Construc- tion Common/Deck Common. In many cases, Construction grades are used for decking while Architectural Clear is used for handrails.

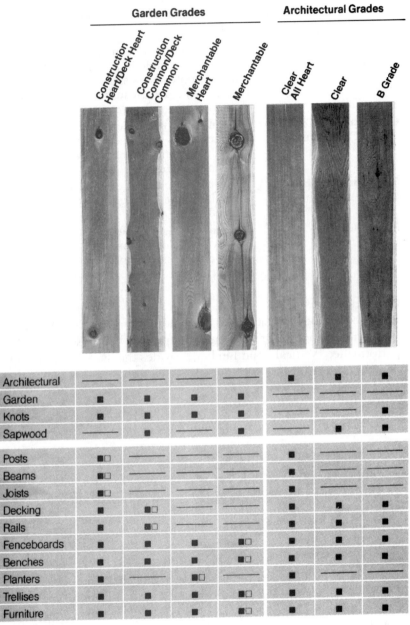

	Garden Grades				Architectural Grades		
	Construction Heart/Deck Heart	Construction Common/Deck Common	Merchantable Heart	Merchantable	Clear All Heart	Clear	B Grade
Architectural	—	—	—	—	■	■	■
Garden	■	■	■	■	—	—	—
Knots	■	■	■	■	—	—	■
Sapwood	—	■	—	■	—	■	■
Posts	■□	—	—	—	■	—	—
Beams	■□	—	—	—	■	—	—
Joists	■□	—	—	—	■	—	—
Decking	■	■□	—	—	■	■	■
Rails	■	■□	—	—	■	■	■
Fenceboards	■	■	■	■□	■	■	■
Benches	■	■	■	■□	■	■	■
Planters	■	—	■□	—	■	—	—
Trellises	■	■	■	■□	■	■	■
Furniture	■	■	■	■□	■	■	■

■ Suitable grade for use.
□ Most economical grade for use.

2-1 *Knowing lumber grades helps when purchasing redwood products, and you appear well informed for potential customers.* California Redwood Association

Of course, a lot depends on what is available in your geographical area. Garden grades consist of:

Construction Heart/ Deck Heart
All heartwood containing knots. Deck Heart is available in 2" × 4" and 2" × 6" widths only and is similar in appearance to Construction Heart but is graded for strength.

Construction Common/ Deck Common
Similar to Construction Heart/Deck Heart but contains sapwood. Deck Common is graded for strength and is available in 2" × 4" and 2" × 6" only.

Merchantable Heart
Most economical of the All-Heartwood grades. Contains large knots and some knotholes.

Merchantable
Similar to Merchantable Heart but contains sapwood. Not recommended for decking but can be cut up and used for planters, benches, etc.

Characteristics

Redwood lumber has either flat or vertical grain (Fig. 2-2). When it is used for decking, flat grain should be applied "bark side up" for best performance. Vertical grain lumber provides the smoothest finish for benches and railings.

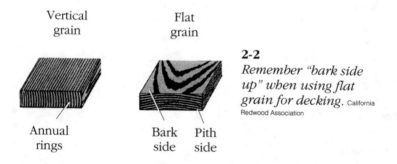

Vertical grain   Flat grain

Annual rings   Bark side   Pith side

2-2
Remember "bark side up" when using flat grain for decking. California Redwood Association

Redwood can be ordered in standard dimension lumber sizes, and orders for Clear All Heart and Clear may specify a grain. You also may choose between kiln-dried (KD), air-dried (AD), and unseasoned stock, but dry material is easier to work with, especially when establishing tight joints. Consult the dealer in your area for more information.

According to reports from the Forest Products Laboratory of the U.S. Department of Agriculture, redwood has less volumetric and tangential shrinkage than other common domestic softwoods. This means redwood stays flat and straight with minimal warping, cupping, or checking in exterior uses.

Redwood's natural resistance to insect infestation, fungal growth, and water damage is present throughout the heartwood lumber, not just on the surface. Redwood's open-celled structure, which contains little or no pitch or resins, allows redwood to absorb and retain all types of finishes. This doesn't mean that redwood is impervious to stains, however. Ordinary or inexpensive fasteners in conjunction with moisture can react with redwood's natural extractives (a complex assortment of chemicals such as tannic acid) and cause staining. Prevent stains by using aluminum alloy, stainless steel, or double hot-dipped zinc-coated fasteners.

For further information on redwood, contact the California Redwood Association at the address shown in Appendix C.

Cedar

Western red cedar is a native of the Pacific Northwest and British Columbia; however, its growth range extends into the inland forests of both the United States and Canada. Its quality values are quite similar to that of redwood but it has its own characteristics: beauty brought out by its unusual and unique grain patterns around knots and its distinctive color palette ranging from reddish-brown to light yellow to the almost pure white of sapwood. With this combination of features, you can create a knotty-looking deck with a rustic appeal.

Cedar's density enhances its insulation value and makes it a lightweight product to transport and handle, and it has a strong and pleasant aroma. Also available are Incense cedar, Alaska cedar, and Port-Orford cedar (limited). Alaska cedar is a beautiful yellow wood and is often used for park benches and bleachers in open stadiums. Western red cedar harvested from the Inland Region, east of the crest of the Cascade mountain range, is often marketed as Inland red cedar.

Cedar grades

Western red cedar immediately presents a choice: clear or knotty? Both perform well and look good. Cedar is available in structural and appearance grade products. Structural grades, with assigned design values, include Select Structural Numbers 1, 2, and 3, and Construction, Standard, Utility, Standard and Stud. Appearance grades include the Selects, Commons, and special Western Red Cedar, Select Knotty, and Quality Knotty Grades. Clear Heart and Clear Vertical Grain Heart can be specified for the highest grades. Select grades include B and Better, C, and D Select. These are the highest quality appearance grades and can be used to create a formal look. Select Knotty and Quality Knotty cedar grades are less expensive and ideally suited to a more casual or rustic design.

Examples of appearance grades in Western red cedar are shown in Fig. 2-3. Notice the grading rules as they have been applied to 1" × 4", 1" × 6", and 1" × 8". These grades may be used for a variety of applications and are often run-to-pattern for siding and paneling products.

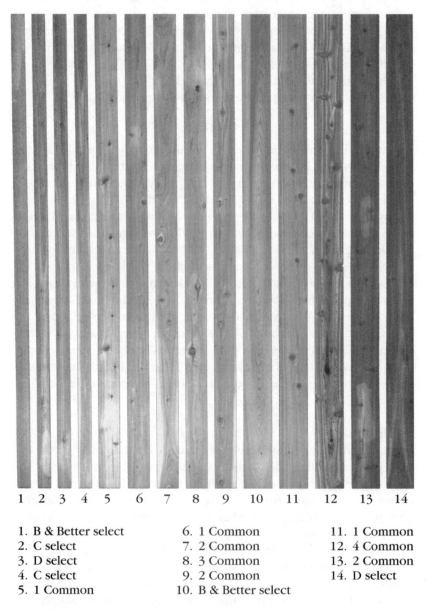

1 2 3 4 5 6 7 8 9 10 11 12 13 14

1. B & Better select
2. C select
3. D select
4. C select
5. 1 Common

6. 1 Common
7. 2 Common
8. 3 Common
9. 2 Common
10. B & Better select

11. 1 Common
12. 4 Common
13. 2 Common
14. D select

2-3 *Western red cedar is the largest of all cedars, slow growing and long-lived.* Western Wood Species Book, Vol. 2., Western Wood Products Association

The Western Red Cedar Lumber Association (WRCLA) has developed deck grading categories so you can specify a particular category for your project. These proprietary grading categories, also referred to as marketing names, are described as follows:

WRCLA Architect Clear   Vertical grain all-heartwood, free of knots (Fig. 2-4)

WRCLA Custom Clear   A mixture of vertical and flat grain Heartwood that could contain sapwood. Minimum defects (Fig. 2-5)

WRCLA Architect Knotty   A mixture of vertical and flat grain heartwood and sapwood with selected sound and tight inner-grown knots (Fig. 2-6)

WRCLA Custom Knotty   A mixture of vertical and flat grain heartwood and sapwood with a combination of knot sizes but free of knotholes (Fig. 2-7)

2-4 *WRCLA Architect Clear.* Western Red Cedar Lumber Association

2-5 *WRCLA Custom Clear.* Western Red Cedar Lumber Association

2-6 *WRCLA Architect Knotty.* Western Red Cedar Lumber Association

2-7 *WRCLA Custom Knotty.* Western Red Cedar Lumber Association

Performance
Compared to redwood, cedar's total performance is quite close; however, advantages are sometimes noted in the following areas:
- Freedom from warping, twisting, and checking
- Decay resistance (heartwood)
- Paint holding
- Freedom from pitch (resin)
- Workability

If you intend to use cedar for structural purposes, make certain you use the correct grade and size for its function. This is important for all species because strength and performance capabilities vary by species.

I have found that screws (rather than nails) achieve the best results for deck construction with cedar. To prevent surface staining, use aluminum alloy stainless steel or double, hot-dipped zinc-coated fasteners. Inexpensive electroplated or copper fasteners can rust and disintegrate and react adversely with the natural preservatives present in cedar, resulting in stains and streaks.

A mixture of redwood and cedar makes an interesting deck. For example, you could use cedar for skirting and balusters (spindles), and redwood for decking and handrails. Use your imagination to design interesting structures with these two woods in combination.

Pressure-treated wood

Nothing is more annoying than to revisit your deck masterpiece a few years later only to see it under attack from insect and fungal growth. Fungi need four conditions to live, breathe, and cause total destruction:

- Temperature (45°F to 100°F)
- Moisture content (in excess of 19 percent)
- Oxygen
- Food (wood fiber; e.g., deck material)

Wood products containing chemical preservatives have been used for more than 60 years to resist insect attack or fungal growth and to assure the durability and longevity of lumber projects. These waterborne preservative chemicals are forced into the wood's cells under pressure within a closed cylinder. A chemical reaction combines the preservative and wood fibers to form an insoluble compound. Chemical fixation occurs during the drying process, permanently adhering the preservative within the wood's fibers. Other pressure treatments include creosote or pentachlorophenol, but these products are used primarily in railroad ties, utility poles, and nonresidential projects.

This overall process creates a product commonly referred to as *treated lumber.* (All references to *treated lumber* in this book refer to lumber treated with waterborne preservatives, not creosote or pentachlorophenol.) Before choosing any treated lumber, be sure you know its intended use because treated lumber can be purchased with different levels of preservative retention.

Retention level refers to the amount of preservative remaining in the cell structure after pressurizing is completed. Retention levels are expressed in pounds of preservative per cubic foot (pcf) of wood: the higher the number, the harsher the condition to which the wood can be exposed. Table 2-1 details standard retentions.

Not all lumber can be pressure treated. Those species that cannot accept the chemical preservatives as easily as other species are *incised.* During this process, little slits are cut into and along the grain of the wood. These slits allow the chemicals to penetrate the wood to maintain a uniform retention level. The depth of penetration is significant because the chemical barrier must be thick enough so that any checking or splitting does not expose untreated wood to decay or insect infestation.

The appearance of the incised wood presently available might not be acceptable to many consumers. The depth of the cuts and the gaps between them are the focus of ongoing developmental work while the industry seeks an optimum combination of treatment effectiveness, appearance, and production efficiency. Most producers guarantee the life of their treated lumber, even without incisions, in above-ground applications.

Table 2-1. Standard Retentions

Application	Retention (lbs/cu. ft.)	Typical Uses
Above-ground uses	0.25	Decking, fencing, sills, railings, joists
Soil or freshwater contact	0.40	Timbers, grape stakes, retaining walls
Soil or freshwater contact (structural)	0.60	Wood foundations, building poles
Piles—soil or freshwater contact (structural)	0.80	Foundation piles
Saltwater contact	2.5	Timbers, pilings, bulkheads, groins

Adapted from: American Wood-Preservers' Association.

Treatable wood species break down into three categories: Southern pine, Imported or Eastern species, and Western species. Each category is further expanded in Table 2-2.

Preservatives

There are a number of wood preservatives on the market, but only one is in extensive use in residential and commercial construction. It is known in the trade as CCA (chromated copper arsenate). Others are ACZA (ammoniacal copper zinc arsenate) and ACQ (ammoniacal copper quaternary). These preservatives are "waterborne," i.e., they use water as a solvent or carrier. Most products leave the treated surface relatively clean, paintable, and odor-free.

Copper is an ingredient in these preservatives, so as the lumber dries and reacts to the sun's UV (ultraviolet) rays, it oxidizes and turns green. This chemical reaction is part of the fixation process binding the preservatives to the wood. Green lumber is a familiar sight on the East Coast, but many West Coast consumers find it objectionable. To improve marketability, a color additive stain or dye can be added (before and/or after the pressure-treating process) that turns the green to brown for cosmetic appeal. Depending on the process, the brown could fade over a period of time. If your customer objects to the color, I recommend using treated lumber for the deck structure and cedar, redwood, or a material specified in your area to complete the top portion (decking and railing systems).

Many licensed lumber treaters feature their own brand-name preservatives, and you might be familiar with some already. The most common ones are described here.

Table 2-2. Treatable Wood Species

Southern Pine	Imported or Eastern Species	Western Species
Loblolly pine	Caribbean pine (aka Ocote or Honduras pine)[2]	Douglas fir[1]
Longleaf pine	Eastern white pine (aka Northern white pine)	Engelmann spruce
Shortleaf pine	Jack pine[1]	Hem-fir[1]
Slash pine	Radiata pine[2,3]	Idaho white pine
	Red pine	Incense cedar
	Scotch pine (aka European redwood)	Lodgepole pine
		Ponderosa pine
		Redwood
		Sitka spruce
		Sugar pine
		Western larch[1]
		Western red cedar

[1]To secure penetration of preservatives in these species, incise (or puncturing) the lateral surfaces of the wood. This requirement might only apply to structural pieces rather than cosmetic pieces such as would be used for decking surfaces or handrails.

[2]Imported.

[3]Monterey pine grown primarily in the Southern Hemisphere. Most Radiata available in the United States is from New Zealand, Chili, or Brazil. Radiata pine is graded under Western rules.

Adapted from: Hickson Corporation, American Wood-Preservers' Association and Western Wood Products Association.

Osmose Sunwood (Osmose) This is a CCA product with color additives forced into the wood during the pressure treatment to achieve an appearance similar to redwood or cedar. (It is not stained or color-coated.) The color fades to simulate the weathering characteristics of natural wood species. The Osmose brand product is green. Their Weathershield brand product is a water-repellent pressure-treated lumber. Weathershield provides unique protection in two ways: It minimizes the initial shock of outdoor exposure by slowing the rate of drying, and it provides wood with long-term resistance against water absorption, minimizing recurring swelling and shrinking cycles. All products carry a lifetime limited warranty when used in specified applications outlined in the terms of the warranty.

Wolmanized (Hickson Corporation) This is also a green CCA product and is available nationwide in a variety of retentions and lumber grades. Outdoor Wood, a form of Wolmanized wood, is produced only with #1 grade lumber for applications where appearance is important. It is pressure treated to a retention level of 0.40 pcf, which makes it appropriate for ground contact as well as above-ground use. Eastern species of wood are treated with a water repellent and dried after treatment, while Western species are factory stained a rich brown color. Wolmanized Extra has a "built-in" water repellency that enables it to resist warping and cracking caused by moisture damage to the wood. The wood is pressure treated with a specially formulated emulsion along with a preservative. All products carry a lifetime limited warranty when used in specified applications outlined in the terms of the warranty.

UltraWood (Chemical Specialties, Inc. (CSI)) This is a green CCA product with water-repellent solutions to fight checking, splitting, and warping. It is backed by a 50-year limited warranty.

SupaTimber (CSI) This is also a green CCA product. It carries a lifetime limited warranty.

DesignWood SupaTimber (CSI) This product, available on the West Coast, is brown.

ACQ Preserve (CSI) This is a new product (introduced within the last four years) that is an environmentally advanced pressure-treated wood for use in above- or below-ground construction. It contains no arsenic, chromium, or any EPA-listed hazardous compounds. Even though the product is green, it weathers to a natural brown tone. It carries a lifetime limited warranty.

To learn more about these products, contact the appropriate companies at the addresses listed in Appendix C.

Treated lumber quality marks

When you purchase lumber, it is important to know what you are getting. Insist that pressure-treated wood bear the quality mark of an approved independent testing agency. The stamp or end tag must indicate compliance with standards of the American Wood-Preservers' Association (AWPA) and bear the identification of the approving agency. On January 14, 1993, the American Lumber Standard Committee (ALSC) began the quality control functions formerly provided by the American Wood Preservers Bureau (AWPB). Figure 2-8 is included to help you interpret the quality mark on pressure-treated wood products.

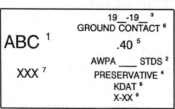

Interpreting a Quality Mark

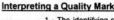

19 -19 ³
GROUND CONTACT ⁶

ABC ¹

.40 ⁵

AWPA ___ STDS ²

XXX ⁷   PRESERVATIVE ⁴

KDAT ⁸

X-XX ⁹

1 - The identifying symbol, logo or name of the accredited agency.
2 - The applicable American Wood Preservers' Association (AWPA) commodity standard.
3 - The year of treatment if required by AWPA standard.
4 - The preservative used, which may be abbreviated.
5 - The preservative retention.
6 - The exposure category (e.g. Above Ground, Ground Contact, etc.).
7 - The plant name and location; or plant name and number; or plant number.
8 - If applicable, moisture content after treatment.
9 - If applicable, length, and/or class.

As specified below for particular agencies, some or all of the following American Wood Preservers' Association commodity standards are used by American Lumber Standard Committee accredited agencies which supervise facilities which pressure treat wood products:

C1   All Timber Products--Preservative Treatment by Pressure Processes
C2   Lumber, Timbers, Bridge Ties and Mine Ties--Preservative Treatment by Pressure Processes
C3   Piles--Preservative Treatment by Pressure Processes
C4   Poles--Preservative Treatment by Pressuer Processes
C5   Fence Posts--Preservative Treatment by Pressure Processes
C6   Crossties and Switch Ties-Preservative Treatment by Pressure Process
C9   Plywood--Preservative Treatment by Pressure Processes
C15   Wood for Commercial-Residential Construction--Preservative Treatment by Pressure Processes
C17   Playground Equipment Treated with Inorganic Preservatives--Preservative Treatment by Pressure Processes
C18   Standard for Pressure Treated Material in Marine Construction
C22   Lumber and Plywood for Permanent Wood Foundations--Preservative Treatment by Pressure Processes
C23   Round Poles and Posts used in Building Construction--Preservative Treatment by Pressure Processes
C24   Sawn Timber Piles Used for Residential and Commercial Building
C25   Sawn Crossarms-Preservative Treatment by Pressure Process
C28   Standard for Preservative Treatment of Structural Glued Laminated Members and Laminations Before Gluing of Southern Pine, Pacific Coast Douglas Fir, Hemfir and Western Hemlock by Pressure Processes
C31   Lumber Used Out of Contact With the Ground and Continuously Protected from Liquid Water--Treatment by Pressure Processes

As specified below for particular agencies, some or all of the following preservatives are available for use:

chromated copper arsenate - CCA   ammoniacal copper zinc arsenate - ACZA   acid copper chromate - ACC
ammoniacal copper arsenate - ACA   copper naphthenate   pentachlorophenol
creosote solutions   creosote   borate

2-8 *Treated lumber quality marks, which the ALSC oversees.* American Lumber Standard Committee

Safety precautions

Wood treated with an Environmental Protection Agency (EPA) registered pesticide containing inorganic arsenicals for protection against insect attack should be used only where such protection is important; exposure to these chemicals may present certain hazards. These pesticides penetrate deeply and remain in pressure-treated wood for a long time. Therefore, the following precautions, provided courtesy of the American Wood Preservers Institute (revised November 1985), should be observed when handling or disposing of treated wood.

• Wood that has been pressure treated with waterborne arsenical preservatives may be used inside residences as long

as all sawdust and construction debris are cleaned up and disposed of after construction.
- Do not use treated wood under circumstances where the preservative might become a component of food or animal feed. Examples of such sites would be structures or containers for storing silage or food.
- Do not use treated wood for cutting boards or countertops.
- Only treated wood that is visibly clean and free of surface residue should be used for patios, decks and walkways.
- Do not use treated wood for construction of those portions of beehives which might come into contact with the honey.
- Treated wood should not be used where it might come into direct or indirect contact with public drinking water, except for uses involving incidental contact such as docks and bridges.
- Dispose of treated wood by ordinary trash collection or burial.
- Treated wood should not be burned in open fires or in stoves, fireplaces, or residential boilers because toxic chemicals might be produced as part of the smoke and ashes. Treated wood from commercial or industrial use (e.g., construction sites) may be burned only in commercial or industrial incinerators or boilers in accordance with state and Federal regulations.
- Avoid frequent or prolonged inhalation of sawdust from treated wood. When sawing and machining treated wood, wear a dust mask. Whenever possible, these operations should be performed outdoors to avoid indoor accumulations of airborne sawdust from treated wood.
- When power-sawing and machining, wear goggles to protect eyes from flying particles.
- After working with the wood, and before eating, drinking, and use of tobacco products, wash exposed areas thoroughly.
- If preservatives or sawdust accumulate on clothes, launder before reuse. Wash work clothes separately from other household clothing.

Environmental concerns

In today's market, consumers are more aware of products and their impact on the environment. Products using chemicals such as CCA (chromated copper arsenate) are of concern to them. Are there alternative products? Do decking products made from recyclable materials really help our environment? What happens when the demand for the product outweighs the supply of recyclable components? These are all questions of interest to consumers and professionals.

Lumber that has been pressure-treated with CCA is very stable. Even though this chemical is forced into the wood in a water solution, it does not leach out when the wood gets wet. According to the experts, the chromium salts combine with the wood sugar to form an insoluble compound that renders the CCA preservative nonleachable. Several decades of field testing yielded insignificant amounts of leaching of the arsenic, copper, and chromium components.

Alternative products are being developed every day. One preservative that has been on the market a few years is an ACQ product marked under the brand name ACQ Preserve by Chemical Specialties, Inc. They claim this preservative contains no arsenic, chromium, or any other EPA-listed hazardous compounds. Extensive independent testing has shown that ACQ Preserve offers the same durability, strength, and protection as other pressure-treated products.

Pressure-treated wood is also safe for gardens. The forest industry and the U.S. Forest Service have conducted research for over 40 years to determine whether or not preservatives from treated wood migrate into the soil. Stake tests have shown no evidence that sufficient depletion occurs to pose significant risks to human health or the environment. Treated wood is therefore an excellent choice for use in gardening and provides many years of service.

Incidental contact of treated wood with drinking water, like that of piling, docks, piers, or bridges is acceptable. While treated wood should never be built into a kitchen or used as a cutting board, it is suitable for a picnic table because a picnic table is primarily used for serving prepared food while a countertop is used as a cutting surface for raw food. CCA-treated wood can be used for animal drinking water troughs but it should not be used where it is likely to become a component of food or animal feed; that is, where the wood is likely to mix with foodstuffs.

Is there reason to be concerned about the environment when using treated wood? After a lengthy special review, the EPA determined that the benefits of the three major preservatives used for the treatment of wood outweighed potential risks. The wood preserving industry and private research laboratories continue to check and test pressure-treated wood to ensure safe use.

Some of the information contained in this section on pressure-treated wood products was obtained from the American Wood Preservers Institute. To be more informed on the use of treated wood products, not only for yourself but also for your customers, request a copy of AWPI's book, *Answers to Often-Asked Questions About Treated Wood*, for $35. Write to:

American Wood Preservers Institute
1945 Old Gallows Road, Suite 150
Vienna, VA 22182

Contact the following organizations for their publications; their addresses are listed in Appendix C.

- *Technical Guidelines for Construction with Treated Round Timber Piling*, available from the National Timber Piling Council, Inc.
- *Pressure Treated Southern Pine* (for $1.30) and *Marine Construction Manual for Southern Pine* (for $1) are available from the Southern Forest Products Association
- *Guide to the Characteristics, Use and Specifications of Pressure Treated Wood*, single copy complimentary of the Western Wood Preservers Institute

Grading

From time to time, pieces of lumber pass through your hands that look as if they were graded incorrectly. It is important to understand whether the lumber was graded for structural performance or visual appearance. Lumber grades are established by the American Lumber Standard Committee (ALSC). Write to ALSC for a list of accredited rules-writing agencies. Accredited agencies such as the Western Wood Products Association, Redwood Inspection Service, etc., are approved to write, publish, and maintain grading rules and provide inspection services covering a variety of lumber species.

Characteristics and lumber grading

Lumber is visually inspected and graded, and machine stress rated (MSR) lumber is also mechanically tested, before the grade is assigned. Structural lumber, whether it is visually inspected or mechanically tested, is graded for its strength and structural performance; its appearance is not a controlling factor. Appearance lumber is graded for how it looks (from the very beautiful to the utilitarian) and its structural capabilities are not a controlling factor in the grade. Structural lumber is always grade stamped, whereas appearance lumber might not have a stamp as it would mar the beauty of the piece. Natural characteristics affect both performance and beauty. These, along with manufacturing imperfections, are considered in both structural and appearance grade categories.

Knots are the most common of the natural characteristics. They are classified by quality, occurrence, form, and size. Generally knot quality rather than the other three characteristics affects the grade. Quality is based on soundness, firmness, and tightness. In occurrence, knots may be well spaced, well scattered, or clustered. In form, knots are defined as round (cut at right angles to the limb), oval (cut at slightly more a right angle to the limb), or spike (cut lengthwise or diagonally).

Defects, imperfections, blemishes, or defacing of lumber caused by the manufacturing process include torn grain, skips, burns, holes, or other manufacturing irregularities.

The grade is calculated according to a complex set of rules that considers the type, size, closeness, frequency, and location of all characteristics and imperfections within a piece. It is the lumber grader's responsibility to judge visually the total effect of the various combinations according to limitations set forth in the grading rules for each grade and species. The grade stamp assures the buyer that the piece meets the criteria set forth for that grade.

The characteristics and imperfections involved in grading, whether natural or artificial, are shown in Figs. 2-9 through 2-12.

Spike knot	Compression wood	Intergrown knot
Sloughed knot	Checked knot	Unsound knot
Tight black knot	Not firmly fixed knot	Knot hole

2-9 *Characteristics of knots.* Western Wood Products Association

Knots are the most frequently encountered characteristic. Illustrated here are the more common types as they appear on the lumber face in cross-section:

Round knot hole
through
two wide faces

Sound, encased knot
through
two wide faces

Sound, star-checked,
intergrown knot
through two wide faces

Sound, intergrown
knot through two
narrow faces

Sound, intergrown
knot through all
four faces

Sound, intergrown
knot through three
faces

2-9 *Continued.*

To learn more about standard sizes and requirements for development and coordination of the lumber grades of softwood lumber, write for a free copy of the *American Softwood Lumber Standard, Voluntary Product Standard PS 20-94* at

American Lumber Standard Committee
P.O. Box 210
Germantown, MD 20875-0210

For a copy of the *Western Wood Species Book* (Volume 1, Dimension Lumber; Volume 2, Selects-Finish/Commons-Boards), write to

Western Wood Products Association
522 SW Fifth Avenue
Portland, OR 97204-2122

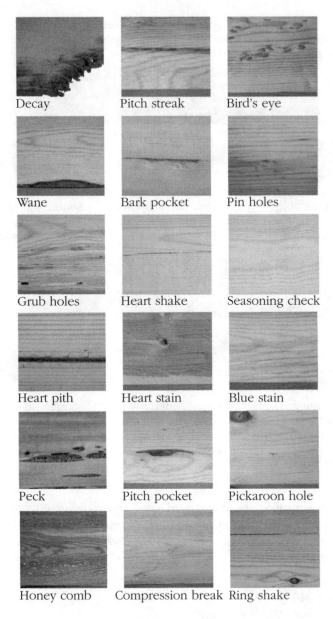

Decay   Pitch streak   Bird's eye

Wane   Bark pocket   Pin holes

Grub holes   Heart shake   Seasoning check

Heart pith   Heart stain   Blue stain

Peck   Pitch pocket   Pickaroon hole

Honey comb   Compression break Ring shake

2-10 *Natural imperfections.* Western Wood Products Association

Grade stamps

Understanding the grade stamped on the lumber helps prevent expensive mistakes if the wrong material is delivered. Take the time to

Machine burn Machine gouge Skips in dressing

Torn grain (planer) Raised grain Wavy dressing

Torn grain (saw) Dog hole Roller check

2-11 *Manufacturing imperfections.* Western Wood Products Association

learn the grades, the wood species, and the moisture content of the product (Fig. 2-13).

Lumber grades and usage

Although pressure treating enables wood to resist fungal decay and termite attack, it does not alter physical properties such as strength, elasticity, and fiber stress in bending, nor characteristics such as knots, wane, and so on, found in wood. Always specify the proper grade for a particular project as well as the treating standard if that is also pertinent.

Any grade of lumber can be pressure treated, and grades are determined by certified graders at the sawmill before treatment. Grades specific to redwood and cedar are explained earlier in this chapter. Descriptions of other commonly available grades suitable for deck projects follow.

Common grades Commons are the standard board grades and are useful for a multitude of applications. Appearance is the controlling factor.

Wane is the presence of bark or lack of wood from any cause on the edge or corner of a piece of lumber.

Shake is a lengthwise separation of the wood which usually occurs between or through the annual growth rings.

Splits are similar to checks except the separations of the wood fibers extend completely through a piece, usually at the ends.

White Speck and Honeycomb are caused by a fungus in the living tree. White Speck is small white pits or spots. Honeycomb is similar but the pits are deeper or larger. Neither is subject to further decay unless used under wet conditions.

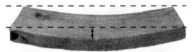

Bow is a deviation from a flat plane of the wide face of a piece of lumber from end to end.

Crook is a deviation from a flat plane of the narrow face of a piece of lumber from end to end.

Decay is a disintegration of the wood substance due to action of wood-destroying fungi. It also may be called dote, rot or unsound wood.

Twist is a deviation from the flat planes of all four faces by a spiraling or torsional action, usually the result of seasoning.

Checks are separations of the wood fibers, normally occurring across or through the annual growth rings, and usually as a result of seasoning. They may occur anywhere on a piece. (Not shown)

Cup is a deviation from the flat plane, edge to edge. (Not shown)

Other characteristics include burl, compression wood, pitch, slope of grain, pitch streak, pith, pocket, sapwood and stain.

Manufacturing imperfections include chipped, torn, raised or loosened grain, skips in surfacing, undersize, mismatch, wavy dressing and machine caused burns, chips, bite or knife marks.

2-12 *Other defects.* Western Wood Products Association

No. 1 Common	Tight-knotted, sound stock considered watertight; defects limited in size
No. 2 Common	Considered tight-grain stock; larger defects allowed
No. 3 Common	Occasional knotholes plus larger and coarser defects than those found in No. 2 stock

Select grades Select grades are stock that can be finished with good results. These are appearance grades used primarily for fence boards and residential accessories.

a. WWPA certification mark. Certifies Association quality supervision. (W)® is a registered trademark.

b. Mill identification. Firm name, brand or assigned mill number. WWPA can be contacted to identify an individual mill whenever necessary.

c. Grade designation. Grade name, number or abbreviation.

d. Species identification. Indicates species by individual species or species combination. New species identification marks for groups to which design values are assigned are:

e. Condition of seasoning. Indicates condition of seasoning at time of surfacing:

MC-15 – 15% maximum moisture content

S-DRY – 19% maximum moisture content

S-GRN – over 19% moisture content (unseasoned)

2-13 *Most grade stamps, except those for rough lumber or heavy timbers, contain five basic elements.* Western Wood Products Association

Grade B and BTR	Almost entirely free of defects; might contain a few blemishes or small defects; can be given a natural finish
Grade C	Limited number of blemishes or small defects that can be hidden by painting
Western Species Radius Edge (eased edges) Patio Decking	Manufactured to be used flat for load-bearing applications where spans are 16" on center (OC); available in two grades surfaced in either 1" (with ¼" eased edges) or 1$\frac{5}{32}$" (with ⅜" eased edges) thick by 5½" wide; available primarily in cedar and ponderosa species
Patio 1	Good appearance, limited allowable characteristics

Patio 2	Between a No. 2 and a No. 3 Common in terms of allowable characteristics
Southern Pine Radius Edge (eased edges) Decking	Special grading rules combining appearance and structural considerations established for ¾ (¼" eased edges) lumber
Premium	Medium surface checks; infrequent holes; small, sound knots
Standard	Larger checks, holes, and knots than Premium grade

Heartwood vs. sapwood

For some applications, the portion of the tree from which the lumber is cut can be an important consideration. Be sure to consult your local building department for specifics. Typically, heartwood (the center part of the tree) can be quite dense and less porous than sapwood (the younger, outer portion of the tree). Heartwood is naturally more resistant to attack by insects, but it is also less accepting of preservatives. Therefore, in marine conditions, for example, where wood-destroying organisms are a threat, it is wise to specify wood with a minimum of heartwood exposed (seawall grade) to be assured of adequate preservative protection.

Similarly, even with naturally durable species like redwood, cedar, and cypress, heartwood grade must be specified for construction where decay and insect attack are likely. If sapwood grades of redwood or cedar are selected for such applications, they should be pressure treated, since sapwood does not have the natural protection of heartwood. (This information was provided by the Hickson Corporation.)

Supreme Decking

The manufacturer of Supreme Decking (Supreme Decking Inc.) re-mills select redwood, cedar, and pine to eliminate most of the defects, creating a smoother, cleaner decking material that is refreshing to install. Each re-milled decking board has a 1¼" finished edge height, while the height in the middle of the board is 1⅜". This ⅛" crown helps to keep the surface dry because it allows water to drain, discouraging surface puddling and cupping, and thus extending the life of the boards.

The decking boards feature lengthwise relief cuts on their undersides (similar to hardwood flooring) to help keep them flat. These cuts also allow the wood to breathe and adjust to temperature and humidity changes, minimizing warping, cupping, and twisting (Fig. 2-14). Supreme Decking is a very high-quality product. It offers one of the smoothest finished surfaces available on the market today.

2-14 *Remilling ensures quality by eliminating some of the allowable defects that make consumers unhappy. Call (800) 532-1323 for a sample.* Supreme Decking Inc.

Seasoning

It is good practice to stack and season your lumber, protected both from rain and from moisture under the stack such as wet ground, to allow it to acclimate to the surrounding air of its final location. Stacking the lumber on 2" × 4" sleepers keep it off the ground. Stickering allows air to circulate between the boards: placing 1" × 2" strips (stickers) at intervals between the layers of lumber create air spaces. The 1" × 2" stickers prevent each layer of boards from sagging, and heavy blocks on top of the pile help stabilize the upper pieces.

Since lumber expands and contracts and can release or absorb moisture in transport or storage, it is wise to give wood an opportunity to stabilize before installation. This is particularly important for green as well as pressure-treated lumber, but all wood benefits from this technique. Stickering allows the lumber to air-dry (releasing or absorbing) evenly on all sides, thus giving it a chance to stabilize to the climate of its new location before installation. If the lumber is too dry for its surrounding atmosphere prior to installation, it expands and tightens joints as it acclimates. If the lumber is too wet (green) when installed, it shrinks and opens joints as it seasons to the moisture content of the surrounding atmosphere. Stable lumber also allows you to gap the decking boards more precisely.

Stickering works well in warmer temperatures because the warm conditions help to evaporate excess water and season the lumber to the environment. Lumber can be stacked and stickered in an open garage or other covered area or protected with a loose tarp just about anywhere where it will be used for exterior installations. (Place the tarp on the top of the stack only—don't "tent" the stack. Tenting traps moisture from the stack as well as the ground.) Lumber for interior applications should be acclimated indoors.

Finishes

As with all wood products, decks require regular maintenance and upkeep to preserve their natural look. As a professional, you need to stress to customers that preventive measures (especially when it comes to decks) should be taken both to maintain the integrity of the structure and to prevent surface deterioration.

Within a short time after installation, new decking boards swell as they absorb moisture and shrink as that moisture is pulled out by the sun. Due to this constant expansion and contraction, wood warps, splits, or cups (Fig. 2-15). The sun's UV rays break down the cellular

2-15 *Good example of a well-weathered pressure-treated deck.* Wolman Wood Care Products

structure of the exposed wood cells, and the infrared rays speed up the drying process. Therefore, it is important during the first year to apply a treatment that slows this process of swelling and shrinking. You should use and promote such treatment products to encourage customers to take care of their newly constructed decks.

Don't be fooled into thinking that pressure-treated lumber doesn't require any precautions against weather. The chemicals used in pressure-treated lumber protect against insect and fungal attacks; weather is another matter. Water alone cannot damage wood, but in combination with other natural weathering elements, such as harsh sunlight, problems can occur.

Almost all new pressure-treated lumber used for construction swells because of water used in the pressure-treatment process. When exposed to warm air and direct sunlight, new pressure-treated lumber dries out very rapidly, releasing the water added during treatment. This initial rapid drying and shrinking cycle begins to degrade the lumber. Therefore, an immediate and ongoing protection against moisture absorption is a must to help prevent cracking, checking, grain-lifting, and twisting.

Cleaning new decks

Many professionals clean their decks (especially redwood or cedar) before applying a protective coating. Before using any chemicals for cleaning, however, make sure that the chemicals you choose have not been banned in your area.

To remove iron stains, mildew, and extractive staining, try one cup of household bleach in one gallon of water. You can also use oxalic acid crystals, which bring back more of the natural color. Dissolve 4 ounces of the crystals in 1 gallon of warm water. After scrubbing the deck, allow the wood to dry and then rinse with water to flush away any residue of oxalic solution. Several applications might be necessary in cases of severe discoloration, but be sure to allow the wood to dry between applications. To prevent streaking, the solution should be applied to an entire board or area at one time.

Oxalic acid is toxic; use it with care, and be sure to follow the manufacturer's recommendations. By all means, make sure there are no children or pets in the area. Protect your skin from burns and wear gloves and eye protection. Protect any lawn, shrubs, and trees around the area you are cleaning.

Treated lumber

Most pressure-treated lumber intended for residential use carries a lifetime limited warranty. For Western species of wood, however, the warranty is null and void unless all cuts, including ends and bore holes, are coated before installation (in some cases) or during construction with a suitable wood preservative. Follow the manufacturer's guidelines. If you are using a Western product that has a color additive (brown), be sure to select a preservative containing a matching colorant. Some species do not require end-cut solution to validate the warranty. When you purchase pressure-treated lumber, be sure to check with your dealer on the terms and conditions of the warranty offered for that particular product.

Sealers

It is important during the first years to slow down the process of swelling and shrinking. Sealers can help. They are penetrating coatings (clear or lightly tinted) that repel moisture. Some sealers have preservatives added. To provide ongoing protection against moisture absorption and to reflect UV rays and maintain a fresh appearance, use a wood finish that is a UV inhibitor and contains other transparent solids. The protection of such a finish lasts longer than standard waterproofing sealers. Some manufacturers claim an effective six years while standard sealers only last one to two years. Generally, manufacturers recommend an annual reapplication with standard sealers.

Check the label before purchasing any sealer; some cannot be stained or painted over, while others make good undercoats for stains or good preprimers for paints. Some sealers might have a time period during which stains or paints should be applied. If this is not your area of expertise, consult the manufacturer of the product you would like to use or subcontract this part of the job to a qualified subcontractor who specializes in this area.

Stains

Oil-based semitransparent stains work best when applied to dry weathered wood rather than new wood. This gives the stain a chance to penetrate the wood to the recommended ⅛".

If you choose to use a stain, apply a sealer first, following in a couple of weeks with two coats of the stain. Apply the second coat before the first coat has dried. Remember that darker stains absorb more solar radiation than lighter shades and also develop wear patterns quickly. Semitransparent stains are still an excellent option, even with this slight limitation. Choose a color that best fits the surrounding environment of the project.

Bleaching oils

For those customers who want an instantly weathered-looking deck, consider using a bleaching oil. Bleaching oils minimize the initial darkening process and accelerate the natural color change of cedar or redwood to a final driftwood gray. Use one or two coats according to the manufacturer's recommendations. Even though some of these bleaching oils contain light pigmentation, fungicides, and water-repellent agents, an additional application of water repellents (with fungicidal additives) will be required when the initial application begins to wear off.

Since the bleaching action depends upon both moisture and sunlight, it is helpful occasionally to flush the surface with cold water. This cleans off any dirt and helps keep the reaction even until a weathered look is achieved. Reapplication of bleaching oil is necessary only if the surface shows signs of darkening.

Applications

All of these products can be brushed, rolled, or sprayed. Because of their low solid/pigment content, they can be applied easily with a low-pressure garden sprayer (although some of the products might gum up the sprayer). One exception is CWF-UV and toners by the Flood Company, which must be applied by an airless sprayer. Be sure to follow the manufacturer's recommendations. After each job, thoroughly clean the sprayer and relubricate all parts. Depending on the time available and your level of expertise, you might prefer to have a subcontractor handle this.

Sealer sources

A variety of sealer products are currently on the market and include the following:

Oil-Based Formulas:
- Plain Water Repellent Sealers and/or New Wood Protection
  ~Cabot Clear Solution (Samuel Cabot Inc.)
  ~Cabot Decking Clear (Samuel Cabot Inc.)
  ~Cabot PTW Clear (Samuel Cabot Inc.)
  ~Seasonite (The Flood Company)
  ~Wolman Rain Coat Water Repellent Clear (Wolman Wood Care Products)
- Water Repellent Preservatives or Finishes with Ultraviolet Light Inhibitors
  ~CWF-UV (The Flood Company)

~Wolman F&P (Premium Wood Finish-Preservative, Wolman Wood Care Products)
- Water Repellent Preservatives or Finishes
~CWF Clear Wood Finish (The Flood Company)
~Osmose Clear Wood Preservative (Osmose Wood Preserving, Inc.)
~Osmose Clear Water Repellent (Osmose Wood Preserving, Inc.)
~Wolman Clear Wood Preservative (Wolman Wood Care Products)
- Semi-Transparent Stains with or without Water Repellent
~Cabot PTW Stains for Pressure-Treated Wood (Samuel Cabot, Inc.)
~Cabot Decking Stains (Samuel Cabot Inc.)
~Cabot Decking Stains (350 VOC, Samuel Cabot Inc.)
~Cabot Clear Solution (Samuel Cabot Inc.)
~Cabot Clear Solution (350 VOC, Samuel Cabot Inc.)
~CWF-UV Toners (The Flood Company)
~Osmose Semi-Transparent Stain (Osmose Wood Preserving, Inc.)
~Wolman Rain Coat Water Repellent with Natural Wood Toners (Wolman Wood Care Products)
- For Field Cuts and Drill Holes
~Osmose Green EndCoat Wood Preservative (Osmose Wood Preserving, Inc.)
~SupaTimber (Chemical Specialties, Inc.)

Water-Based Acrylic Formulas:
- Plain Water Repellent Sealers
~Osmose-BetterEarth Products Wood Sealer (Osmose Wood Preserving, Inc.)
~Wolman Rain Coat Water Repellent Clear VOC (Wolman Wood Care Products)
- Semi-Transparent Stains with Water Repellent
~Osmose-BetterEarth products Wood Toner (Osmose Wood Preserving, Inc.)
~Osmose-BetterEarth Products Sunwood Toner (Osmose Wood Preserving, Inc.)
~Wolman Deck Stain with Rain Coat Water Repellent (Wolman Wood Care Products)

Note that "Clear" does not necessarily mean clear; the product could have a slight tint or amber color. Also, for those areas of the country where coatings must meet federal or state environmental volatile organic compound (VOC) regulations, be sure to read labels carefully. The addresses for all companies listed are contained in Appendix C.

Alternative products

It is important that you stay abreast of all products currently on, or just coming to, the market. Check their track records and how the companies warrant their products. Verify that they have undergone safety testing, structural integrity evaluation, establishment of quality assurance standards, and long-term field performance tests. Don't forget to check the written warranty. Today's customers are open to new ideas and approaches that would better suit their particular needs or lifestyles. As a professional, you will be expected to educate them, so stay informed and request information and samples of the products mentioned in this chapter. It could make the difference between closing a sale or not.

TREX

TREX is an innovative product that is interesting to work with. It is fairly new, but it has a good track record. Roger Wittenberg (the developer) first introduced this product to the market in the 1980s, and it was produced under the name Rivenite until 1991. When Mobil Chemical Company (Composite Products Division) purchased the technology, its name was changed to Timbrex. Since then, the product has been refined and the name simplified to TREX.

TREX, a wood composite lumber, is made from recycled and/or reclaimed plastic (grocery bags and industrial stretch film) and waste wood (wood fiber from sawdust and used pallets), and it contains no virgin wood or preservatives. It resists moisture (including saltwater) as well as UV rays, insects, and solvents, so it will not rot or deteriorate. This has made an impact on the commercial market: boardwalks (in Spring Lake, New Jersey), playgrounds, marina docks, landscaping decks, an outside dance floor (The Neptune Beach Club in Southampton, Long Island), and amphitheater seating (Mohican State Park) are some of the installations that have used TREX, and the list continues to grow.

If you soak a sample for 10 minutes in hot water, TREX appears to absorb the water—but it really doesn't. Within minutes, the material is completely dry and returns to its original color. Produced with a slight crown (similar to Supreme Decking), TREX sheds water. This product is not structurally designed and is therefore not intended for use as columns, beams, joists, stringers, or other primary load-bearing members.

TREX is available in two colors: natural, a light brown that fades to gray, and dark brown, which is color-fast. It comes in 8', 12', and 16' lengths and in dimensions of 2" × 4", 2" × 6", 2" × 8", and ¾ × 6" (1¼" × 5½"). Several other less commonly used profiles are also available. The product has no grain or knots, is very dense, and features bull-nosed edges. It will not check, crack, or splinter and it is not necessary to predrill, even when deck screws are placed close to the edge (but I recommend you predrill anyway). If you countersink a screw, the material lifts up around the head; tapping this area with a hammer flattens the raised portion. If you barely cut the surface with the countersink bit, the screw will then pull itself and the decking material down flush to the surface, giving a clean, countersunk look.

The product sands, routs, and cuts like natural wood, but since it is very dense, you cannot cut through it as easily as redwood or cedar. A 40-tooth carbide saw blade gives a clean cut, but the manufacturer recommends an 18- or 24-tooth carbide blade to keep both the blade and the material cooler.

TREX appears to be maintenance-free. Sealants are not required. It readily accepts paint and stain and is splinter- and knot-free. At this time, the company offers a 10-year fully transferable limited warranty.

There are a few points to consider when working with a TREX product. TREX expands and contracts due to temperature changes. In colder temperatures, the manufacturer recommends a ³⁄₁₆" gap (based on two 16' boards) between ends. I recommend having the material delivered to the job site at least a week before installation so you can sticker the pile (every two feet and as level as possible). In temperatures of 70° and above, the product expands to 80 or 90 percent capacity. If you install the boards at this temperature, you can butt the joints relatively tight.

When working with ¾ materials, the manufacturer recommends at 125 psf (pounds per square foot) live load to place the joists at 16" OC. I found that placing the joists on 12" centers (especially on the hottest side of a house) and bridging each joist with blocks stabilized the TREX between joists and prevented deflection. The extra joist helps keep the decking boards in place, which keeps the ends of the boards tight (provided you use screws, not nails).

I recommend two people to handle this product, especially the 16' pieces. After you have had time to work with TREX and feel you understand its characteristics, you should be able to cut your labor time in half.

If you can start from the house in full width, the following doesn't apply, but if you trim the board to fit and it is less than 3" wide, string a line so this first piece is installed straight, otherwise it will conform to irregularities on the house and every board will follow suit. (This practice should be followed with any product less than 3" wide.)

TREX balusters, caps, and bottom rails are available, but combining TREX with natural wood (cedar or redwood) railings produces an attractive deck.

Re-Source Lumber

Re-Source Lumber is another product made from 100 percent recycled waste, such as plastic milk containers. A synthetic ridged plastic consisting of HDPE (high-density polyethylene) resins, UV-inhibited pigment systems, foaming compounds, and selected process additives, it carries a 20-year limited warranty not to rot, split, crack, or splinter. With no painting or sealing required, this truly is a maintenance-free product (Fig. 2-16).

2-16 *When mixed with timbers or other natural woods, Re-Source Lumber makes an interesting and attractive entertainment area.* Re-Source Building Products

Manufactured in many dimensional lumber sizes, shapes, and colors, Re-Source Lumber can be installed with standard woodworking tools. A 72-tooth carbide blade cuts through it with ease and routing is simple. In fact, a newly routed edge blends in with the rest of the material. When using a router bit with a roller bearing, be sure to check the bearing and clean off the plastic film that will wrap around it. The plastic film removes easily.

I recommend using a countersink bit before installing screws. It is not necessary to fasten through the surface if you use the grooved planks, since decking clips are available. This attachment system allows for improved expansion and contraction tolerance of the decking surface. An 8' piece might expand or contract ¼" over a 50° temperature change. For example, if the deck material is installed at 50°F and the temperature increases to 100°F, the material will expand ¼". Also available are tongue-and-groove boards for even easier installation. Because of the minimal shrinkage, it is now possible to have outdoor structures without gaps between the boards. The tongue-and-groove boards are not 100 percent watertight, so water will either run through or run off. Water left on the surface is actually beneficial since the product provides a better grip when it's wet than when it has a coating of dry dust.

Re-Source products are too flexible to be used for joists or supporting members. When you use it in a railing system, use blocks under the bottom rail and between the posts, which should not be more than 3' apart. Proper precautions during installation prevent sagging during hot weather: Re-Source expands and contracts with temperature changes. The ¾" × 5½" planks should be installed on a joist system that is 12" OC. The manufacturer recommends that you bridge joists with blocking material to tighten and secure the entire framing system. They have also introduced galvanized joists and structural lumber with an aluminum core. The galvanized joist along with Re-Source is virtually maintenance-free, and the structural lumber with the aluminum core delivers a rigid support system, especially when used in a railing system.

When fastening through the surface, use Re-Source color-coordinated screws. The manufacturer recommends that white be used in the railing system but not in the decking surface because white shows dirt very quickly and needs regular washing with soap and water. This product might work well to cosmetically tie into a mobile home or a home with vinyl siding. It comes in weathered redwood, light oak, cedar, gray, and white, which gives your customers the opportunity to create color accents that blend with the rest of the home.

Dreamdeck

When Dreamdeck was first introduced to the market, it was intended for use in dock construction, but it has slowly been making its way into decks. Both Dreamdeck and Dreamdock are manufactured by Thermal Industries, Inc. It is noteworthy that the main portion of the material used to make the substrate of these products comes from recycled waste from their 100 percent polyvinyl chloride (PVC) window division.

The substrate is covered with a textured weatherable PVC (not re-cycled). The four "feet" on the bottom of the substrate are lined along the length of the plank with flexible materials that add cushion and prevent squeaking. Dreamdeck is durable and maintenance free, mildew- and UV-resistant, splinter-free, has a slip-resistant surface, and is aesthetically appealing.

The surface material is available in two colors: earth tone and white. Stock lengths are 12', 16', and 20' (the manufacturer can ac-commodate special lengths) and 1⅜" thick × 5½" wide. Once the joists are in place (12" or 16" OC) and level, then simply screw down the snap-on connector to the joist. Snap the Dreamdeck PVC lumber down over the snap connector, leaving no visible nail or other fas-tening devices on the walking surface. The exposed ends can be cos-metically finished with a U-channel, which is fastened from the underside with pan-head screws (Fig. 2-17).

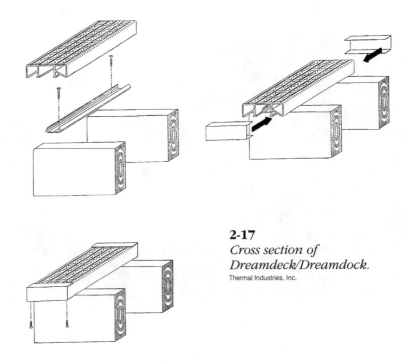

2-17
*Cross section of
Dreamdeck/Dreamdock.*
Thermal Industries, Inc.

Because you will be cutting the PVC lumber to specific lengths, consider leaving the joists long until you know exactly where the piece will land. You can finish the perimeter with natural wood in 1× or 2× instead of using a U-channel. In any case, this material, when used for a deck or a dock, does not require maintenance or finishing, nor will your customers have the cleaning problems that can occur with a wooden surface. This product is worthy of attention.

E-Z Deck

E-Z Deck uses new rather than recycled materials. It is a composite made from glass fiber and a resin matrix, which is quite similar to fiberglass.

The full-width boards are commonly available in 2" × 4" (1½" × 3⅞") and 2" × 6" (1½" × 5⅞") and in Classic Grey, Sandalwood, and Arctic White colors. The joist spacing is recommended at 16" OC. E-Z Deck is also available in custom lengths of 8' to 40' in even 2' intervals; rails are 8' to 40' in even 4' intervals. This particular product is not fastened through the top but rather snapped into place over retaining clips (available in 8' lengths) that have been fastened to the top of the joist (Fig. 2-18). This product is so easy to install it could become the decking material of the future.

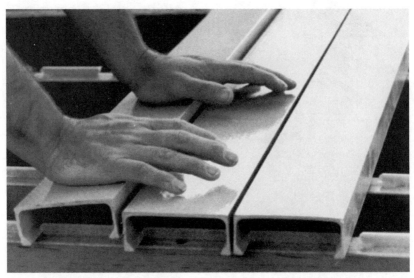

2-18 *Hook bottom edge of deck profile on clips, then press down to snap it into place.* ZCL Mfg. Canada Inc. (E-Z Deck)

What I found unique about this product is its complete Hand/Guard Rail System made of the same material. The balusters (43" and 50" in length) are placed in precut slots located on the bottom rail, which also acts as a fascia board. The top rail is placed over the balusters and fastened with self-tapping screws at 45 degree angles upward through the underside of the deck rail at the groove's location (Fig. 2-19).

2-19 *Drill two ¼" holes through rail and baluster, securing with 3" lag screws and washers.* ZCL Mfg. Canada Inc. (E-Z Deck)

Other products

Phoenix Recycled Plastics manufactures plastic lumber for all your outdoor needs from 100 percent recycled plastics. They offer four grades of plastic to help meet a wide range of customer needs. Each grade has special characteristics that suit it for particular applications. Write to them for samples and assistance with a particular project you might have in mind.

The color is the same all the way through these recycled products, and they are manufactured with a built-in "wood grain" texture. Available are the standard colors of white, black, gray, teak, weathered teak, and redwood as well as custom colors. Most nominal sizes are available (about the same as dimensional wood products) for decking boards, tongue and groove, round and square posts, and structural fiberglass-reinforced lumber in lengths up to 40'. If you are considering this product for structural applications, be sure to consult a customer service representative before you begin.

With all these colors and sizes available, you may want to consider the product for the following uses:

- Decks
- Boardwalks
- Docks

- Bulkheads
- Handrails
- Benches
- Tables
- Furniture
- Trim
- Landscaping
- Sheds
- Fencing
- Acid areas
- Pallets
- Truck flooring

Outwater Plastic/Industries, Inc., carries recycled plastic lumber in sizes such as 1" × 4", 1" × 6", 2" × 2", 2" × 4", 2" × 6", and 4" × 4" as well as tongue-and-groove recycled plastic decking in 1" × 6" and 2" × 6" and in standard lengths of 8', 12', and 16' with custom lengths up to 40'. Also available are the following products manufactured in recycled plastic:

- Adirondack chairs
- Trash receptacles
- Landscape timbers
- Speed bumps
- Car stops
- Picnic tables
- Hexagonal tables
- Classic park benches
- Mall benches

If you are looking for a 100 percent maintenance-free product in decking or outdoor products, write Outwater for their catalog. They offer a complete line of products that might suit your next deck, gazebo, or arbor project.

Have an open mind toward the new alternative products entering the market. Your customers might already be aware of these products and eager to put them to use. Don't lose a sale because you are not aware of the latest in alternative products or are unwilling to work with them. You must remain adaptable and flexible to stay on top of the competition.

3

Hardware

New hardware products that can make deck installation easier are continually introduced into the market. As with decking material, it's important to stay abreast of the latest in hardware, fasteners, and alternative building materials. These products are essential to the deck-building process and can help expedite your project and produce the professional-looking job your customers expect and deserve.

Fasteners

Whether you use nails or screws, lag screws, machine bolts, or carriage bolts, all are compatible with wood, and in most construction uses, few corrosion problems occur. However, you can expect corrosion when there is a high moisture content in the wood surrounding the fasteners. Fastener corrosion can contribute to wood deterioration, leading to loss of strength in joints and in the structural integrity of the assembly. Therefore, it is important to choose the correct fastener for a particular application. This chapter helps you to understand the materials so you can choose appropriate fasteners.

Nails

If you are still using nails, be aware that they are generally only temporary fasteners. Nails tend to split (or wedge) wood fibers apart as they enter the wood, and the hammer marks left by pounding them in are unattractive. Nail-popping is yet another problem. As wood dries, it shrinks, and nails become loose and protrude or even fall out altogether.

Screws are a permanent solution. If you are not yet totally convinced of the advantages of using screws in deck construction, then be sure the nails you use are the very best you can purchase and are the correct nail for the application.

There are four major processes for applying zinc to steel nails:

Electroplating These nails are bright and shiny and have a very thin zinc coating.

Mechanical plating Also called "peen-plating" and "golden galvanizing," mechanical plating gives nails a thin zinc coating as well.

Tumbler or barrel hot galvanizing Also called just "hot galvanizing," this process does not hot dip the nails but coats them with zinc chips in a hot tumbler, which delivers an uneven coating.

Hot dipping in molten zinc In this process, the nails are completely immersed in a vat of molten zinc. Nails coated by this process outperform all other types of galvanized nails for exterior applications.

To install decking boards, try Stormguard "PTL" (Pressure Treated Lumber) nails by Maze Nails. The T44-A series (Anchor-Down) and T44-S series (Screw-Down) are double hot-dipped, zinc-coated nails (Fig. 3-1). With their shank design, these nails provide superior holding power to reduce nail pop-ups. Their slimmer shanks also help to reduce wood splits, and a protective zinc coating prevents staining. According to the manufacturer, there has not been a single verified report in the last 60 years of stains or streaks due to rust.

If you are still in doubt, you can always use stainless steel nails. The Anchor-Down stainless steel nails (SS series) are available from 6d to 20d.

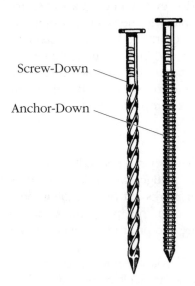

Screw-Down

Anchor-Down

3-1
Pressure-treated lumber nails.
Maze Nails

Screws

Even though improved nails are on the market, I highly recommend that you use screws in deck construction and avoid nail-related problems altogether. The correct screw can form a permanent bond so it is important to select screws to fit a particular application. Selecting the right screw can make a difference on callbacks, and warranty calls cut into profits.

Construction professionals often use some kind of power screwdriver to install screws and have at one time or another stripped or snapped the heads off of a few screws. Here are some practices you can adopt that might eliminate some of these mishaps:

- Drill pilot holes before installing screws. With pilot holes, your driver is subjected to less strain, and this helps eliminate snapping a screw or splitting the wood.
- Use square recess (Bugle) heads instead of Philips recess screws. It actually takes less downward pressure to keep the screw bit lip engaged in a square recess than in a Philips head screw.
- Use a screw gun instead of a drill. A drill can overdrive a screw, twist the head off, or strip the head. A screw gun with a built-in clutch can help. Don't misunderstand, a screw gun can strip the head just as easily, but in most cases, it's the operator's fault.
- Use 10-gauge instead of 8-gauge screws. The 10-gauge is heavier so it delivers a higher shear strength (depending, of course, on the type of metal used).
- Never use drywall screws. They are not designed for deck installation.

There are all types of screws on the market today with different finishes or coatings. Some of these finishes cannot withstand destructive elements like saltwater, chemicals, sunlight, and industrial pollutants such as acid rain. Others might react with the chemicals in certain woods (tannic acids in redwood and cedar and copper salts used in the waterborne preservatives of pressure-treated lumber) and cause staining. Check with the dealer to see if the fasteners you plan to use are warranted for exterior use. Also make sure they have gone through the Hesternich and/or salt spray tests and meet or exceed ASTM (American Society for Testing and Materials) Standards.

Hesternich test The Hesternich test is conducted under German Industrial Standard DIN 50018. This test involves repeated condensation and drying cycles, simulating the atmosphere commonly found in industrial cities, to see how well a screw holds up under polluted conditions and acid rain.

Salt spray test The salt spray test is a commonly accepted testing method to determine the corrosion resistance of plating, finishes, and fasteners. This test incorporates an atmospheric mixture of distilled water and sodium chloride, and values are expressed in hours. It determines the percentage of corrosion (red rust) of the screw under simulated marine conditions.

The following list shows, in ascending order, how well the various screw coatings held up (in hours) before reaching the 5 percent red rust corrosion limit under the salt spray test. These common products feature different thicknesses of platings and coatings that could affect the corrosion level of a fastener.

Time (hours)	Coating	Description
12	Phosphate	Most common plating for drywall screws usually gray or black
24	Clear Zinc	A chrome-colored plating
48	Yellow Zinc	Also known as Zinc Dichromate; yellowish to gold, commonly used as an exterior fastener but recommended for interior use for cosmetic purposes
300	Dacrotized	Battleship gray
1000	GrabberGard	A chemical-coated layer encased in a ceramic layer

Stainless steel screws are a very good choice but they can be expensive. Stainless steel is a combination of nickel (chromium) and carbon; however, all stainless steel screws are not the same, so check out the percentages of each element in the screws you purchase. The higher the percentage of nickel, the lower the corrosion factor. Because nickel is a soft metal, carbon is used to strengthen the fastener, but too much carbon decreases the level of protection. I suggest you deal directly with the fastener manufacturer or a dealer in your area to obtain nickel and carbon percentages.

So which screw should you choose? Consider Woodys by Grabber. This screw is designed specifically for wood and features a very flat head and ribbed underside (collar) to ensure a flush countersink (Fig. 3-2). Heads are available in square or Philips recess and in 8 or 10 gauge for extra strength and durability. They have 8 TPI (threads per inch) for increased holding power. The choice of coatings includes clear zinc, yellow zinc, and the GrabberGuard finish (a chemical layer encased in a ceramic layer). There has been talk of replacing the ceramic with a polymer ("space age plastic") that offers an even harder finish, and this product might be on the market by the time you read this book. As of this writing, many professionals currently consider GrabberGuard the ultimate deck fasteners, preferring them to galvanized and even stainless screws.

3-2 *Woodys by Grabber can be used out-doors wherever you need a superior weather-resistant screw.* Grabber Construction Products, Division of John Wagner Associates, Inc.

For more information on corrosion of metals by wood products, contact

Forest Products Laboratory
One Gifford Pinchot Drive
Madison, WI 53705-2398

Specifically request the following:
Baker, A. J. 1974. *Degradation of Wood by Products of Metal Corrosion*

_____ 1980. *Corrosion of Metals in Wood Products*
_____ 1988. *Corrosion of Metals in Preservative-Treated Wood*

Anchor systems

At some point during your deck-building career, you will need to fasten ledger board, conduit straps, joist hangers, or some other product to concrete. The correct fastener and tools can help make this process smooth and efficient.

Installing fasteners in concrete can be difficult. Sanko Fastem USA, Inc., has developed the SanTap Drive Tool, a one-piece drill/drive unit that allows for fast, easy, one-person installation of their SanTap masonry screws (Fig. 3-3). If you prefer to use a Philips screw, you can install a Philips bit into the end of the socket. SanTap masonry screws are self-tapping anchors that cut their own threads into concrete, hollow blocks, or bricks. They are useful when installing joist and beam hangers, duct straps, conduit straps, and so on. Their kits include case, tool, and screws.

If your particular project requires heavy-duty concrete applications, such as joining structural supports to concrete, fastening electrical and plumbing systems, or installing angle iron, then check out the All-Anchor (C-Type), a hammer-driven anchor also manufactured by Sanko. Especially designed for concrete applications, the hot-rolled steel body is encased with yellow zinc dichromate for corrosion resistance. The body has a tensile strength of 60,000 psi (pounds per square inch) minimum.

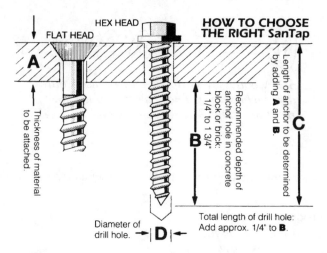

HOW TO CHOOSE THE RIGHT SanTap

HEX HEAD

FLAT HEAD

A

B

C

Thickness of material to be attached.

Recommended depth of anchor hole in concrete block or brick: 1 1/4" to 1 3/4".

Length of anchor to be determined by adding **A** and **B**.

Diameter of drill hole. →| **D** |←

Total length of drill hole: Add approx. 1/4" to **B**.

TYPICAL APPLICATIONS WITH SanTap CONCRETE SCREWS

CURTAIN WALL   PARTITIONS   WOOD SLEEPERS

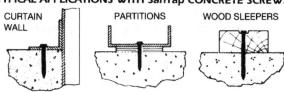

1. Simply attach SanTap DRIVE TOOL to your 3/8" variable speed drill, set bit and drill hole.

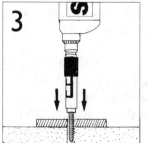

2. After holes are drilled through material to be attached and into masonry object, retract bit. Insert SanTap CONCRETE SCREW into the socket head of DRIVE TOOL and drive into hole.

3. Drive SanTap CONCRETE SCREW into hole and tighten until material is firmly attached.

3-3 *A one-piece unit that allows fast, easy, one-person installation.* Sanko Fastem USA, Inc.

The hardened pin is formed from hot-wrought carbon steel and has a tensile strength of 80,000 psi minimum. The effective and simple design allows the anchor to expand in concrete and masonry just by hammering down the hardened steel center pin. This product is also available in stainless steel, ranging from ¼" to ¾" in diameter and 1⅛" to 7½" in length, depending on the model (Fig. 3-4).

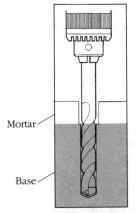

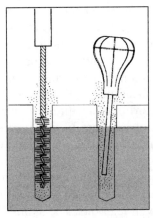

Mortar

Base

Drill hole through fixture to be fastened for desired diameter and depth. Use proper drill and bit.

Clean hole using wire brush and blow-out bulb or compressed air.

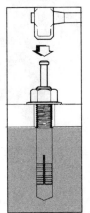

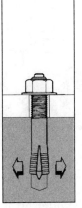

Insert anchor through fixture and hammer center pin flush until it is aligned with top of the bolt.

Installation completed. Slotted legs expand in four directions by the center pin and maximize holding power.

3-4 *Installing the All-Anchor by Sanko. Deeper embedment is suggested if installation requires mortar between fixture and base.* Sanko Fastem USA, Inc.

Brackets

One area that is always of concern in deck building is the ledger board, the area where the deck is attached to the house. If the ledger board is incorrectly attached to the house, water can become trapped, and if there is no way for the water to drain out or dry, the ledger board begins to deteriorate. Of course, this scenario depends on factors such as whether there is a roof covering the deck and whether the siding is embedded into caulk that lies directly on the deck platform. Alternative construction methods are discussed later in this book, but you should know that hardware is available to create an air space between the backside of the ledger board and the face of the siding or sheathing on the house.

Crawford manufactures an aluminum deck bracket that provides a space and moisture barrier between the deck and the structure to which the deck is attached to help prevent sill rot and insect damage. The bracket (Fig. 3-5) measures 8" wide on the backside (the side facing the house) and 4" wide on the front side (the backside of the ledger). It is 5" high and 4" deep and designed to be attached to the rim joist with lag bolts. The siding fits around the neck of the bracket and the area is then caulked.

3-5 *Weather-resistant aluminum bracket that can be used on new or existing construction.* C.R.S., Inc.

A multipurpose bracket manufactured by P. A. Stratton & Co., Inc. is easy to use and a great problem-solver. The Stratton bracket, like Crawford's, is designed to keep moisture away from the side of the house, but the difference is that it gives you the option of building the entire deck framework on the ground and then lifting the frame up and into the brackets. Although this process might require extra hands, it eliminates the need to attach a ledger board to the house and to cut the siding before installing the brackets (Fig. 3-6).

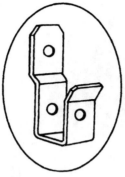 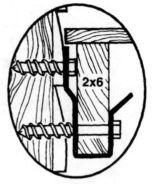

3-6 *A starter kit contains both hanger brackets and lag bolts.* P. A. Stratton & Co. Inc.

The manufacturer recommends spacing the brackets 6" to 12" in from the ends of the ledger board. Intermediate brackets should be 48" OC for 2" × 6" construction, 24" OC for a 2" × 8", and 16" OC for a 2" × 10" or 2" × 12". Even though these brackets were designed to meet or exceed the National Building Code, consult your local building department to learn their required bracket spacing.

Stratton's system allows you to shift the framework within the bracket to center and square it to the house. It also allows air to circulate between the house, decking, and ledger board, thus preventing water build-up that could cause rot or decay or permit bug infestation. In addition, it allows the ledger board to expand and contract with the seasons without adverse effects.

If you are designing a temporary installation, this bracket is perfect. The bracket has many other uses as well: stair and flower box installation, mounting solid shutters over windows, creating a collapsible workbench, and providing door security for a 2" × 4" cross door. I found it great to use on concrete walls. The Stratton bracket is very versatile; you will probably find other uses for it as well.

Framing connectors

As any deck builder already knows, a joist hanger is one piece of hardware you must have. If you need to install many joists, you might consider using the Boss by Advanced Connector Systems (ACS). This metal connector was designed for compatibility with pneumatic nailers or air palm nailers. The funnel shape guides the nail directly into the hole in a fraction of a second (Fig. 3-7). You will need a nail gun adapter, and models are available that fit over the nose of Hitachi or

3-7 *Metal connectors designed for pneumatic nailers or air palm nailers eliminate hand nailing.* Advanced Connector Systems

Halstead framing nailers. Attachments are also available for other nail guns; contact your ACS distributor for more information. A system like this can trim your workload considerably.

Advanced Connector Systems has other framing connectors that can be incorporated into your projects (Figs. 3-8 through 3-11). These are heavy-duty specialty items with a steel thickness of ¾₆" to ⅜" and are painted with a corrosion-resistant primer. Perhaps these connectors can provide some ideas or solutions for your next deck project.

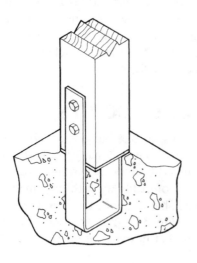

3-8
Column base provides a download-bearing plate as well as uplift resistance for wood column members.
Advanced Connector Systems

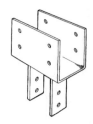

3-9
Column cap provides a good way to secure a laminated beam (or structure support material) to a column post. Advanced Connector Systems

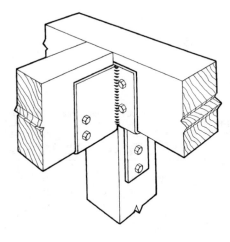

3-10
This column cap allows a beam to intersect a structure support within the same bracket and still be secured to a column post. Advanced Connector Systems

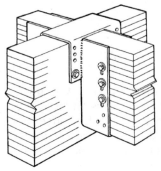

3-11
Glulam Saddle Hanger allows a main support to be intersected on both sides and carry the loads of the secondary supports. Advanced Connector Systems

When you use joist hangers or other connectors, *you must use the nails that were specially designed for them.* Joist hanger nails are short in length but have a high shear strength (Fig. 3-12). The conversion chart and nail hole identification comes in handy when choosing and working with connectors (Fig. 3-13).

Framing connectors solve wood-to-wood and wood-to-concrete connection problems. They were developed specifically to make wood construction easier, faster, and simpler, and to ensure a stronger, safer, better-looking structure. One company that has met wood frame build-

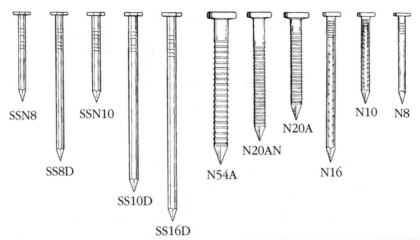

MODEL NO.	DESCRIPTION	METRIC EQUIVALENT (mm)	FINISH [4]	NAILS PER CWT	DOUG FIR-LARCH/SO. PINE ALLOWABLE LOADS [1]				SPRUCE-PINE-FIR ALLOWABLE LOADS [1]			
					LIGHT GAUGE		3 GAUGE		LIGHT GAUGE		3 GAUGE	
					SHEAR (100)	GAUGE	SHEAR (100)		SHEAR (100)	GAUGE	SHEAR (100)	
N8	(8d) 10¼ ga x 1½" SMOOTH SHANK	3.3 x 38.1	HDG	15200	86	14	105		74	16	90	
SSN8	(8d) 0.131 x 1½" SMOOTH SHANK	3.3 x 38.1	SS	15200	86	14	105		74	16	90	
SS8D	(8d) 0.131 x 2½" SMOOTH SHANK	3.3 x 63.5	SS	9400	92	20	131		80	18	112	
SD8X1.25	#8 x 1¼" SCREW	4.1 x 31.7	EG	9926	76	18	—		65	18	—	
N10	(10d) 9 ga x 1½" SMOOTH SHANK	3.8 x 38.1	HDG	11900	92	14	112		79	16	97	
SSN10	(10d) 0.148 x 1½" SMOOTH SHANK	3.8 x 38.1	SS	12200	92	14	112		79	16	97	
SS10D	(10d) 0.148 x 3" SMOOTH SHANK	3.8 x 76.2	SS	6700	112	18	158		96	20	136	
N16	(16d) 8 ga x 2½" SMOOTH SHANK	4.1 x 63.5	BRIGHT	6300	134	18	187		115	20	163	
SS16D	(16d) 0.162 x 3½" SMOOTH SHANK	4.1 x 88.9	SS	4400	134	18	187		115	20	163	
N20AN	(20d) 0.192 x 2⅛" ANNULAR RING	4.9 x 54.0	BRIGHT	6300	145	14	174		125	18	152	
N20A	(20d) .192 x 1¾" ANNULAR RING	4.9 x 44.5	BRIGHT	6300	119	14	140		103	18	122	
N54A	.250 x 2½" ANNULAR RING	6.4 x 63.5	BRIGHT	2700	167	14	188		145	18	164	

1. Allowable loads are based on the 1991 NDS. Adjustments are made for use with metal side plates, F_{es} = 45 ksi. Loads under light gauge are for gauge listed through 22 gauge. Allowable loads for gauges not indicated must be calculated according to the code. Contact factory for more details.
2. N16, N20, N20AN and N54A fasteners may be ordered galvanized; specify EG; for example N16EG.
3. Metric equivalents are listed by Diameter × Length.
4. EG = electro-galvanized;
   HDG = hot-dipped galvanized;
   SS = stainless steel;
   Bright = no finish.

3-12 *Nails and fasteners.* Simpson Strong-Tie Company, Inc.

Metric Conversion

IMPERIAL	METRIC
1 in	25.40 mm
1 ft	0.3048 m
1 lb	4.448N
1 Kip	4.448 kN
1 psi	6895 Pa

Bolt Diameters

in	mm
3/8	9.5
1/2	12.7
5/8	15.9
3/4	19.1
7/8	22.2
1	25.4

Optional nails for face mount hangers and straight straps

CATALOG NAIL	REPLACEMENT NAIL	ALLOWABLE LOAD ADJUSTMENT FACTOR
16d COMMON	10d×1½	0.64
16d COMMON	10d COMMON	0.84
16d COMMON	16d SINKER	0.84
16d COMMON	16d×2½	1.00
10d COMMON	10d×1½	0.77
10d COMMON	16d SINKER	1.00

1. 10d×1½" nails may not be substituted for joist nails in double shear hangers (i.e. LUS, HUS, HHUS). Contact factory for exception.
2. 10d×1½" nails may not be substituted for face nails on skewed LSU and LSSU hangers.
3. This table does not apply to specials (see Hanger Options) or steel thicker than 10 gauge.

U.S. Standard Steel Gauge Equivalents in Nominal Dimensions

GAUGE	APPROXIMATE DIMENSIONS		DECIMALS (in)		
	in	mm	UNCOATED STEEL	GALVANIZED STEEL (G60)	Z-MAX
3	1/4	6.0	0.239	—	—
7	3/16	4.5	0.179	—	—
10	9/64	3.4	0.134	0.138	0.140
11	1/8	3.0	0.120	0.123	0.125
12	7/64	2.7	0.105	0.108	0.110
14	5/64	2.0	0.075	0.078	0.080
16	1/16	1.5	0.060	0.063	0.065
18	3/64	1.2	0.048	0.052	0.054
20	1/32	1.0	0.036	0.040	0.042

Slope Conversion

RISE/RUN	SLOPE
1/12	5°
2/12	10°
3/12	14°
4/12	18°
5/12	23°
6/12	27°
7/12	30°
8/12	34°
9/12	37°
10/12	40°
11/12	42°
12/12	45°

Positive Angle Nailing (PAN)
Provided when wood splitting may occur, and to speed installation.

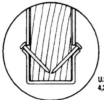

U.S. Patent 4,291,996

Speed Prongs
Used to temporarily position and secure the connector for easier and faster installation.

Double Shear Nailing
The nail is installed into the joist and header, distributing the load through two points on each joist nail for greater strength.

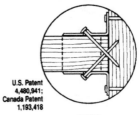

U.S. Patent 4,480,941; Canada Patent 1,193,418

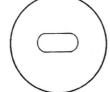

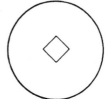

Triangle Holes
Provided on some products in addition to round holes. Round and triangle holes must be filled to achieve the published maximum load value.

Obround Holes
Used to provide easier nailing access in tight locations.

Diamond Holes
Optional holes to temporarily secure connectors to the member during installation.

3-13 *Conversion charts and nail hole identification.* Simpson Strong-Tie Company, Inc.

ing challenges is Simpson Strong-Tie Company, Inc. Simpson has led the industry since 1956 with innovative framing connectors. Even if you are familiar with their products already, it helps to have the information at your fingertips when discussing a project with a prospective customer. Other connectors that are used in other sections of a deck project are explored in the appropriate chapters (Figs. 3-14 through 3-19). Table 3-1 lists face mount hangers available for a selection of joist sizes.

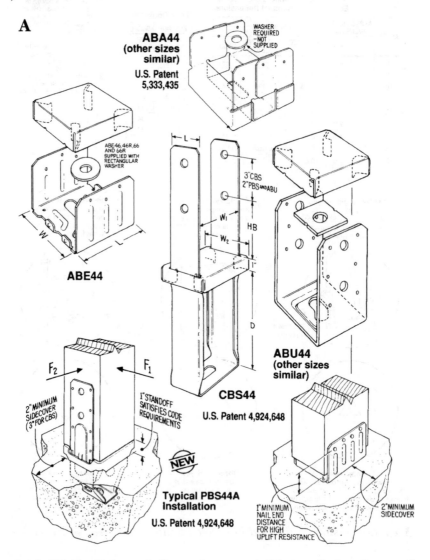

3-14 *(A) Typical standoff post bases and (B) installation for rough lumber.* Simpson Strong-Tie Company, Inc.

MODEL NO.	NOMINAL POST SIZE	MATERIAL		DIMENSIONS					FASTENERS				UPLIFT AVG ULT	ALLOWABLE LOADS						
		BASE	STRAP	W_1	W_2	D	L	HB	ANCHOR DIA	POST				UPLIFT (133)		F_1 (133)		F_2 (133)		DOWN (100)
										NAILS	BOLTS			NAILS	BOLTS	NAILS	BOLTS	NAILS	BOLTS	
											QTY	DIA								
ABA44	4×4	16 ga	16 ga	3 9/16	3 1/2	—	3 1/2	—	1/2	6-10d	—	—	2120	555	—	—	—	—	—	6000
ABE44	4×4	16 ga	16 ga	3 9/16	3 1/2	—	3 1/2	—	1/2	6-10d	—	—	1893	520	—	—	—	—	—	6665
ABU44	4×4	16 ga	12 ga	3 9/16	3 1/2	—	3	1 3/4	5/8	12-16d	2	1/2	7833	2200	2200	—	—	—	—	6665
PBS44	4×4	12 ga	14 ga	3 9/16	3 1/2	3 1/2	2 1/4	3 7/16	—	14-16d	2	1/2	7730	2400	2400	1165	230	885	885	6665
PBS44A	4×4	12 ga	14 ga	3 9/16	3 1/2	3 1/2	2 1/4	3 7/16	—	14-16d	2	1/2	7733	2400	2400	1165	230	885	885	6665
CBS44	4×4	12 ga	10 ga	3 9/16	3 1/2	7 1/8	2 1/4	4 5/16	—	—	2	5/8	16667	—	5335	—	—	—	—	9665
ABA44R	RGH 4×4	16 ga	16 ga	4 1/16	3 5/8	—	3 1/2	—	1/2	6-10d	—	—	2120	555	—	—	—	—		8000
ABE44R	RGH 4×4	16 ga	16 ga	4	3 1/2	—	3 1/2	—	1/2	6-10d	—	—	1893	400	—	—	—	—	—	6665
ABE46	4×6	12 ga	16 ga	3 9/16	5 3/8	—	5 7/16	—	5/8	8-16d	—	—	5167	810	—	—	—	—	—	7335
PBS46	4×6	12 ga	14 ga	3 9/16	5 3/8	3 1/2	2 1/4	3 7/16	—	14-16d	2	1/2	7733	2400	2400	1165	360	885	885	9335
ABA46	4×6	14 ga	14 ga	3 9/16	5 1/2	—	5 1/4	—	5/8	8-16d	—	—	2967	935	—	—	—	—	—	9435
CBS46	4×6	12 ga	10 ga	3 9/16	5 7/16	7 7/8	3	4 1/2	—	—	2	5/8	16667	—	5335	—	—	—	—	10000
ABU46	4×6	12 ga	12 ga	3 9/16	5 3/8	—	5	2 5/8	5/8	12-16d	2	1/2	8633	2200	2300	—	—	—	—	10335
ABE46R	RGH 4×6	12 ga	16 ga	4 1/16	5 3/8	—	5 7/16	—	5/8	8-16d	—	—	4350	810	—	—	—	—	—	7335
ABA46R	RGH 4x6	14 ga	14 ga	4 1/16	5 1/2	—	5 1/4	—	5/8	8-16d	—	—	2967	935	—	—	—	—	—	12000
PBS66	6×6	12 ga	12 ga	5 1/2	5 3/8	5	2 1/4	3 7/16	—	14-16d	2	1/2	13100	2630	3560	1865	570	1700	1700	9335
ABA66	6×6	14 ga	14 ga	5 1/2	5 1/2	—	5 1/4	—	5/8	8-16d	—	—	3050	985	—	—	—	—	—	10665
CBS66	6×6	12 ga	10 ga	5 1/2	5 7/16	6 7/8	3	4 1/2	—	—	2	5/8	24000	—	5560	—	—	—	—	13000
ABE66	6×6	12 ga	14 ga	5 1/2	5 1/2	—	5 7/16	—	5/8	8-16d	—	—	4833	880	—	—	—	—	—	15000
ABU66	6×6	12 ga	10 ga	5 1/2	5 3/8	—	5	2 3/4	5/8	12-16d	2	1/2	8900	2300	2300	—	—	—	—	15000
ABA66R	RGH 6x6	14 ga	14 ga	6	5 1/2	—	5 1/4	—	5/8	8-16d	—	—	3050	985	—	—	—	—	—	12665
ABE66R	RGH 6x6	12 ga	14 ga	6 1/16	5 1/2	—	5 7/16	—	5/8	8-16d	—	—	5367	900	—	—	—	—	—	15000

1. Uplift and lateral loads have been increased 33% for wind or earthquake loading; no further increase allowed. Reduce by 33% for normal loading.
2. Downloads may not be increased for short-term loading.
3. For higher downloads, solidly pack grout under 1″ standoff plate before installing CBS into concrete. Base download on post or concrete, according to the code.

3-14 *Continued*

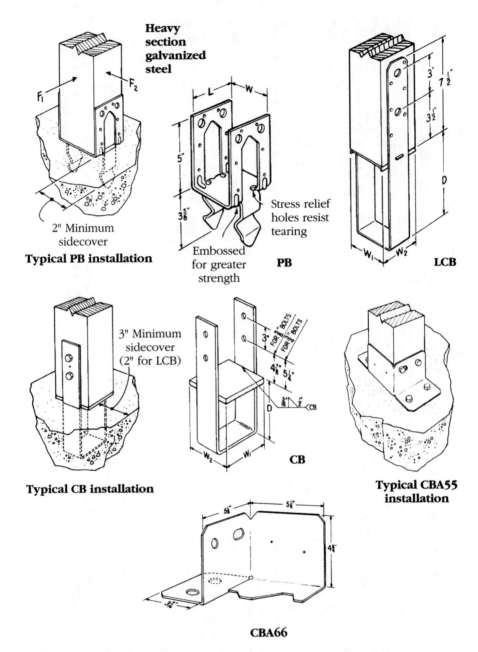

3-15 *Post and column bases.* Simpson Strong-Tie Company, Inc.

MODEL NO.	NOMINAL POST SIZE	MATERIAL		DIMENSIONS			POST FASTENERS			UPLIFT AVG ULT	ALLOWABLE LOADS	
		STRAP	BASE	W₁	W₂	D	NAILS	BOLTS			UPLIFT (133)	
								QTY	DIA		NAILS	BOLTS
LCB44	4×4	12 ga ×2	16 ga	3⁹⁄₁₆	3½	6½	12-16d	2	½	11267	2255	3545
CB44	4×4	7 ga ×2	7 ga	3⁹⁄₁₆	3⁹⁄₁₆	8	—	2	⅝	14350	—	4200
LCB46	4×6	12 ga ×2	16 ga	3⁹⁄₁₆	5½	6½	12-16d	2	½	11267	2255	3530
CB46	4×6	7 ga ×2	7 ga	3⁹⁄₁₆	5½	8	—	2	⅝	14350	—	4200
CB48	4×8	7 ga ×2	7 ga	3⁹⁄₁₆	7½	8	—	2	⅝	14350	—	4200
CB5	GLULAM	7 ga ×3	7 ga	5¼	SPEC	8	—	2	⅝	14350	—	4200
LCB66	6×6	12 ga ×2	16 ga	5½	5½	5½	12-16d	2	½	11267	2255	3525
CB66	6×6	7 ga ×3	7 ga	5½	5½	8	—	2	⅝	14350	—	4200
CBA66	6×6, 6×6R	10 gauge		See illustration			—	2	⅝	13000	—	3000
CB68	6×8	7 ga ×3	7 ga	5½	7½	8	—	2	⅝	14350	—	4200
CB86	6×8	3 ga ×3	7 ga	7½	5½	8	—	2	¾	20650	—	6650
CB7	GLULAM	3 ga ×3	7 ga	6⅞	SPEC	8	—	2	¾	20650	—	6650
CB88	8×8	3 ga ×3	7 ga	7½	7½	8	—	2	¾	20650	—	6650
CB9	GLULAM	3 ga ×3	7 ga	8⅞	SPEC	8	—	2	¾	20650	—	6650
CB1010	10×10	3 ga ×3	3 ga	9½	9½	8	—	2	¾	20650	—	6650
CB1012	10×12	3 ga ×3	3 ga	9½	11½	8	—	2	¾	20650	—	6650
CB1212	12×12	3 ga ×3	3 ga	11½	11½	8	—	2	¾	20650	—	6650

1. Uplift loads have been increased 33% for wind or earthquake loading; no further increase allowed.
2. CBA load applies only when installed in pairs. Use 4-¾" anchor bolts. Specify and design anchor bolt type, length, embedment to resist uplift forces.

MODEL NO.	DIMENSIONS		UPLIFT AVG ULT	ALLOWABLE LOADS			
	W	L		12-16d NAILS			2–½ MB
				UPLIFT (133)	F₁ (133)	F₂ (133)	UPLIFT (133)
PB44	3⁹⁄₁₆	3¼	4333	1365	765	1325	—
PB44R	4	3¼	4333	1365	765	1325	—
PB46	5½	3¼	4333	1365	765	1325	—
PB66	5½	5⅜	5143	1640	765	1325	1640
PB46R	6	3⅜	4333	1365	765	1325	1640
PB66R	6	5⅜	5143	1640	765	1325	1640

1. Allowable loads have been increased 33% for wind or earthquake loading, with no further increase allowed.

3-15 *Continued*

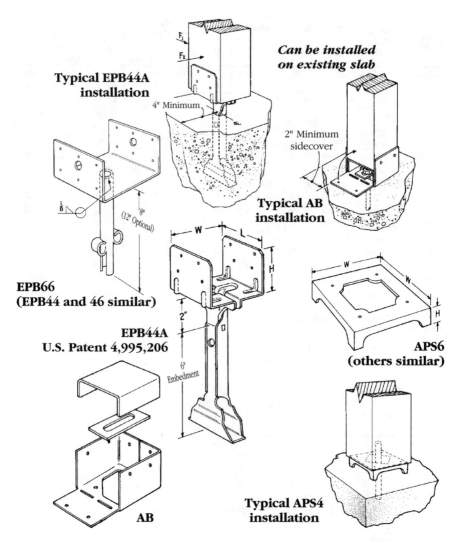

Typical EPB44A installation

Can be installed on existing slab

4" Minimum

2" Minimum sidecover

Typical AB installation

EPB66
(EPB44 and 46 similar)

EPB44A
U.S. Patent 4,995,206

$\frac{1}{8}$ 8"
(12" Optional)

W   L

2"

H

6" Embedment

W   W

H

APS6
(others similar)

AB

Typical APS4 installation

Elevated Post Bases

MODEL NO.	W	L	H	NAILS	UPLIFT AVG ULT	ALLOWABLE LOADS			
						UPLIFT (133)	F₁ (133)	F₂ (133)	DOWN (100)
EPB44A	3⁹⁄₁₆	3	2³⁄₈	8-16d	3600	1100	815	935	2670
EPB44	3⁹⁄₁₆	3¼	2⁵⁄₁₆	8-16d	3600	1070	800	800	3465
EPB46	5½	3⁵⁄₁₆	3	8-16d	3600	1070	800	800	3465
EPB66	5½	5½	3	12-16d	—	1610	800	800	3465

1. Loads may not be increased for short-term loading.
2. EPB44 and EPB46 have extra nail holes; only eight must be filled to achieve table loads.

3-16 *Typical specs and installation for elevated, ad-justable, and stand-off post bases.* Simpson Strong-Tie Company, Inc.

Adjustable Post Bases

MODEL NO.	DIMENSIONS		ALLOWABLE DOWNLOADS (100)
	W	L	
AB44	3⁹⁄₁₆	3⁹⁄₁₆	4065
AB46	3⁹⁄₁₆	5½	4165
AB44R	4	4	4065
AB46R	4	6	4165
AB66	5½	5½	5335
AB66R	6	6	5335

1. Loads may not be increased for short-term loading.

Aluminum Post Standoff

MODEL NO.	POST COLUMN SIZE	DIMENSIONS	
		W	H
APS4	4×4	3¼	1
APS5	5×5	4⅜	1
APS6	6×6	5⅛	1
APS8	8×8	8	1¼
APS10	10×10	9¾	1½
APS12	12×12	11¾	1½

3-16 *Continued*

LPC Post Caps

MODEL NO.	FASTENERS[1]		UPLIFT AVG ULT	ALLOWABLE LOADS[2,3] (133)	
	BEAM	POST		UPLIFT	LATERAL[4]
LPC4	8-10d	8-10d	2333	760	325
LPC6	8-10d	8-10d	2817	915	490

1. Fastener quantities are for two LPCs.
2. Allowable loads have been increased 33% for wind or earthquake loading with no further increase allowed.
3. Loads apply only when product is installed in pairs.
4. Lateral load is in the direction of the beam's axis.

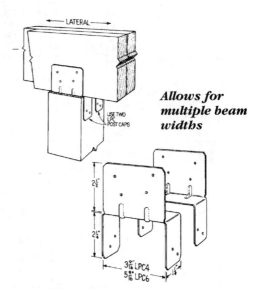

Allows for multiple beam widths

3-17 *Installation for various post and base caps.* Simpson Strong-Tie Company, Inc.

AC Post Caps

MODEL NO.	DIMENSIONS		FASTENERS (TOTAL 2 PIECES)		UPLIFT AVG ULT	ALLOWABLE LOADS (133)	
	W	L	BEAM	POST		UPLIFT	LATERAL
AC4	3⁹/₁₆	6¹/₂	12-16d	8-16d	4467	1080	715
AC4R	4	6¹/₂	12-16d	8-16d	4467	1080	715
ACE4	—	4¹/₂	8-16d	6-16d	—	810	715
AC6	5¹/₂	8¹/₂	12-16d	8-16d	4667	1080	715
AC6R	6	8¹/₂	12-16d	8-16d	4667	1080	715
ACE6	—	6¹/₂	8-16d	6-16d	—	810	715

1. Allowable loads have been increased
33% for wind or earthquake loading
with no further increase allowed;
reduce for other load durations
according to the code.
2. Loads apply only when
used in pairs.

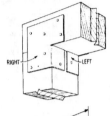

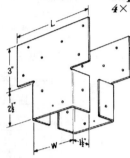

*Allows for
all post widths
4× and greater*

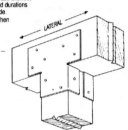

BC Post Caps/Bases

MODEL NO.	DIMENSIONS						FASTENERS (EACH SIDE)			UPLIFT AVG ULT	ALLOWABLE LOADS (133)[1]	
	W₁	W₂	L₁	L₂	H₁	H₂	SURFACE A	SURFACE B	SURFACE C		UPLIFT	LATERAL
CAPS												
BC4	3⁹/₁₆	3⁹/₁₆	2⁷/₈	2⁷/₈	3	3	3-16d	3-16d	—	3100	980	1000
BC46	3⁹/₁₆	5¹/₂	4⁷/₈	2⁷/₈	3¹/₂	2¹/₂	6-16d	3-16d	—	3100	980	1000
BC4R	4	4	4	4	3	3	6-16d	6-16d	—	3100	980	1000
BC6	5¹/₂	5¹/₂	4³/₈	4³/₈	3³/₈	3³/₈	6-16d	6-16d	—	6100	1330	2000
BC6R	6	6	6	6	3	3	6-16d	6-16d	—	6100	1330	2000
BC8	7¹/₂	7¹/₂	7¹/₂	7¹/₂	4	4	6-16d	6-16d	—	5600	1800	2000
BASES												
BC4O	3⁹/₁₆	—	3¹/₄	—	2¹/₄	—	3-16d	—	4-16d	—	—	535
BC4OR	4	—	4	—	3	—	4-16d	—	4-16d	—	—	535
BC46O	5¹/₂	—	3³/₈	—	3	—	4-16d	—	4-16d	—	—	535
BC6O	5¹/₂	—	5¹/₂	—	3	—	6-16d	—	4-16d	—	—	535
BC6OR	6	—	6	—	3	—	6-16d	—	4-16d	—	—	535

1. Allowable loads have been increased 33% for wind or
earthquake loading with no further increase allowed;
reduce for other load durations according to the code.

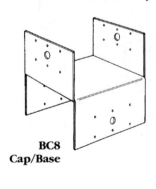

**BC8
Cap/Base**

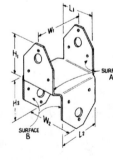

**BC4
Cap/Base**

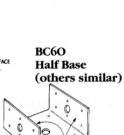

**BC6O
Half Base
(others similar)**

JOIST OR RAFTER	ALLOWABLE SHEAR					
	100		115		125	
	DFL	SPF	DFL	SPF	DFL	SPF
2×4	332	245	382	282	415	306
2×6	522	385	600	443	653	481
2×8	688	508	792	584	860	635
2×10	878	648	1010	745	1098	810

1. DFL = Doug Fir-Larch; SPF = Spruce-Pine-Fir.
2. F_V = 95 psi for Doug Fir-Larch, 70 psi for Spruce-Pine-Fir.
3. The 115 and 125 loads are 115% and 125% of the 100 column, according to the code for short-term loading.

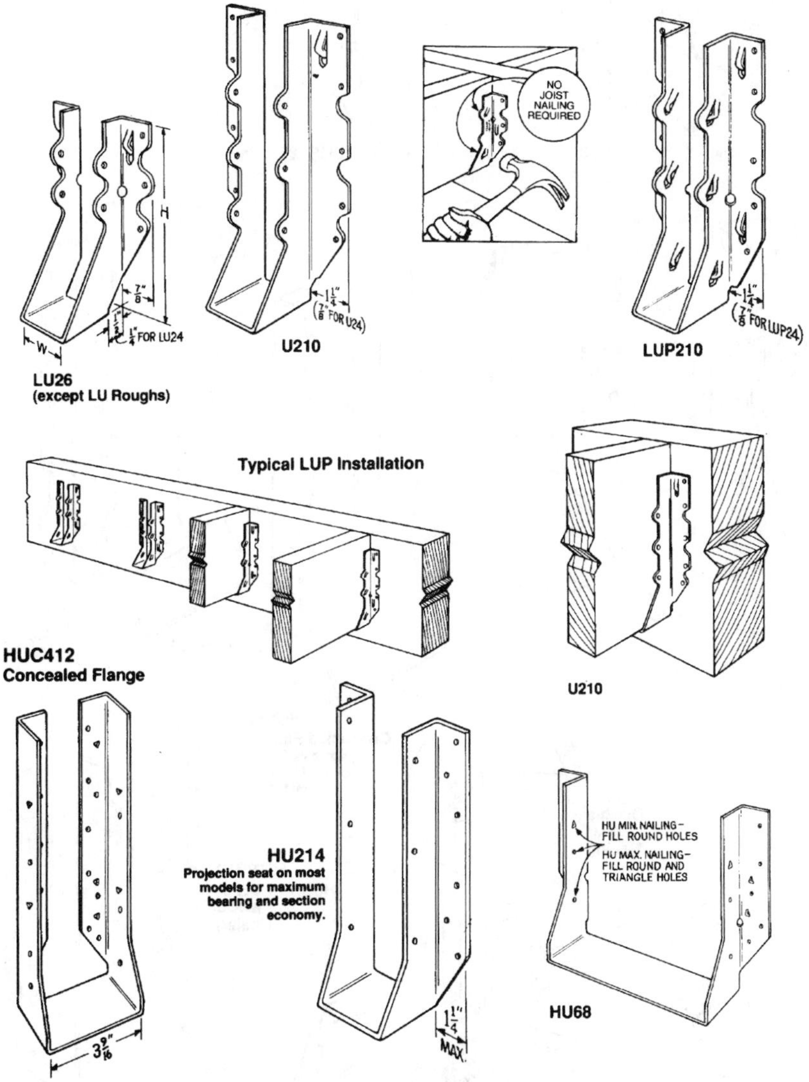

H
7/8"
1/2"
1/4" FOR LU24
W
LU26
(except LU Roughs)
1 1/4"
(7/8" FOR U24)
U210
NO JOIST NAILING REQUIRED
1 1/4"
(7/8" FOR LUP24)
LUP210
Typical LUP Installation
HUC412
Concealed Flange
U210
3 9/16"
HU214
Projection seat on most models for maximum bearing and section economy.
1 1/4"
MAX.
HU MIN. NAILING – FILL ROUND HOLES
HU MAX. NAILING – FILL ROUND AND TRIANGLE HOLES
HU68

3-18 *Various face mount hangers. Shown are standard joist hangers and double shear joist hangers.* Simpson Strong-Tie Company, Inc.

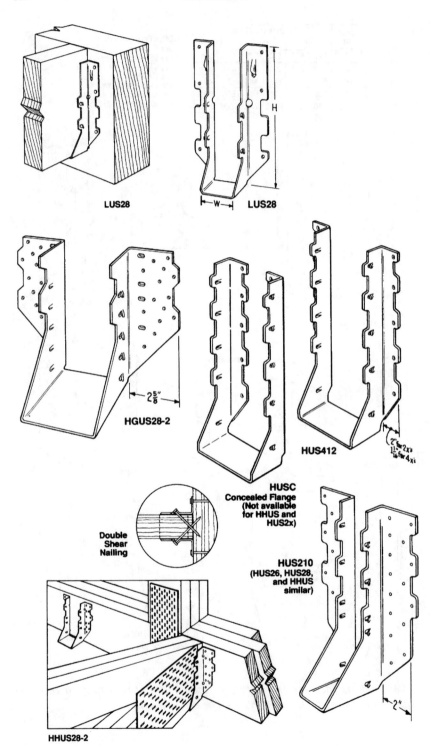

LUS28

LUS28

HGUS28-2

HUS412

HUSC
Concealed Flange
(Not available
for HHUS and
HUS2x)

Double
Shear
Nailing

HUS210
(HUS26, HUS28,
and HHUS
similar)

HHUS28-2

3-18 *Continued*

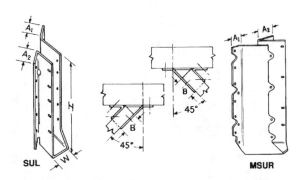

MSULC Available for
double 2x and 4x models only.

SUL

MSUR

MODEL NO.	JOIST SIZE	DIMENSIONS					FASTENERS[1]		DOWN AVG ULT	ALLOWABLE LOADS		
		W	H	B	A₁	A₂	HEADER	JOIST		UPLIFT[2] (133)	FLOOR[3] (100)	ROOF[3] (125)
SUR/L24	2×4	1⁹⁄₁₆	3⅛	2	1	1⅜	4-16d	4-10d×1½	2817	450	530	665
SUR/L26	2×6,8	1⁹⁄₁₆	5	2	1	1⅜	6-16d	6-10d×1½	4067	720	800	1000
SUR/L210	2×10,16	1⁹⁄₁₆	8⅛	2	1	1⅜	10-16d	10-10d×1½	8717	1200	1330	1660
SUR/L214	2×14,16	1⁹⁄₁₆	10	2	1	1⅜	12-16d	12-10d×1½	8717	1440	1595	1995
SUR/L26-2	(2) 2×6,8	3⅛	4¹⁵⁄₁₆	2⁷⁄₁₆	1¼	2³⁄₁₆	8-16d	4-16d×2½	4067	710	1065	1330
MSUR/L26-2	(2) 2×6,8	3⅛	4¹⁵⁄₁₆	2⁷⁄₁₆	1¼	2³⁄₁₆	8-N20AN	4-16d×2½	5283	715	1145	1430
SUR/L210-2	(2) 2×10,12	3⅛	8¹¹⁄₁₆	2⁷⁄₁₆	1¼	2³⁄₁₆	14-16d	6-16d×2½	7558	1065	1860	2330
MSUR/L210-2	(2) 2×10,12	3⅛	8¹¹⁄₁₆	2⁷⁄₁₆	1¼	2³⁄₁₆	14-N20AN	6-16d×2½	7500	1070	2000	2500
SUR/L214-2	(2) 2×14,16	3⅛	12¹¹⁄₁₆	2⁷⁄₁₆	1¼	2³⁄₁₆	18-16d	8-16d×2½	7833	1420	2395	2500
MSUR/L214-2	(2) 2×14,16	3⅛	12¹¹⁄₁₆	2⁷⁄₁₆	1¼	2³⁄₁₆	18-N20AN	8-16d×2½	15983	1430	2575	3220
SUR/L46	4×6,8	3⁹⁄₁₆	4¾	2⁷⁄₁₆	1	2³⁄₁₆	8-16d	4-16d	4067	710	1065	1330
MSUR/L46	4×6,8	3⁹⁄₁₆	4¾	2⁷⁄₁₆	1	2³⁄₁₆	8-N20AN	4-16d	5283	715	1145	1430
SUR/L410	4×10,12	3⁹⁄₁₆	8½	2⁷⁄₁₆	1	2³⁄₁₆	14-16d	6-16d	7558	1065	1860	2330
MSUR/L410	4×10,12	3⁹⁄₁₆	8½	2⁷⁄₁₆	1	2³⁄₁₆	14-N20AN	6-16d	7500	1070	2000	2500
SUR/L414	4×14,16	3⁹⁄₁₆	12½	2⁷⁄₁₆	1	2³⁄₁₆	18-16d	8-16d	7833	1420	2395	2500
MSUR/L414	4×14,16	3⁹⁄₁₆	12½	2⁷⁄₁₆	1	2³⁄₁₆	18-N20AN	8-16d	15983	1430	2575	3220

1. N20AN fasteners are furnished with the hangers; others are not.
2. Uplift loads have been increased by 33% for wind or earthquake loading with no further increase allowed; reduce for other load conditions as required by code.
3. Roof loads are 125% of floor loads unless limited by other criteria. Floor loads may be adjusted for other load durations according to the code, provided they do not exceed those in the roof column.

3-19 *Standardized and code-listed 45 degree skewed hangers make installing nails quick and easy.* Simpson Strong-Tie Company, Inc.

Deck fastening systems

It is not enough to choose the finest product for the decking surface if you intend to fasten through the tops of those expensive boards with screws or nails. Not only can the head of the fastener cause surface staining, depending on the fasteners you select, but water can seep into the wood surrounding the fasteners and cause the wood to rot.

Once the decking material is damaged by a fastener, its surface is no longer completely protected. One way to get around this and to leave the surface unmarred by fasteners, hammer dents, or unnecessary holes caused when a screw gun slips is to install a fastening system that eliminates the need for fastening through the top surface.

Table 3-1. Face Mount Hangers

How to use this table:

1. Select the joist size required.
2. Match the loads required with the allowable loads table.
3. Select the most cost-effective hanger using the Installed Cost Index (ICI). Hangers are listed by relative installed cost, from low to high. The "Lowest" hanger has the lowest installed cost in each Joist Size group.
4. The ICI gives comparative cost, and includes labor fastener and hanger costs. Material and labor charges may vary. **Do not use the ICI for job costing.**
5. Refer to Simpson's Installed Cost Guide for relative installed costs.

JOIST SIZE	MODEL NO.	GA	W	H	B	HEADER 10d	HEADER 16d	JOIST	DOWN AVG ULT	UPLIFT (133)	FLOOR (100) 10d	FLOOR (100) 16d	SNOW (115) 10d	SNOW (115) 16d	ROOF (125) 10d	ROOF (125) 16d	INSTALLED COST INDEX (ICI)
								SAWN LUMBER SIZES									
2x4	LUP24	18	1 9/16	3 1/8	1 1/2	4-10d	4-16d	2 PRONG	2817	—	445	530	510	610	555	665	Lowest
	LU24	20	1 9/16	3 1/8	1 1/2	4-10d	4-16d	2-10dx1 1/2	2333	245	445	530	510	610	555	665	+3 %
	LUS24	18	1 9/16	3 1/8	1 3/4	4-10d	—	2-10d	3850	470	640	—	735	—	800	—	+10 %
	U24	16	1 9/16	3 1/8	1 1/2	4-10d	4-16d	2-10dx1 1/2	4117	240	445	530	510	610	555	665	+52 %
	HU26	14	1 9/16	3 1/16	1 1/2	—	4-16d	2-10dx1 1/2	5270	240	—	535	—	615	—	670	+296 %
DBL 2x4	LUS24-2	18	3 1/8	3 1/8	2	—	4-16d	2-16d	5303	565	—	765	—	880	—	960	Lowest
	U24-2	16	3 1/8	3	2	4-10d	4-16d	2-10d	4117	295	445	530	510	610	555	665	+30 %
	HU24-2	14	3 1/8	3 1/16	2	—	4-16d	2-10d	5270	300	—	535	—	615	—	670	+161 %
2x6	LUS26	18	1 9/16	4 3/4	1 3/4	4-10d	—	4-10d	5167	935	835	—	960	—	1045	—	Lowest
	LUP26	18	1 9/16	4 3/4	2	6-10d	6-16d	4 PRONG	3937	—	665	800	765	920	830	1000	+0 %
	LU26	20	1 9/16	4 3/4	1 1/2	6-10d	6-16d	4-10dx1 1/2	3217	490	665	800	765	920	830	1000	+8 %
	U26	16	1 9/16	4 3/4	2	6-10d	6-16d	4-10dx1 1/2	4950	480	665	800	765	920	830	1000	+31 %
	HU26	14	1 9/16	3 1/16	2	—	4-16d	2-10dx1 1/2	5270	240	—	535	—	615	—	670	+164 %
	HUS26	16	1 5/8	5 1/8	3	—	14-16d	6-16d	10000	1550	—	2565	—	2950	—	3205	+249 %
DBL 2x6	LUS26-2	18	3 1/8	4 7/8	2	—	4-16d	4-16d	6076	1140	—	1000	—	1150	—	1250	Lowest
	U26-2	16	3 1/8	5	2	8-10d	8-16d	4-10d	7033	590	890	1065	1020	1225	1110	1330	+42 %
	HUS26-2	14	3 1/8	5 3/16	2	—	8-16d	4-16d	8033	1080	—	1005	—	1155	—	1255	+139 %
	HU26-2 MIN	14	3 1/8	5 3/8	2	—	8-16d	4-10d	9474	605	—	1070	—	1235	—	1340	+185 %
	HU26-2 MAX	14	3 1/8	5 3/8	2	—	12-16d	6-10d	11383	905	—	1610	—	1850	—	2010	+203 %
TPL 2x6	LUS26-3	18	4 5/8	4 1/8	2	4-10d	4-16d	4-16d	6433	1140	1000	—	1150	—	1250	—	*
	U26-3	16	4 5/8	4 1/4	2	8-10d	8-16d	2-10d	7033	295	890	1065	1020	1225	1110	1330	*
	HU26-3 MIN	14	4 11/16	5 1/2	2	—	8-16d	4-10d	9474	605	—	1070	—	1235	—	1340	*
	HU26-3 MAX	14	4 11/16	5 1/2	2	—	12-16d	6-10d	11383	905	—	1610	—	1850	—	2010	*
	LUS26	18	1 9/16	4 3/4	1 3/4	4-10d	—	4-10d	5167	935	835	—	960	—	1045	—	Lowest
	LUP26	18	1 9/16	4 3/4	2	6-10d	6-16d	4 PRONG	3937	—	665	800	765	920	830	1000	+0 %
	LU26	20	1 9/16	4 3/4	1 1/2	6-10d	6-16d	4-10dx1 1/2	3217	490	665	800	765	920	830	1000	+8 %
	LUS28	18	1 9/16	6 5/8	1 3/4	—	—	4-10d	6067	940	1015	—	1170	—	1270	—	+27 %

Group	Model																
2x8	LUP28	18	1 9/16	6 5/8	2	8-10d	8-16d	6 PRONG	6167	—	890	1065	1020	1225	1110	1330	+29%
	U26	16	1 9/16	4 3/4	2	6-10d	6-16d	4-10dx1½	4950	480	665	800	765	920	830	1000	+31%
	LU28	20	1 9/16	6 3/8	1½	8-10d	8-16d	6-10dx1½	4017	735	890	1065	1020	1225	1110	1300	+38%
	HU28	14	1 9/16	5 1/4	2	—	6-16d	4-10dx1½	6683	480	—	805	—	925	—	1005	+229%
	HUS26	16	1 5/8	5 1/8	3	—	14-16d	6-16d	10000	1550	—	2565	—	2950	—	3205	+249%
	HUS28	16	1 5/8	7	3	—	22-16d	8-16d	13167	2000	—	3585	—	3700	—	3775	+375%
	LUS26-2	18	3 1/8	4 7/8	2	—	4-16d	4-16d	6076	1140	—	1000	—	1150	—	1250	Lowest
	LUS28-2	18	3 1/8	7	2	—	6-16d	4-16d	7750	1075	—	1265	—	1455	—	1585	+17%
	U26-2	16	3 1/8	5	2	8-10d	8-16d	4-10d	7033	590	890	1065	1020	1225	1110	1330	+42%
DBL 2x8	HUS28-2	14	3 1/8	7 3/16	2	—	6-16d	6-16d	11190	1550	—	1505	—	1730	—	1885	+157%
	HU28-2 MIN	14	3 1/8	7	2	—	10-16d	4-10d	11383	605	—	1340	—	1540	—	1675	+237%
	HU28-2 MAX	14	3 1/8	7	2	—	14-16d	6-10d	14566	905	—	1875	—	2155	—	2345	+255%
TPL 2x8	LUS28-3	18	4 5/8	6 1/4	2	—	6-16d	4-16d	7500	1140	—	1265	—	1455	—	1585	*
	U26-3	16	4 5/8	4 1/4	2	8-10d	8-16d	2-10d	7033	295	890	1065	1020	1225	1110	1330	*
2x10	LUS28	18	1 9/16	6 5/8	1¾	6-10d	—	4-10d	6067	940	1015	—	1170	—	1270	—	Lowest
	LUP28	18	1 9/16	6 5/8	2	8-10d	8-16d	6 PRONG	6167	—	890	1065	1020	1225	1110	1330	+1%
	LU28	20	1 9/16	6 3/8	1½	8-10d	8-16d	6-10dx1½	4017	735	890	1065	1020	1225	1110	1300	+8%
	LUS210	18	1 9/16	7 13/16	1¾	8-10d	—	4-10d	7750	935	1280	—	1470	—	1600	—	+12%
	LUP210	18	1 9/16	7 13/16	2	—	10-16d	6 PRONG	6533	—	—	1330	—	1530	—	1660	+15%
	LU210	20	1 9/16	7 13/16	1½	10-10d	10-16d	6-10dx1½	6250	735	1110	1330	1275	1530	1390	1660	+22%
	U210	16	1 9/16	7 13/16	2	10-10d	10-16d	6-10dx1½	5583	720	1110	1330	1275	1530	1390	1660	+54%
	HU210	14	1 5/8	7 7/8	2	10-10d	8-16d	4-10dx1½	9474	480	1110	1070	1275	1235	1390	1340	+203%
	HUS210	16	3 1/8	9	3	—	30-16d	10-16d	18833	2845	—	3775	—	3920	—	4020	+377%
DBL 2x10	LUS28-2	18	3 1/8	7	2	—	6-16d	4-16d	7750	1075	—	1265	—	1455	—	1585	Lowest
	LUS210-2	18	3 1/8	9	2	—	8-16d	6-16d	10906	1550	—	1765	—	2030	—	2210	+20%
	U210-2	16	3 1/8	8 1/2	2	—	14-16d	6-10d	11000	890	1555	1860	1785	2140	1940	2330	+58%
	HUS210-2	14	3 1/8	9 3/16	2	14-10d	8-16d	8-16d	14550	2160	—	2010	—	2310	—	2510	+143%
	HU210-2 MIN	14	3 1/8	8 13/16	2	—	14-16d	6-10d	14566	905	—	1875	—	2155	—	2345	+251%
	HU210-2 MAX	14	3 1/8	8 13/16	2	—	18-16d	10-10d	15166	1505	—	2410	—	2775	—	3015	+271%
TPL 2x10	LUS28-3	18	4 5/8	6 1/4	2	—	6-16d	4-16d	7500	1140	—	1265	—	1455	—	1585	*
	LUS210-3	18	4 5/8	8 9/16	2	—	8-16d	6-16d	7500	1710	—	1765	—	2030	—	2210	*

Table 3-1. Continued

SAWN LUMBER SIZES

JOIST SIZE	MODEL NO.	GA	W	H	B	HEADER 10d	HEADER 16d	JOIST	DOWN AVG ULT	UPLIFT (133)	FLOOR (100) 10d	FLOOR (100) 16d	SNOW (115) 10d	SNOW (115) 16d	ROOF (125) 10d	ROOF (125) 16d	INSTALLED COST INDEX (ICI)
TPL 2x10	U210-3	16	4⁵⁄₈	7³⁄₄	2	14-10d	14-16d	6-10d	11000	890	1555	1860	1785	2140	1940	2330	*
	HU210-3 MIN	14	4¹¹⁄₁₆	8⁹⁄₁₆	2	—	14-16d	6-10d	14566	905	—	1875	—	2155	—	2345	*
	HU210-3 MAX	14	4¹¹⁄₁₆	8⁹⁄₁₆	2	—	18-16d	10-10d	15166	1505	—	2410	—	2775	—	3015	*
2x12	LUS210	18	1⁹⁄₁₆	7¹³⁄₁₆	1³⁄₄	8-10d	—	4-10d	7750	935	1280	—	1470	—	1600	—	Lowest
	LUP210	18	1⁹⁄₁₆	7¹³⁄₁₆	2	10-10d	10-16d	6 PRONG	6533	—	1110	1330	1275	1530	1390	1660	+3 %
	LU210	20	1⁹⁄₁₆	7¹³⁄₁₆	1¹⁄₂	10-10d	10-16d	6-10dx1½	6250	735	1110	1330	1275	1530	1390	1660	+9 %
	U210	16	1⁹⁄₁₆	7¹³⁄₁₆	2	10-10d	10-16d	6-10dx1½	5583	720	1110	1330	1275	1530	1390	1660	+38 %
	HU212	14	1⁹⁄₁₆	9	2	—	10-16d	6-10dx1½	11383	720	—	1340	—	1540	—	1675	+212 %
	HU210	16	1⁵⁄₈	9	3	—	30-16d	10-16d	18833	2845	—	3775	—	3920	—	4020	+326 %
DBL 2x12	LUS210-2	18	3¹⁄₈	9	2	—	8-16d	6-16d	10906	1550	—	1765	—	2030	—	2210	Lowest
	LUS214-2	18	3¹⁄₈	10¹⁵⁄₁₆	2	—	10-16d	6-10d	12750	1550	—	2030	—	2335	—	2540	+16 %
	U210-2	16	3¹⁄₈	8¹⁄₂	2	14-10d	14-16d	6-10d	11000	890	1555	1860	1785	2140	1940	2330	+32 %
	HUS210-2	14	3¹⁄₈	9³⁄₁₆	2	—	8-16d	8-16d	14550	2160	—	2010	—	2310	—	2510	+102 %
	HUS212-2	14	3¹⁄₈	10³⁄₄	2	—	10-16d	10-16d	18033	2700	—	2510	—	2885	—	3140	+136 %
	HU212-2 MIN	14	3¹⁄₈	10⁹⁄₁₆	2	—	16-16d	6-10d	14316	905	—	2145	—	2465	—	2680	+265 %
	HU212-2 MAX	14	3¹⁄₈	10⁹⁄₁₆	2	—	22-16d	10-10d	15933	1505	—	2950	—	3390	—	3685	+287 %
TPL 2x12	LUS28-3	18	4⁵⁄₈	6¹⁄₄	2	—	6-16d	4-16d	7500	1140	—	1265	—	1455	—	1585	*
	U210-3	16	4⁵⁄₈	7³⁄₄	1³⁄₄	14-10d	14-16d	6-10d	11000	890	1555	1860	1785	2140	1940	2330	*
2x14	LUS210	18	1⁹⁄₁₆	7¹³⁄₁₆	1³⁄₄	8-10d	—	4-10d	7750	935	1280	—	1470	—	1600	—	Lowest
	LUP210	18	1⁹⁄₁₆	7¹³⁄₁₆	1³⁄₄	10-10d	10-16d	6 PRONG	6533	—	1110	1330	1275	1530	1390	1660	+3 %
	LU210	20	1⁹⁄₁₆	7¹³⁄₁₆	1¹⁄₂	10-10d	10-16d	6-10dx1½	6250	735	1110	1330	1275	1530	1390	1660	+9 %
	U210	16	1⁹⁄₁₆	7¹³⁄₁₆	2	10-10d	10-16d	6-10dx1½	5583	720	1110	1330	1275	1530	1390	1660	+38 %
	U214	16	1⁹⁄₁₆	10	2	12-10d	12-16d	8-10dx1½	8335	960	1330	1595	1530	1835	1665	1995	+86 %
	HU214	14	1⁹⁄₁₆	10¹⁄₈	2	—	12-16d	6-10dx1½	11383	720	—	1610	—	1850	—	2010	+300 %
DBL 2x14	LUS214-2	18	3¹⁄₈	10¹⁵⁄₁₆	2	—	10-16d	6-16d	12750	1550	—	2030	—	2335	—	2540	Lowest
	U210-2	16	3¹⁄₈	8¹⁄₂	2	14-10d	14-16d	6-10d	11000	890	1555	1860	1785	2140	1940	2330	+14 %
	HUS212-2	14	3¹⁄₈	10³⁄₄	2	—	16-16d	6-10d	18033	2700	—	2510	—	2885	—	3140	+104 %
	HU212-2 MIN	14	3¹⁄₈	10⁹⁄₁₆	2	—	16-16d	6-10d	14316	905	—	2145	—	2465	—	2680	+222 %
	HU212-2 MAX	14	3¹⁄₈	10⁹⁄₁₆	2	—	22-16d	10-10d	15933	1505	—	2950	—	3390	—	3685	+234 %
	HU214-2 MIN	14	3¹⁄₈	12¹³⁄₁₆	2	—	18-16d	8-10d	15166	1205	—	2410	—	2775	—	3015	+253 %
	HU214-2 MAX	14	3¹⁄₈	12¹³⁄₁₆	2	—	24-16d	12-10d	18196	1810	—	3215	—	3700	—	4020	+271 %

TPL 2x14	U210-3	16	4⅝	7¾	2	14-10d	14-16d	6-10d	11000	890	1555	1860	1785	2140	1940	2330	•
2x16	U214	16	1⁹⁄₁₆	10	2	12-10d	12-16d	8-10d×1½	8335	960	1330	1595	1530	1835	1665	1995	Lowest
	HU214	14	1⁹⁄₁₆	10⅛	2	—	12-16d	6-10d×1½	11383	720	—	1610	—	1850	—	2010	+115%
DBL 2x16	HUS212-2	14	3⅛	10¾	2	—	10-16d	10-16d	18033	2700	—	2510	—	2885	—	3140	Lowest
	HU216-2 MIN	14	3⅛	13⅞	2	—	20-16d	8-10d	15933	1205	—	2680	—	3080	—	3350	+96%
	HU216-2 MAX	14	3⅛	13⅞	2	—	26-16d	12-10d	18196	1810	—	3485	—	4005	—	4355	+105%
3x4	U34	16	2⁹⁄₁₆	3⅜	2	4-10d	4-16d	2-10d×1½	4117	240	445	530	510	610	555	665	•
	HU34	14	2⁹⁄₁₆	3⅜	2	—	4-16d	2-10d×1½	5270	240	—	535	—	615	—	670	•
3x6	U36	16	2⁹⁄₁₆	5⅜	2	8-10d	8-16d	4-10d×1½	7033	480	890	1065	1020	1225	1110	1330	•
	HU36	14	2⁹⁄₁₆	5⅜	2	—	8-16d	4-10d×1½	9474	480	—	1070	—	1235	—	1340	•
3x8	U36	16	2⁹⁄₁₆	5⅜	2	8-10d	8-16d	4-10d×1½	7033	480	890	1065	1020	1225	1110	1330	•
	HU38	14	2⁹⁄₁₆	7⅛	2	—	10-16d	4-10d×1½	11383	480	1555	1340	—	1235	—	1675	•
3x10	U310	16	2⁹⁄₁₆	7⅞	2	14-10d	14-16d	6-10d×1½	11000	720	1555	1860	1785	2140	1940	2330	•
	HU310	14	2⁹⁄₁₆	8⅞	2	—	14-16d	6-10d×1½	14566	720	—	1875	—	2155	—	2345	•
3x10	U310	16	2⁹⁄₁₆	8⅞	2	14-10d	14-16d	6-10d×1½	11000	720	1555	1860	1785	2140	1940	2330	•
3x12	HU312	14	2⁹⁄₁₆	10⅝	2	—	16-16d	6-10d×1½	14316	720	—	2145	—	2465	—	2680	•
3x14	U314	16	2⁹⁄₁₆	10½	2	16-10d	16-16d	6-10d×1½	11000	720	1775	2130	2040	2445	2220	2660	•
	HU314	14	2⁹⁄₁₆	12⅜	2	—	18-16d	8-10d×1½	15166	960	—	2410	—	2775	—	3015	•
3x16	U314	16	2⁹⁄₁₆	10½	2	16-10d	16-16d	6-10d×1½	11000	720	1775	2130	2040	2445	2220	2660	•
	HU316	14	2⁹⁄₁₆	14⅛	2	—	20-16d	8-10d×1½	15933	960	—	2680	—	3080	—	3350	•
4x4	LUS44	18	3⁹⁄₁₆	3	2	—	4-16d	2-16d	5303	540	445	765	510	880	555	960	Lowest
	U44	16	3⁹⁄₁₆	2⅞	2	4-10d	4-16d	2-10d	4117	295	—	530	—	610	—	665	+12%
	HU44	14	3⁹⁄₁₆	2⅞	2	—	4-16d	2-10d	5270	300	—	535	—	615	—	670	+141%
4x6	LUS46	18	3⁹⁄₁₆	4¾	2	—	4-16d	4-16d	6076	1075	—	1000	—	1150	—	1250	Lowest
	U46	16	3⁹⁄₁₆	4⅞	2	8-10d	8-16d	4-10d	7033	590	890	1065	1020	1225	1110	1330	+24%
	HUS46	14	3⁹⁄₁₆	5	2	—	4-16d	4-16d	8033	1080	—	1005	—	1155	—	1255	+139%
	HU46 MIN	14	3⁹⁄₁₆	5³⁄₁₆	2	—	8-16d	4-10d	9474	605	—	1070	—	1235	—	1340	+163%
	HU46 MAX	14	3⁹⁄₁₆	5³⁄₁₆	2	—	12-16d	6-10d	11383	905	—	1610	—	1850	—	2010	+182%

Table 3-1. Continued

JOIST SIZE	MODEL NO.	GA	W	H	B	HEADER 10d	HEADER 16d	JOIST	DOWN AVG ULT	UPLIFT (133)	FLOOR (100) 10d	FLOOR (100) 16d	SNOW (115) 10d	SNOW (115) 16d	ROOF (125) 10d	ROOF (125) 16d	INSTALLED COST INDEX (ICI)
								SAWN LUMBER SIZES									
4×8	LUS46	18	3-9/16	4-3/4	2	–	4-16d	4-16d	6076	1075	–	1000	–	1150	–	1250	Lowest
	U46	16	3-9/16	4-7/8	2	8-10d	8-16d	4-10d	7033	590	890	1065	1020	1225	1110	1330	+24 %
	LUS48	18	3-9/16	6-3/4	2	–	6-16d	4-16d	7750	1075	–	1265	–	1455	–	1585	+28 %
	HUS48	14	3-9/16	7	2	–	6-16d	6-16d	11190	1550	–	1505	–	1730	–	1885	+185 %
	HU48 MIN	14	3-9/16	6-13/16	2	–	10-16d	4-10d	11383	605	–	1340	–	1540	–	1675	+217 %
	HU48 MAX	14	3-9/16	6-13/16	2	–	14-16d	6-10d	14566	905	–	1875	–	2155	–	2345	+236 %
4×10	LUS48	18	3-9/16	6-3/4	2	–	6-16d	4-16d	7750	1075	–	1265	–	1455	–	1585	Lowest
	LUS410	18	3-9/16	8-3/4	2	–	8-16d	6-16d	10906	1550	–	1765	–	2030	–	2210	+15 %
	U410	16	3-9/16	8-3/8	2	14-10d	14-16d	6-10d	11000	890	1555	1860	1785	2140	1940	2330	+48 %
	HUS410	14	3-9/16	9	2	–	8-16d	8-16d	14550	2160	–	2010	–	2310	–	2510	+155 %
	HU410 MIN	14	3-9/16	8-5/8	2	–	14-16d	6-10d	14566	905	–	1875	–	2155	–	2345	+173 %
	HU410 MAX	14	3-9/16	8-5/8	2	–	18-16d	10-10d	15166	1505	–	2410	–	2775	–	3015	+193 %
4×12	LUS410	18	3-9/16	8-3/4	2	–	8-16d	6-16d	10906	1550	–	1765	–	2030	–	2210	Lowest
	U410	16	3-9/16	8-3/8	2	14-10d	14-16d	6-10d	11000	890	1555	1860	1785	2140	1940	2330	+28 %
	LUS414	18	3-9/16	10-3/4	2	–	10-16d	6-16d	12750	1550	–	2030	–	2335	–	2540	+40 %
	HUS410	14	3-9/16	9	2	–	8-16d	8-16d	14550	2160	–	2010	–	2310	–	2510	+121 %
	HUS412	14	3-9/16	10-9/16	2	–	10-16d	10-16d	18033	2700	–	2510	–	2885	–	3140	+135 %
	HU412 MIN	14	3-9/16	10-5/16	2	–	16-16d	6-10d	14316	905	–	2145	–	2465	–	2680	+210 %
	HU412 MAX	14	3-9/16	10-5/16	2	–	22-16d	10-10d	15933	1505	–	2950	–	3390	–	3685	+231 %
4×14	LUS410	18	3-9/16	8-3/4	2	–	8-16d	6-16d	10906	1550	–	1765	–	2030	–	2210	Lowest
	LUS414	18	3-9/16	10-3/4	2	–	10-16d	6-16d	12750	1550	–	2030	–	2335	–	2540	+40 %
	U414	16	3-9/16	10	2	16-10d	16-16d	6-10d	11000	890	1775	2130	2040	2445	2220	2660	+71 %
	HUS412	14	3-9/16	10-9/16	2	–	10-16d	10-16d	18033	2700	–	2510	–	2885	–	3140	+135 %
	HU414 MIN	14	3-9/16	12-5/8	2	–	18-16d	8-10d	15166	1205	–	2410	–	2775	–	3015	+247 %
	HU414 MAX	14	3-9/16	12-5/8	2	–	24-16d	12-10d	18196	1810	–	3215	–	3700	–	4020	+268 %
4×16	U414	16	3-9/16	10	2	16-10d	16-16d	6-10d	11000	890	1775	2130	2040	2445	2220	2660	Lowest
	HUS412	14	3-9/16	10-9/16	2	–	10-16d	10-16d	18033	2700	–	2510	–	2885	–	3140	+37 %
	HU416 MIN	14	3-9/16	13-5/8	2	–	20-16d	8-10d	15933	1205	–	2680	–	3080	–	3350	+137 %
	HU416 MAX	14	3-9/16	13-5/8	2	–	26-16d	12-10d	18196	1810	–	3485	–	4005	–	4355	+149 %

6×6	U66	16	5 1/2	5	2	8-10d	8-16d	4-10d	7033	590	890	1065	1020	1225	1110	1330	*
	HU66 MIN	14	5 1/2	4 3/16	2	—	8-16d	4-16d	9474	715	—	1070	—	1235	—	1340	*
	HU66 MAX	14	5 1/2	4 3/16	2	—	12-16d	6-16d	11383	1070	—	1610	—	1850	—	2010	*
6×8	U66	16	5 1/2	5	2	8-10d	8-16d	4-10d	7033	590	890	1065	1020	1225	1110	1330	*
	HU68 MIN	14	5 1/2	5 13/16	2	—	10-16d	4-16d	11383	715	—	1340	—	1540	—	1675	*
	HU68 MAX	14	5 1/2	5 13/16	2	—	14-16d	6-16d	14566	1070	—	1875	—	2155	—	2345	*
6×10	U610	16	5 1/2	8 1/2	2	14-10d	14-16d	6-10d	11000	890	1555	1860	1785	2140	1940	2330	*
	HU610 MIN	14	5 1/2	7 5/8	2	—	14-16d	6-16d	14566	1070	—	1875	—	2155	—	2345	*
	HU610 MAX	14	5 1/2	7 5/8	2	—	18-16d	8-16d	15166	1430	—	2410	—	2775	—	3015	*
6×12	HU612 MIN	14	5 1/2	9 3/8	2	—	16-16d	6-16d	14316	1070	—	2145	—	2465	—	2680	*
	HU612 MAX	14	5 1/2	9 3/8	2	—	22-16d	8-16d	15933	1430	—	2950	—	3390	—	3685	*
6×14	HU614 MIN	14	5 1/2	11 5/8	2	—	18-16d	8-16d	15166	1430	—	2410	—	2775	—	3015	*
	HU614 MAX	14	5 1/2	11 5/8	2	—	24-16d	12-16d	18196	2145	—	3215	—	3700	—	4020	*
6×16	HU616 MIN	14	5 1/2	12 11/16	2	—	20-16d	8-16d	15933	1430	—	2680	—	3080	—	3350	*
	HU616 MAX	14	5 1/2	12 11/16	2	—	26-16d	12-16d	18196	2145	—	3485	—	4005	—	4355	*
8×8	HU88 MIN	14	7 1/2	6 5/8	2	—	10-16d	4-16d	11383	715	—	1340	—	1540	—	1675	*
	HU88 MAX	14	7 1/2	6 5/8	2	—	14-16d	6-16d	14566	1070	—	1875	—	2155	—	2345	*
8×10	HU810 MIN	14	7 1/2	8 3/8	2	—	14-16d	6-16d	14566	1070	—	1875	—	2155	—	2345	*
	HU810 MAX	14	7 1/2	8 3/8	2	—	18-16d	8-16d	15166	1430	—	2410	—	2775	—	3015	*
8×12	HU812 MIN	14	7 1/2	10 1/8	2	—	16-16d	6-16d	14316	1070	—	2145	—	2465	—	2680	*
	HU812 MAX	14	7 1/2	10 1/8	2	—	22-16d	8-16d	15933	1430	—	2950	—	3390	—	3685	*
8×14	HU814 MIN	14	7 1/2	11 7/8	2	—	18-16d	8-16d	15166	1430	—	2410	—	2775	—	3015	*
	HU814 MAX	14	7 1/2	11 7/8	2	—	24-16d	12-16d	18196	2145	—	3215	—	3700	—	4020	*
8×16	HU816 MIN	14	7 1/2	13 5/8	2	—	20-16d	8-16d	15933	1430	—	2680	—	3080	—	3350	*
	HU816 MAX	14	7 1/2	13 5/8	2	—	26-16d	12-16d	18196	2145	—	3485	—	4005	—	4355	*
PLATED TRUSS SIZES																	
1 PLY	HUS26	16	1 5/8	5 1/8	3	—	14-16d	6-16d	10000	1550	—	2565	—	2950	—	3205	*
	HUS28	16	1 5/8	7	3	—	22-16d	8-16d	13167	2000	—	3585	—	3700	—	3775	*
	HUS210	16	1 5/8	9	3	—	30-16d	10-16d	18833	2845	—	3775	—	3920	—	4020	*

Table 3-1. Continued

JOIST SIZE	MODEL NO.	GA	W	H	B	HEADER 10d	HEADER 16d	JOIST	DOWN AVG ULT	UPLIFT (133)	FLOOR (100) 10d	FLOOR (100) 16d	SNOW (115) 10d	SNOW (115) 16d	ROOF (125) 10d	ROOF (125) 16d	INSTLL COST INDEX (ICI)
								PLATED TRUSS SIZES									
2 PLY	HGUS26-2	12	3 7/16	4 1/2	4	—	20-16d	8-16d	14667	2255	—	3695	—	4250	—	4620	*
	HHUS26-2	14	3 7/16	5	3	—	14-16d	6-16d	14667	1065	—	2580	—	2965	—	3225	*
	HGUS28-2	12	3 7/16	6 1/2	4	—	36-16d	10-16d	25180	2820	—	6140	—	7060	—	7675	*
	HHUS28-2	14	3 7/16	6 7/8	3	—	22-16d	8-16d	19850	2000	—	3885	—	4465	—	4855	*
	HGUS210-2	12	3 7/16	8 1/2	4	—	46-16d	12-16d	28333	3385	—	7750	—	8665	—	8665	*
	HHUS210-2	14	3 7/16	8 7/8	3	—	30-16d	10-16d	22167	2855	—	5190	—	5900	—	5900	*
	HUS212-2	14	3 1/8	10 3/4	2	—	10-16d	10-16d	18033	2700	—	2510	—	2885	—	3140	*
3 PLY	HGUS26-3	12	5 1/8	4 1/2	4	—	20-16d	8-16d	25180	2255	—	3695	—	4250	—	4620	*
	HGUS28-3	12	5 1/8	6 3/4	4	—	36-16d	10-16d	25180	2820	—	6140	—	7060	—	7675	*
	HGUS210-3	12	5 1/8	8 3/4	4	—	46-16d	12-16d	28333	3385	—	7750	—	8665	—	8665	*
4×	HGUS46	12	3 5/8	4 7/16	4	—	20-16d	8-16d	25180	2255	—	3695	—	4250	—	4620	*
	HHUS46	14	3 5/8	5 1/8	3	—	14-16d	6-16d	14667	1065	—	2580	—	2965	—	3225	*
	HGUS48	12	3 5/8	6 7/16	4	—	36-16d	10-16d	25180	2650	—	6140	—	7060	—	7675	*
	HHUS48	14	3 5/8	7	3	—	22-16d	8-16d	19850	2000	—	3885	—	4465	—	4855	*
	HGUS410	12	3 5/8	8 7/16	4	—	46-16d	12-16d	28333	3385	—	7750	—	8665	—	8665	*
	HHUS410	14	3 5/8	9	3	—	30-16d	10-16d	22167	2855	—	5190	—	5900	—	5900	*
	HGUS412	12	3 5/8	10 7/16	4	—	56-16d	14-16d	35000	3945	—	9365	—	10400	—	10400	*
	HGUS414	12	3 5/8	12 7/16	4	—	66-16d	16-16d	35000	4510	—	10260	—	10640	—	10640	*
								GLULAM AND MANUFACTURED LUMBER SIZES (LVL, PSL)									
1 3/4 LAM	HUS1.81/10	16	1 13/16	8 7/8	3	—	30-16d	10-16d	18833	2845	—	4900	—	5045	—	5145	*
3 1/8 LAM	HU212-2 MIN	14	3 1/8	10 9/16	2	—	16-16d	6-10d	14316	905	—	2145	—	2465	—	2680	*
	HU212-2 MAX	14	3 1/8	10 9/16	2	—	22-16d	10-10d	15933	1505	—	2950	—	3390	—	3685	*
	HU216-2 MIN	14	3 1/8	13 7/8	2	—	20-16d	8-10d	15933	1205	—	2680	—	3080	—	3350	*
	HU216-2 MAX	14	3 1/8	13 7/8	2	—	26-16d	12-10d	18195	1810	—	3485	—	4005	—	4355	*
5 1/8 LAM	HU5.125/12	14	5 1/4	10 1/4	2	—	22-16d	8-16d	15933	1430	—	2950	—	3390	—	3685	*
	HU5.125/16	14	5 1/4	13 7/8	2	—	26-16d	12-16d	18196	2145	—	3485	—	4005	—	4355	*

PSL	HGUS2.75/10	12	$2\frac{3}{4}$	$8\frac{15}{16}$	4	—	46-16d	12-16d	28333	3385	—	7750	—	8135	—	8135	*
	HGUS2.75/12	12	$2\frac{3}{4}$	$10\frac{15}{16}$	4	—	56-16d	14-16d	35000	3945	—	8040	—	8370	—	8370	*
	HGUS2.75/14	12	$2\frac{3}{4}$	$12\frac{15}{16}$	4	—	66-16d	16-16d	35000	4510	—	8230	—	8610	—	8610	*
PSL or LVL	HGUS5.50/10	12	$5\frac{1}{2}$	$8\frac{7}{16}$	4	—	46-16d	12-16d	28333	3385	—	7750	—	8665	—	8665	*
	HGUS5.50/12	12	$5\frac{1}{2}$	$10\frac{7}{16}$	4	—	56-16d	14-16d	35000	3665	—	9365	—	10770	—	11335	*
	HGUS5.50/14	12	$5\frac{1}{2}$	$12\frac{7}{16}$	4	—	66-16d	16-16d	35000	3665	—	10980	—	11335	—	11335	*
	HGUS7.25/10	12	$7\frac{1}{4}$	$8\frac{7}{16}$	4	—	46-16d	12-16d	29667	3385	—	7750	—	8915	—	9665	*
	HGUS7.25/12	12	$7\frac{1}{4}$	$10\frac{7}{16}$	4	—	56-16d	14-16d	29667	3945	—	9365	—	9665	—	9665	*
	HGUS7.25/14	12	$7\frac{1}{4}$	$12\frac{7}{16}$	4	—	66-16d	16-16d	29667	4510	—	9665	—	9665	—	9665	*
ROUGH LUMBER SIZES																	
2×4 (R)	LU24R	20	2	$2\frac{13}{16}$	$1\frac{1}{2}$	—	4-16d	2-10d×$1\frac{1}{2}$	2233	245	—	530	—	610	—	665	†
	U24R	16	2	$3\frac{5}{8}$	2	4-10d	4-16d	2-10d×$1\frac{1}{2}$	4117	240	445	530	510	610	555	665	†
2×6 (R)	LU26R	20	2	$4\frac{9}{16}$	$1\frac{1}{2}$	—	6-16d	4-10d×$1\frac{1}{2}$	5270	485	—	800	—	920	—	1000	†
	U26R	16	2	$5\frac{5}{8}$	2	8-10d	8-16d	4-10d×$1\frac{1}{2}$	7033	480	890	1065	1020	1225	1110	1330	†
2×8 (R)	LU28R	20	2	$6\frac{3}{8}$	$1\frac{1}{2}$	—	8-16d	6-10d×$1\frac{1}{2}$	5157	730	—	1065	—	1225	—	1330	†
	U26R	16	2	$5\frac{5}{8}$	2	8-10d	8-16d	4-10d×$1\frac{1}{2}$	7033	480	890	1065	1020	1225	1110	1330	†
2×10 (R)	LU210R	20	2	$7\frac{5}{16}$	2	—	10-16d	6-10d×$1\frac{1}{2}$	6250	730	—	1330	—	1530	—	1660	†
	U210R	16	2	$9\frac{1}{8}$	2	14-10d	14-16d	6-10d×$1\frac{1}{2}$	11000	720	1555	1860	1785	2140	1940	2330	†
2×12 (R)	U210R	16	2	$9\frac{1}{8}$	2	14-10d	14-16d	6-10d×$1\frac{1}{2}$	11000	720	1555	1860	1785	2140	1940	2330	†
2×14 (R)	U210R	16	2	$9\frac{1}{8}$	2	14-10d	14-16d	6-10d×$1\frac{1}{2}$	11000	720	1555	1860	1785	2140	1940	2330	†
4×4 (R)	U44R	16	4	$2\frac{5}{8}$	2	4-10d	4-16d	2-16d	4117	355	445	530	510	610	555	665	†
4×6 (R)	U46R	16	4	$4\frac{5}{8}$	2	8-10d	8-16d	4-16d	7033	710	890	1065	1020	1225	1110	1330	†
4×8 (R)	U46R	16	4	$4\frac{5}{8}$	2	8-10d	8-16d	4-16d	7033	710	890	1065	1020	1225	1110	1330	†
4×10 (R)	U410R	16	4	$8\frac{1}{8}$	2	14-10d	14-16d	6-16d	11000	1065	1555	1860	1785	2140	1940	2330	†
4×12 (R)	U410R	16	4	$8\frac{1}{8}$	2	14-10d	14-16d	6-16d	11000	1065	1555	1860	1785	2140	1940	2330	†
4×14 (R)	U410R	16	4	$8\frac{1}{8}$	2	14-10d	14-16d	6-16d	11000	1065	1555	1860	1785	2140	1940	2330	†
6×6 (R)	U66R	16	6	5	2	8-10d	8-16d	4-16d	7033	710	890	1065	1020	1225	1110	1330	†
6×8 (R)	U66R	16	6	5	2	8-10d	8-16d	4-16d	7033	710	890	1065	1020	1225	1110	1330	†
6×10 (R)	U610R	16	6	$8\frac{1}{2}$	2	14-10d	14-16d	6-16d	11000	1065	1555	1860	1785	2140	1940	2330	†
6×12 (R)	U610R	16	6	$8\frac{1}{2}$	2	14-10d	14-16d	6-16d	11000	1065	1555	1860	1785	2140	1940	2330	†
6×14 (R)	U610R	16	6	$8\frac{1}{2}$	2	14-10d	14-16d	6-16d	11000	1065	1555	1860	1785	2140	1940	2330	†

* Hangers do not have an Installed Cost Index as they are for specialty applications.

† Rough lumber sizes have similar installed costs to the corresponding models for Swan Lumber.

Keep in mind that these systems are not 100 percent "surface free." There are a few situations where you will have to fasten through the surface. In addition, the cost of the hardware is higher and so is the cost of labor; fastening systems require more installation time than conventional methods of installing decking boards. However, these systems also help to hold the entire structure together to minimize the movement of dry deck boards. The solid end result is worth the extra time and money, and your customers will appreciate the beauty of a clear decking surface.

A Deck-Tie Connector (Simpson) is set on the edge of a deck board by the locator prongs of the connector. It is then held in place with a 10d × 1½" galvanized hot-dip nail. The connector is placed within 2" of each joist but not on the joist itself. Slide the board forward and toenail the front edge. Then repeat the process for each board. Deck-Tie Connectors are designed for use with 2" × 4" or 2" × 6" (Fig. 3-20) decking boards.

A DeckMaster produces an impressive 22"-long galvanized or stainless steel bracket. It rests on the top and is fastened to the side of the joist. Decking boards are then fastened from the underside, with two screws per board set on an angle. The brackets are installed alternately to the opposite side of each joist from the previous course, which creates a very solid system.

Spray the tops of the brackets with flat black paint to prevent the metal from reflecting between the deck boards. If the deck is accessible from the underside (i.e., the customer is able to walk underneath the deck and view it from below), then spray the brackets prior to installation. If the deck will not be seen from the underside, spray the tops once the brackets are in place because any paint overspray on the joists will not be visible.

For the elegant look of a hardwood floor and a surface almost free of moisture penetration, you might want to investigate these systems (Figs. 3-21 and 3-22).

Additional products

Other deck-related products on the market to give the deck a finishing touch or incorporate privacy are worth your consideration. Still others can be built and presented to your customer as a small "thank you" token; for example, a flower box. These little touches can be a good selling tool, and you'll be surprised at how fast word spreads.

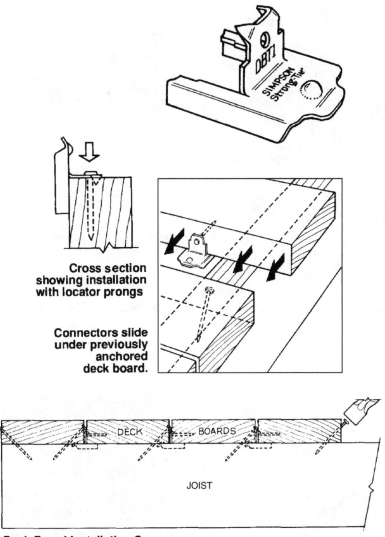

Cross section showing installation with locator prongs

Connectors slide under previously anchored deck board.

DECK BOARDS

JOIST

Deck Board Installation Sequence

3-20 *An 18-gauge, galvanized deckboard tie connector. Material: 18 gauge. Finish: Galvanized. Installation: Position the DBT1 with the locator prongs and install with a single 10d or 10d×1½" nail. As with any deck board fastening system, using dry lumber will minimize deck board movement after installation. Code Number: BOCA, ICBO, SBCCI No. NER-443.* Simpson Strong-Tie Company, Inc.

3-21 *Good example of DeckMaster bracket alternation on the joists. When blocking your framework, cut the top corners on an angle to allow the bracket to slide by.* C.R.S., Inc.

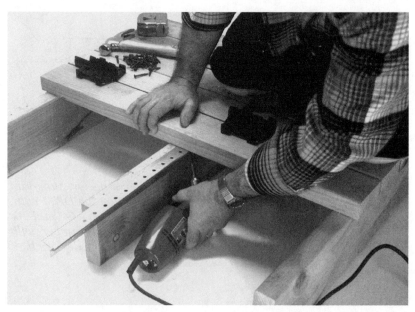

3-22 *You might find it easier to use an angle drill; positioning the drill so it is more comfortable to use will be a trial-and-error process.* C.R.S., Inc.

Privacy

LouveRail products put your imagination into overdrive. When you open the box, it's not immediately clear what the parts are for or how to use them. Basically, LouveRail consists of resin-injected molded parts that offer excellent resistance to moisture, solvents, and UV rays as well as high tensile strength. When you combine these parts with wood (from 4" to 10" wide), you create 180 degree vertical-position louvers that open and close in tandem for privacy, wind control, view, and/or sunshade. The main (LouverLinc) bar comes in 43", 53", and 68" lengths.

There are many possible uses for LouveRail's products: fencing; pool, spa, or hot tub privacy; storm and window shutters; deck railings; patio screening; a plant trellis are only some of the possibilities that come to mind. By adding a motorized LouveRail, you can mount the louvers horizontally as well. Then, with the touch of a button, you can activate louvers over skylights, in awnings mounted over patios or decks, or in a fence. The motorized application works with any Louve-Rail system you install, whether horizontal or vertical (Figs. 3-23 and 3-24).

3-23 *Consider LouveRail when privacy is important in your deck design.* LouveRail

3-24 *LouveRail lets in the sunlight when it's wanted.* LouveRail

Creative timbers

DesignWood Interlocking Timbers by Thompson Industries, Inc., offers many possibilities for adding finishing touches to your customer's deck. These timbers are pressure-treated Southern yellow pine and are available in 4" × 4" and 6" × 6" with lengths of 2', 4', 6', and 8' and have male and female ends that interlock with a joint pin.

Interlocking Timbers allow you to create decorative landscape bordering, planters, and retaining walls (Fig. 3-25). Other projects could include a planter/bench-top combination using their prebuilt 2' × 2' and 2' × 4' bench tops that work with the 4" × 4" timbers, a raised-bed garden, a sandbox/bench top and so forth.

Lattice

Many professionals use standard or architectural grade wood lattice for camouflaging the area underneath a deck or for other decorative purposes. Now vinyl lattice is available for this purpose.

Cross Industries, Inc. produces a durable PVC product they call CROSS VINYLattice. With matching vinyl accessories, it has the appearance of a fine wood product with a flat enamel finish when in-stalled (Fig. 3-26).

Some of the advantages this product offers over traditional wood include:

- Sturdy construction
- No splintering or splitting
- Cleans easily
- Sealed joints
- Standard or custom colors (no need to paint)
- Durable and resistant to both mildew and termites
- Available in different panel lengths, widths, and thicknesses
- Available in many patterns including custom-ordered patterns to fit your design

Vinyl lattice is certainly worth considering for any deck, porch, or utility enclosure. Write to request a sample of this product or any oth-ers discussed in this chapter. Samples increase your understanding of what these products are and how you can use them.

3-25 *The Interlocking Timbers system eliminates the need for cutting and boring holes, is flexible and quick, and allows you to work with the contours of any yard.* Thompson Industries, Inc.

3-26 *Cross VINYLattice creates a traditional looking job and requires less maintenance than wood lattice.*
Cross Industries, Inc.

4

Tools

The main ingredients for building a deck are materials and hardware, but these two items alone are not enough to create a dream deck— tools are the most important component in deck construction. It is essential to use the correct tools in order to complete a job efficiently and at the highest quality possible. Using the correct tools can also expedite the project, saving you time and money.

This chapter introduces you to some tools that save time and work well. Some might be tools you cannot afford, others you might already own, and some are specialty tools or new to the market. If it's your goal to be the best in the deck construction business, then it is important to use the type of tools described in this chapter.

Don't immediately purchase all the tools discussed in this chapter, but take your time and buy only those that you need the most now. You can gradually purchase other tools as the need arises. When purchasing tools, select only those that will work for you— tools that handle well and feel comfortable. In many cases, budget-priced tools are not the most economical, because they can wear out with heavy use. Instead, purchase tools that can become regular workhorses. Take good care of your tools and treat them with respect to maintain them in good working order.

Safety

When working around a customer's home, safety must be your top priority, especially if children are present. The job site should be kept clean at all times. Don't leave cut material scattered about; it's a hazard. Clean up as you work. If the debris includes lumber with nails or screws, remove those nails or screws or bend them over. Find an area in which to store debris until proper disposal is possible, and try to pick a site that expedites its pick-up.

If your particular job site features installed glass near the floor level in the area where you are working, put a piece of plywood in front of the glass. This protects the glass—and anyone who might be standing behind it—in case you slip with a pneumatic gun or a nail ricochets.

Tools themselves can be very dangerous, especially to children who may have been watching you work. Children are very curious about tools you touch and turn on and off. To prevent accidents, unplug your tools, lower blades, and remove extension cords if you will be away from the tool for any length of time. When you practice safety all the time, it soon becomes automatic. Your customers will appreciate your emphasis on safety as well.

First aid kit

Your own safety is as important as others. You have probably been on job sites by yourself when a particle flew into your eye or a sliver into your finger and there was no one around to help. Set yourself up with a first aid kit that can accommodate the unexpected. Purchase the best one you can or assemble one yourself. You never know when you, or someone else on the site, might need help.

One kit you may want to consider is the Workshop Safety & First Aid Kit by Miracle Point. This compact kit includes a dust mask, goggles, earplugs, gloves, a generous supply of basic first aid items, and an adjustable Magna-Point—a 5× magnifying glass attached to stainless steel tweezers in a resealable plastic pouch (Fig. 4-1). This product is great for removing slivers.

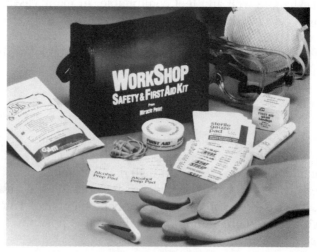

4-1 *No home, workshop, vehicle, or job site should be without a first aid kit.* Miracle Point Inc.

Eyewear

One area of particular concern should be your eyes. When you assemble your first aid kit, be sure to include eye wash. There are so many airborne particles on a job site that it is very easy for some to land in your eyes. Some of these particles are abrasive; do not rub your eye if something gets in it, or you could scratch the surface of the eyeball. Use the eye wash whenever your eye(s) feel irritated. I can't stress this enough—your eyes are important!

A good way to protect your eyes is to wear safety glasses. Choose glasses that are adjustable, comfortable to wear, and provide protection on the top and on the side areas around the eyes as well. Also look for coated lenses to help prevent fogging, static, and scratches and to help protect your eyes from UV radiation.

If you wear prescription glasses, choose eyewear that fits comfortably over your existing glasses. UVEX SAFETY, Inc., sells attractive and stylish protective eyewear to accommodate any particular need you might have (Fig. 4-2).

4-2
The 3000 Series eye protection. UVEX SAFETY, Inc.

Other safety concerns

Hearing protectors, gloves, good work boots (not athletic shoes), and appropriate clothing are also important. I firmly believe that hearing protection should be worn when working with power tools or even working near someone using power tools. However, hearing protection (plugs or muffs) can be hazardous if worn all the time because you cannot hear what is happening around the job site nor remain as alert as you should. When you are through using a power tool or have moved away from someone who is, remove your hearing protection, but don't forget to use it when the power tools fire up again.

Sawhorses

Sawhorses are important in any construction project. Unfortunately, many professionals do not take the time to shop for the very best sawhorses capable of handling the loads they are required to support. If you have replaced, rebuilt, or thrown away sawhorses over the course of your career or even spent time building them from scratch, you might want to consider some alternative products.

Once built, sawhorses are difficult to store. If you plan to purchase fully assembled sawhorses, keep in mind that sawhorses have three basic functions: rough cutting of material such as plywood, load bearing of stacked material, and finish cutting (e.g., cutting the end off a door). The following are a couple of products that work just right for the loads associated with deck projects.

A product I use for direct loads is StowAways, a folding support system by Iowa Manufacturing, Inc. StowAways are complete 16-gauge galvanized steel sawhorses that fold down to 3½" × 5½" × 36" (or 42"), so they are easy to hang on the shop wall or store in your utility truck toolbox. They come in two lengths, 36" and 42", and four heights, 18", 24", 30", and 36". These measurements include an optional 2× you can attach to the top of the cross member, which adds a final 1½". The legs are designed to angle out both sideways and endwise to increase stability as the load increases. Each sawhorse has a safe load capacity of 500 pounds (Fig. 4-3).

To add to the confusion surrounding the selection of sawhorses, there are now new breeds made of synthetic products. They come folded, stationary, and with features that apply to special cutting applications. One unusual but functional product is the Dura Bull Saw-

4-3 *The StowAway sawhorse.* Iowa Manufacturing, Inc.

Buddy by Creative Building Products (SOA). Constructed of HDPE in bright orange, SawBuddy works well for cutting beams, dimension lumber, logs, and pipe. The SawBuddy reminds me of old-fashioned sawbucks used for cutting logs. Any length 2" × 4" can be used as a crossbar and up to a 9½"-wide board securely fits into the X-shaped end pieces to provide sturdy scaffolding, a seat, or a ministep. Because the product is short, it supports one end of a laminated beam in place very well. This means that lifting the beam is kept to a minimum, and you can use just one SawBuddy to prop one end of the beam for cutting. The manufacturer claims this product is stable on uneven ground and has a load rating of 900 pounds per set (Fig. 4-4).

4-4 *The SawBuddy sawhorse is made of synthetic materials.* C.R.S., Inc.

Measuring and leveling tools

Tape measures are heavily used in construction. If you have experienced times when the tape measure blade could have been a hair thicker or extended a couple more feet, or you just didn't have an extra person to run the blade to the other end of the house, some new electronic measuring tools now on the market can help eliminate these frustrations. They work exceptionally well for quick measurements taken to prepare a bid. They can also impress a potential customer during your first appointment.

Sonin Inc. produces the Sonin Combo PRO, which fits on your belt or in your briefcase. The receiver unit runs on a 9-volt battery and has a narrow beam for measurements in tight areas. The beam is about 1' wide for each 10' segment measured, but this width can be reduced by using the accompanying target. It has a 99.5 percent accuracy, which is fine for rough measurements.

The receiver alone can measure 2' to 60'; with the target you can measure 3' up to 250'. This tool measures length, width, and height in feet, meters, decimal feet, and yards. It converts measurements to feet, meters, decimal feet, and yards; computes square footage (area) and cubic footage (volume); and adds and subtracts measurements. It even comes with a carrying case (Fig. 4-5).

4-5
Electronic measuring tools can prevent frustrating mistakes. Sonin Inc.

A good level is an essential to deck construction. Traditional bubble levels only indicate whether surfaces are level or plumb. Now there is a digital electronic level, the SmartLevel Pro Series, that can measure all the angles in a 360° range. These allow you to measure angles four different ways: in degrees, in percent slope, in inches of rise per foot of run, and (for those who insist) as a simulated bubble level. The sensor module runs on a 9-volt battery and can be used as a torpedo level or locked into the handholds of 24", 48", or 78" heavy aluminum rail (made of I-beam clad with ABS plastic). The module is sealed against dirt and water and has no shock-sensitive moving parts.

SmartLevel retains its decimal point accuracy because it can be recalibrated at the touch of a button even after it has been dropped. There is a hold button to "freeze" any angle reading, and it features two levels of accuracy (0.1° or 0.2°). This tool is useful in many phases of deck construction (Fig. 4-6).

An effective addition to your tool collection is an electronic water level. It works well when building decks and fences and for creating landscaping masterpieces. The ElectraLevel Pro by Zircon Corporation comes with a 50' hose and an impact-resistant carrying case. A nice feature of this unit is that it can be used in a "blind" leveling situation (e.g., around corners) without the help of a second person. When you

4-6 *This digital level has a 99.9 percent accuracy.* Macklanburg-Duncan

reach the desired level mark, a distinctive buzzer sounds. All you need to do is install the 9-volt battery and fill the hose with distilled water. Storage is easy: lock the clamps, roll the hose around the built-in carrying handle, and store the unit in its case (Fig. 4-7).

4-7 *To get a good feel for when the buzzer will sound, raise the tube slowly several times. When comfortable, make your mark.* Zircon Corporation

Helping hand tools

On any project, there comes a time when a second pair of hands would be helpful. The tools described in this section are especially helpful when working on a railing system when you need an extra pair of hands.

You can never have too many clamps. I use them when installing handrails to hold the rails in place while I make final adjustments, and they have many other uses. The Jorgensen E-Z HOLD II bar clamp by Adjustable Clamp Company is easy to use and can be operated with one hand. This tool is really two clamps in one: a bar clamp and a spreader clamp. The jaws contain a wide flat surface, and soft plastic pads fit over the jaws to protect the material from clamp marks (Fig. 4-8).

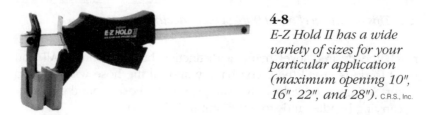

4-8
E-Z Hold II has a wide variety of sizes for your particular application (maximum opening 10", 16", 22", and 28"). C.R.S., Inc.

The Stair Square by Brotherwood LTD has an array of interesting uses, including the accurate placement of a handrail parallel with the skirtboard (stringer) or with the top and bottom tread at the proper height. This unusual-looking tool can help get the measurement and the angle up against one or two surfaces; for example, measuring a stair tread between two skirtboards. It's also useful for making repeated angle cuts like those required when applying siding to the gable end of a house. You can attach the two protractor blades together and use it for laying out roof rafters or stair stringers. Precision-machined of lightweight aircraft aluminum, the Stair Square helps with all these deck-related operations (Fig. 4-9).

There is no sense in straining muscles or sustaining a back injury when hydraulic jacks can help ease framing parts into place. Six-ton

4-9
Adding the level adapter can help you solve a number of problems. C.R.S., Inc.

hydraulic jacks are always useful to have on hand. Build yourself a plywood storage box to hold a pair of jacks along with the handles and hydraulic oil so they are easy to transport to job sites when you need them (Fig. 4-10).

4-10 *Hydraulic jacks save unnecessary strain.* C.R.S., Inc.

Specialized deck tools

The specialized tools described in this section not only increase production but also help you achieve a professional-looking job.

As you already know, decking boards expand and contract as the weather changes over seasons, so it is important that a deck breathe and drain properly. Probably the most frustrating part of installing decking boards is spacing them evenly and consistently. Deck-Mate by Johnson Level & Tool can help this process. Nails or wooden strips can certainly perform this same function, but they can be time wasters as they frequently fall through the cracks. Deck-Mate allows you to space the boards either $\frac{1}{8}$" or $\frac{3}{16}$" apart, and there is no need to worry about losing it through the cracks (Fig. 4-11). It also has notches for marking accurate pilot holes. When working at a joint (e.g., at the center of a

4-11 *Deck-Mate won't fall through the cracks.* C.R.S., Inc.

joist), drill pilot holes with a ⅛" bit at 10° to 15° angles in the ends of
the boards to prevent splitting, to allow the screws to properly penetrate the center of the joist. It is preferable, of course, to eliminate
joints by using full-length decking boards whenever possible.

I have discovered that two Deck-Mate tools are not enough. I use
about a dozen and have set up a carrying pack to hold these specialty
items, plus other tools, for use only when I work on decks. The Soft
Sider Tool Box by Portable Products, Inc., is useful for this purpose.
The bag has 17 exterior tool pockets, a zipper closure, and a shoul-
der strap as well as handles (Fig. 4-12).

If you are not able to get the straightest possible boards or
decking material, The Lumber Jack by T. C. Manufacturing can help
you install crowned or bowed decking material to correct align-
ment errors of up to 1¼". Place the tool on and over the joist, pull
the wire loop (spring) to engage the joist-grabbing steel jaws, pull
the rubber-gripped steel handle to force the decking board into
place, and while holding the handle, install the fasteners (Fig. 4-
13).

The unusual-looking Boardbender by Stanley Tools has many purposes. Like The Lumber Jack, it is used to straighten bowed boards, but
it employs a versatile U-shaped hook that swivels 180°, and is a good
tool for straightening decking boards installed on an angle to the joist.

4-12 *Don't forget to include knee pads in your own kit (also by Portable Products).* C.R.S., Inc.

4-13
Use The Lumber Jack to set bent or bowed material into place. C.R.S., Inc.

The Boardbender is also useful when you need to tweak twisted joists into place: Mount the hook over the joist and then either pull or push on the handle, depending on the hook's position and where you are standing (Fig. 4-14).

4-14
Whether you need to tweak a joist back in place or straighten a deck board, a tool like this can save energy, time, and materials. C.R.S., Inc.

Pneumatic tools

In the last few years I have realized how valuable pneumatic tools can be in the construction process. Of course, pneumatic tools save time, but even more importantly, they prevent the constant shock to my elbow every time I swing a hammer. If you do not already own pneumatic tools, I strongly recommend you make the transition, especially if you plan to go into this business full time. You will soon find how useful pneumatic tools are when constructing the framework.

Before you actually purchase pneumatic tools, you need to choose a compressor. I have been using the T-150ST "ULTRA" and a portable tank dolly, "Air-Pac," by Thomas Industries Inc. The dolly gives me two extra tanks of air (7 gallons total), two storage hangers for the hoses (normally one hanger is used for a tool), and a platform for the compressor (Fig. 4-15). ULTRA is oil-less, which means maintenance-free operation, and it is clearly built with the professional in mind. Replaceable filters and rebuild kits make on-site service easy, and the twin tanks supply a total of 4 gallons of air. Its low current draw won't blow standard 15-amp circuits (depending, of course, on what the customer has on the circuit). Thomas has an entire line of compressors from which to choose.

4-15
*Mobile compressors
such as this one are
easier to cart around
the job site.* C.R.S., Inc.

To prolong the life of your pneumatic tools, install a filter/lubricator on the compressor. This removes moisture and automatically lubricates the tools.

When considering a nailer, you have to choose a pneumatic gun that best fits your personal needs. I have found Hitachi's Model NR 834A nailer to be a comfortable pneumatic gun to use. It's great for heavy-duty construction, especially during the framing portion of a deck. It drives full-head plastic-collated nails at a speed of up to 3 nails per second. Nail sizes range from 2" to 3½" × .113/.120/.131 in smooth-, ring-, and screw-shank styles. The tool is well balanced and weighs only 7.9 pounds (Fig. 4-16).

If a pneumatic nailer is not within your budget, consider the Tradesman Pony air palm nailer by Power Tool Specialists, Inc. This

4-16
*Notice the adapter
(ACS) on the nose of the
Hitachi #NR83A for use
with The Boss metal
connectors; it speeds up
joist hanger
installation.* C.R.S., Inc.

tool weighs just under three pounds but can drive 6d to 50d nails and is custom fitted with a leather work glove for secure handling. It is useful when you are working in areas that are hard to reach or in corners too tight for a hammer, such as when you are installing joist hangers (Fig. 4-17).

4-17
Pneumatic nailers reduce the fatigue associated with swinging a hammer.
C.R.S., Inc.

Porta-tables and accessories

You might have the best miter or table saw in the world but still find yourself handicapped at the job site. Most of the tools used by construction professionals are portable, and a pair of sawhorses and a sheet of plywood generally serve as a work table to support them. However, the table can easily be knocked to the ground because it is not steady or the plywood slips off the sawhorse at one end. The tools in this section address such problems.

The MS-2000 by Trojan Manufacturing Inc. is a well-contained miter saw stand that is a pleasure to use. It works well with most of the miter saws, compound slide saws, and even abrasive chop saws that are currently on the market. The platform is designed to handle most saws but in some cases, where a saw has long rear platform/bench mounting stabilizers (such as the DeWalt DW 705), you might want to replace the medium-density board platform with one that is 4" or more in depth. This way you can push the saw farther back on the platform to maximize the width of the roller on the unit.

The stand is easy to set up. Extended at the first phase, the stand is 8'8" (4'4" on each side of the blade). Pulling out the extension wing yields another 4' total (2' on each side of the blade). If you replace the extension with the MS-2000X extension wing, you can add another 1' on either side of the blade for a maximum of 7'4" on a side. The extension provides both leg supports and another roller, which make it quite a workhorse (Figs. 4-18A and B).

If you choose not to use the MS-2000X extension wing on both sides, you can still get a roller stand. In fact, even extended to 7'4", a roller stand is a good idea, especially when you work with longer material. In my experience, some of the roller stands on the market are

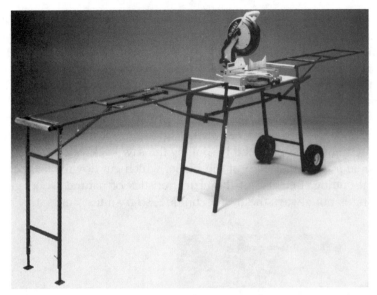

4-18A *Shown with the optional MS-2000X extension wing on the left side.* Trojan Manufacturing Inc.

4-18B
With its 10" pneumatic tires, the MS2000 is easy to move around the job site whether folded or fully set up. C.R.S., Inc.

not very stable and can fall over easily, but Trojan makes great roller stands that stay put and fold flat for easy transport and storage.

I have been using the RS-15 roller stand, which has a 15"-wide galvanized ball bearing roller. The base is made of 1¼" × 1¼" square steel tubing, and it can indeed hold weight. The roller height is adjustable from 24" to 40" and is centered over its extra-wide base for great stability. Two rollers are just right for any job site (Fig. 4-19).

If you build a lot of decks using ¾ material, you might find the next item intriguing. Install a 7¼" or 8¼" circular saw into the Trimtramp Professional 300 by Trimtramp Ltd. to create a precise sliding compound miter saw table. It has the ability to make crosscuts up to 19" and cuts boards up to 2" thick (Fig. 4-20). Cleaner cuts with less splintering can be obtained by pulling the saw backward through the material so the rear teeth of the blade, which cut downward, do the actual cutting. Because of the characteristics of natural wood grain, pulling is not always the best technique, so try a test cut first.

4-19
*The RS-12 has a 12" roller;
the base is made of 1"
square steel tubing.* Trojan
Manufacturing Inc.

4-20 *TrimTramp Pivot Extension Table (Model 301) coupled with the
Model 300 provides a sliding compound miter saw table that can rotate
from −45° to +45° quickly and easily. The extension wings stretch to a
total of 15 feet.* TrimTramp LTD.

Saws

Hand and power saws play a major part in assembling a deck. The best tool paired with the correct blade can help you fit and deliver tight joints. All you need to do is measure twice, check your mark, and cut.

Even when you own power saws, you will still use hand saws. I find it a pleasure to work with a good pull-stroke saw such as the Japanese-style saws; unlike their Western push-stroke counterparts, these are true pull-stroke saws.

One of a new breed of Japanese-style saws, the PULLSAW SharkSaw series by Takagi Tools has replaceable blades and weather-resistant, high-impact ABS plastic handles designed to fit many applications. The handle design provides a comfortable Western-style pistol-grip, and the saw delivers the same fine cut as a traditional Japanese saw. Takagi blades have a combination of crosscut and rip teeth and are made of high-quality spring carbon steel. The teeth are hardened by electric impulse so they'll last longer than conventional saws (Fig. 4-21). The 10-2312 (14 pt.) works well for 2" × 4" or 2" × 6" material as well as ABS or PVC plumbing pipe. The 10-2318 (8 pt.) is good for treated material and dimensional lumber such as 4" × 4", 4" × 8", and so on. If you're open to the pull-saw concept, try the 10-2312 first.

4-21 *The blades are uniquely designed so each tooth has three cutting edges to deliver a straighter, faster, cleaner cut.* Takagi Tools, Inc.

A few years ago, I would not have considered using a cordless saw because I didn't believe it could have the power of an electric saw. However, when I tried DeWalt's 14.4 volt DW 935 model, I was impressed when the 5⅜" thin-kerf blade cut through a 2" × 4" in a single pass. The blade, mounted on the left side of the motor, is the same as for a worm-drive saw. It makes a useful trim saw, or you can use it to cut a piece when you don't want to bother with extension cords (Fig. 4-22). It has been estimated that the DW 935 can cut over 75 2" × 4"s on a single charge.

For those who want power, there is nothing like a 13-amp worm-drive saw powered by 120 volts. Many professionals use a circular

4-22
The DW 935K produces 3000 RPM for faster cutting and can handle bevel cuts up to 50°. DeWalt Industrial Tool Company

saw for both rough framing and finish work. Personally, I prefer a circular saw for finish work and a worm-drive for rough framing. Because of its design, I have better control over the saw, though I let the saw do the work. With the blade on the left side of the motor, I can see the line I am about to cut and am able to keep the saw on the cut side instead of the finish side.

The Skilsaw Magnesium Worm-Drive Saw Model HD 77M is two pounds lighter than its predecessor—and two pounds can make a big difference by the end of the day. I recommend that all professionals have a worm-drive in their collection of tools (Fig. 4-23).

4-23
The design of this saw model allows you to see the line you are cutting.
S-B Power Tool Company

If you are selecting a miter saw, consider the LS1211 by Makita. This 12" slide dual compound miter saw features an innovative dust-proof single-pole design that can make precision bevel cuts 45 degrees left and 45 degrees right with miters up to 60 degrees either way. The pleasure of using this saw is its ability to cut dimensional lumber, especially 4" × 4"s used in handrails. It also has the capability to cut up to 4" × 12"s.

This tool also features positive stops at 15 settings, an electric brake, comes with a 96-tooth 12" carbide-tipped blade, and has a unique removable safety lock-off button to guard against unauthorized use (Fig. 4-24).

4-24 *You will appreciate that the LS1211 cuts compound miters on both the left and right sides.* Makita U.S.A., Inc.

Saw blades

Some professionals mistakenly use the same blade to handle rip, crosscut, fine, and rough cuts. Not all saw blades cut the same way. Because you make different cuts and work with material that has varying grain patterns over which you have no control, it makes sense to use the proper blade for the job. There are several ways to handle this efficiently:

- Set yourself up with more than one saw to do the different cuts with the proper blades.
- Use a blade that closely matches the types of cuts you make the most.
- Purchase the different blades and change them as needed for particular cuts.

Keep in mind that there are specific blades that work with table saws, radial arm saws, and miter saws (slide compound or just compound). Freud tested some specific blades for the different saws in some commonly used materials. Tables 4-1 through 4-3 and Figs. 4-25 through 4-27 contain helpful information from Freud about choosing the right type of Freud blade for specific cutting applications and the type of saw used. The technical information in Figs. 4-28 and 4-29 should help you to better understand saw blades and how and why certain selections were made.

For the table saw, radial arm saw, and miter saw, 10" blades were specified. Other sizes of these blades are available for larger miter saws and smaller table saws.

4-25 *Freud's ripping and crosscutting positive hook "TK" blade.* Freud Inc.

4-26
The LU73M010 is 10" with 60 alternate top bevel (ATB) teeth. Freud Inc.

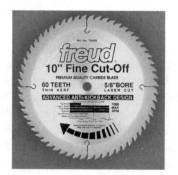

4-27
The TK406 is an example of a fine-rip/crosscut 60-tooth thin kerf blade. Freud Inc.

Table 4-1. Circular Saw

Product	Cut	Blade	Description
TREX	Rip/crosscut	TK103	7¼ × 16 thin kerf, flat top, anti-kickback, positive hook
	Fine rip/crosscut	TK203	7¼ × 24 thin kerf, flat top, anti-kickback, positive hook
Redwood	Rip	TK103	7¼ × 16 thin kerf, flat top, anti-kickback, positive hook
	Crosscut	TK103	7¼ × 16 thin kerf, flat top, anti-kickback, positive hook
	Fine crosscut	TK303	7¼ × 40 thin kerf, flat top, anti-kickback, positive hook
P.T. Pine	Rip	TK103	7¼ × 16 thin kerf, flat top, anti-kickback, positive hook
	Crosscut	TK103	7¼ × thin kerf, flat top, anti-kickback, positive hook
	Fine crosscut	TK303	7¼ × 40 thin kerf, flat top, anti-kickback, positive hook

Source: Freud Inc.

Table 4-2. Miter Saw

Product	Cut	Blade	Description
TREX	Rip/crosscut	LU82M010	10 × 60 triple chip grind—positive hook
	Fine rip/crosscut	LU82M010	10 × 60 triple chip grind—positive hook
Redwood	Crosscut	LU73M010	10 × 60 alt. top bevel—positive hook
	Fine crosscut	LU73M010	10 × 60 alt. top bevel—positive hook
P.T. Pine	Crosscut	LU73M010	10 × 60 alt top bevel—positive hook
	Fine crosscut	LU73M010	10 × 60 alt. top bevel—positive hook

Source: Freud Inc.

Table 4-3. Table Saw/Radial Arm Saw

Product	Cut	Blade	Description
TREX	Rip/crosscut	TK306	10 × 40 thin kerf, flat top, anti-kickback, positive hook
	Fine rip/crosscut	TK406	10 × 60 thin kerf, flat top, anti-kickback, positive hook
Redwood	Rip	TK306	10 × 40 thin kerf, flat top, anti-kickback, positive hook
	Crosscut	TK306	10 × 40 thin kerf, flat top, anti-kickback, positive hook
	Fine crosscut	TK406	10 × 60 thin kerf, flat top, anti-kickback, positive hook
P.T. Pine	Rip	TK306	10 × 40 thin kerf, flat top, anti-kickback, positive hook
	Crosscut	TK306	10 × 40 thin kerf, flat top, anti-kickback, positive hook
	Fine crosscut	TK406	10 × 40 thin kerf, flat top, anti-kickback, positive hook

Source: Freud Inc.

The TREX actually cut easily. It does not show an induced grain pattern and appears to be fairly homogeneous throughout, like chip board. However, with the metal inclusions and the natural tendency of manmade materials to be fairly abrasive, a flat top grind or triple clip is recommended. The miter saw specified is a triple chip with a positive hook, which is less likely to wear as quickly as the ATB blades usually put on miter saws. For the circular saw and table/radial arm saw, the first blade recommended provides a good cut (typically better than that seen on most construction sites) and the second blade gives a smoother cut but does not feed as easily or as quickly. The same holds true for the solid woods listed.

The advantage with solid wood is that the same blade yields a good cut for both ripping and crosscutting. A flat top thin kerf is recommended for a hand-held saw and the table/radial arm saw. This provides maximum blade life and is less likely to follow grain patterns.

Properly Tensioned Blade Bodies for Superior Blade Flatness

Saw blades are subjected to changes in temperature, shocks from cutting, and stresses from turning at high speeds. A blade that starts out flat may not stay flat even after a few hours of use. Freud pretensions its blades to insure many years of smooth operation. This is performed by computer controlled equipment which was designed and built by Freud. This tensioning ring can be seen on most blades as a faint ring about 3/4 the diameter of the blades.

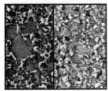

Other Carbide   Freud Carbide

Super Micrograin Carbide with Titanium

Carbide is a metal powder and binder mixture molded at high temperatures and pressures. Wear occurs because grains of the hard metal powders break away. The larger the grain size, the faster the cutting edge dulls, and large grains creates "lakes" of binder which weakens the structure. Binders also break down from the chemical attack from the acids found in wood products. Freud is one of the few saw blade companies who manufacture carbide. Our grain size is smaller than other grades and titanium is added making it more impervious to chemical attack. We produce several carbide mixtures for different cutting requirements, manufacturers who buy their carbide usually have only a few mixtures to choose from and these are usually formulated for metal cutting.

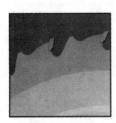

Anti-Kickback Design

Anyone who has been involved with woodworking has experienced saw blade kickbacks from over feeding. These can be very dangerous, and happen so quickly that it is impossible to react before injury occurs. On a table saw, the wood is thrown back violently at you. On a radial arm saw, the blade climbs quickly out of the cut. On a hand held circular saw, the saw is pushed back out of the cut. Freud's Anti-Kickback Design effectively reduces these kickbacks. Each tooth is preceded by a limitator which restricts tooth bite to the maximum safe amount. These have reduced saw accidents of this type in Europe.

Laser Cut, High Strength Blade Bodies

Most manufacturers use stamped bodies. The punch cuts 2/3 of the way through the material and the remaining 1/3 is stretched until it tears. This creates stresses in the body which can cause problems with flatness that may only appear after the blade is used. Also, stamping operations can only be done with steel which is under Rc 30 in hardness (Rc is a designation from Rockwell Hardness Testing Standard on the "C" scale). Metal this soft is too flexible and the blade can wander within the cut when the grain pattern is inconsistent. Freud uses industrial lasers to manufacturer blade bodies. The laser cuts the steel without leaving unwanted stresses. The laser also allows the use of higher strength steel, 40 to 45 Rc. These bodies start and remain truer, even after years of use.

4-28 *Technical information on blades can help you choose the right blade for the job.* Freud Inc.

The use of anti-kickback design blades for the circular, table, and radial arm saws is strongly recommended. The blades specified for the miter saw have a high enough tooth count so the anti-kickback design is not required.

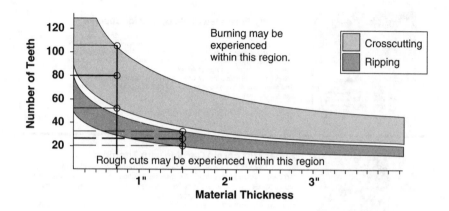

How To Use This Chart - 1. Find the material thickness you will be cutting on the bottom scale. 2. Extend a vertical line up into the shaded area that matches the cut you will be making (ripping or crosscutting). 3. Extend a horizontal line from the point the vertical line enters the shaded area and a line from where it exits the shaded area. These two lines represents the maximum and minimum number of teeth that should be used to make the cut. 4. Extend a horizontal line centered between the first two horizontal lines. This line represents the ideal number of teeth that should be used to make the cut.
Example 1 - How many teeth should be used to crosscut a 3/4" thick board? The heavy solid line is extended vertically into the light gray crosscut region. The two light solid lines are extended horizontally from where the vertical line crosses the boundaries of the crosscut region. The heavy solid line is drawn horizontally from the middle of the crosscut region. The chart shows that the blade to use to crosscut a 3/4" board should have between 56 and 104 teeth and ideally a blade with 80 teeth should be used. You then select the blade closest to the ideal number of teeth. This would be a 80 tooth blade.
Example 2 - How many teeth should be used to rip a 1-1/2" thick board? The heavy dashed line is extended vertically into the dark gray ripping region. The two light dashed lines are extended horizontally from where the vertical line crosses the boundaries of the ripping region. The heavy dashed line is drawn horizontally from the middle of the ripping region. The chart shows that the blade to use to rip a 1-1/2" board should have between 20 and 32 teeth and ideally a blade with 26 teeth should be used. You then select the blade closest to the ideal number of teeth. This would be a 24 tooth blade.

4-29 *Recommended teeth per material thickness. Note: The correct number of teeth is more important than the highest number of teeth.* Freud Inc.

Power drills/impact drivers

The drill plays a major role in deck construction. Whether you are building a railing system or installing decking boards, drills are convenient, efficient, time-saving tools. However, not every drill is appropriate for every application. The next three tools have a single purpose, but they are so useful and important that perhaps they should be added to your shopping list for your next project.

Angle drills

In an earlier chapter I mentioned the DeckMaster brackets. An angle drill is a must for installing those brackets or anything else in difficult to reach or tight areas; for example, when you are installing brackets on joists set 12" OC.

The model shown in Fig. 4-30 is a Milwaukee Model 0379–1½" chuck. What makes this tool unique is that it is 10" long with a 55°

4-30
*Milwaukee's Close Quarter
Drill is an excellent tool for
reaching tight spots.* C.R.S., Inc.

angle. The angled head and chuck measure 3⅜", which provides easy
access in tight places. This close-quarter drill weighs just 3½ pounds,
has a durable high-impact housing, and a grip paddle switch that is
comfortable to operate.

Cordless drills

The convenience of cordless drills cannot be overemphasized. I still
use my corded power drills when they suit the application, but the
advantages of portability and no cord to trip over often make the
cordless drill preferable. I had a mental block about using batteries
rather than 120 volts from an outlet, but discovered that there are
cordless models on the market today that compare quite favorably
with outlet-powered tools. A case in point is DeWalt's Model DW
991K with 14.4 volts. It has plenty of power from a new breed of
high-capacity batteries that have a 25 percent longer running time
than standard batteries. However, these new batteries do require a
high-capacity battery charger.

I recommend using a drill at least during the early phases of
building a deck. I am a firm believer in drilling pilot holds whenever
I install a screw because it helps prevent screws from snapping off
and splitting or cracking the wood, especially when working near the
end or points. Note the compact ergonomic design of the clutch dri-
ver/drill shown in Fig. 4-31, with its anti-slip rubber grip.

Impact drivers

My experience in the field has shown that some drills (including
some of the clutch driver/drills) really don't have the power to drive
screws all day. One tool that I found works quite well, however, is
the impact driver. It's a regular workhorse and can take a lot of abuse.
Because of the internal hammer-striking force that assists the rotation
of the impact driver (perpendicular to the spindle), less strain is put
on the tool as it drives the screw into the material. You still need to
drill pilot holes, but the constant pounding also results in fewer
cracks or splits in the deck boards, and fewer screws snap.

4-31
A well-balanced tool with a heavy-duty keyless chuck and electric brake. C.R.S., Inc.

Hitachi has two cordless impact drivers I have found excellent to use, models WH8DC or WH8DA1 (Fig. 4-32). They are somewhat noisy because of the internal striking force, so I recommend using hearing protection. You will need an extra battery. Two batteries last between six and eight hours, depending on the number of screws installed. It's a good idea, though, to change the first battery at lunch-time.

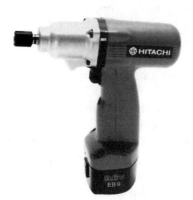

4-32
Cordless tools are more portable, and there is no cord to get in the way. C.R.S., Inc.

Drill bits

Just as using correct saw blades for specific applications makes you more efficient, using proper drill bits can also speed up tasks. You might find the bits shown in Fig. 4-33 of interest. The extra long high speed steel (HSS) twist bits have a 135-degree split-point tip for non-slip starting on hard materials (such as metal) without a center punch. They also feature a black oxide finish for greater wear resistance and longer life as well as a parabolic flute design that provides fast chip removal. Because of their 12" length, you can drill holes in dimensional lumber without an extension. The line is complete with seven

4-33 *These bits are designed for high-performance drilling in metal, wood, and plastic.* DeWalt Industrial Tool Company

bits from ⅛" to ½" in diameter, and two of the bits (⁷⁄₁₆" and ½") have a ⅜" reduced shank for use with drills with ⅜" chucks.

Generator

The day will come when you will be without power. The homeowner might leave and lock the door without your knowing it; if you blow a circuit breaker, there is no way to get into the house. Another possibility is that the deck to be built is 300 feet or more away from any power. Certainly you could string out extension cords if you've got enough, but depending on the amperage rating of the tools, you need a certain wire gauge to prevent a serious voltage drop that could damage your tools.

One way to get around situations like these is to have a gas-powered generator. Once you own one, you will be using it all the time. You won't have to worry about inconveniencing your customer or interruptions to your work in progress.

One generator I enjoy using because of its low noise volume is the G5501R by Makita (Fig. 4-34). A full tank provides about 5 hours of operating time. It has both a recoil starter and an electric starter. Be sure to get a battery because none is included with the package. What's nice about this unit is that you can get both 120-volt and 240-volt power. If you could use one but can't afford to buy it, rent one instead.

4-34 *The 5500 W maximum output is sufficient for most construction equipment.*
Makita U.S.A., Inc.

All the tools described in this chapter and throughout the book are tools I have used and have found to be true assets for deck construction. Of course, other hand and power tools are also essential in order to complete a deck. Remember, you can never have enough tools, but you might need a bigger truck in which to haul them!

5

Project layout

From the time you first set foot on a potential customer's property until you attend to the last detail on that new deck, you will be faced with many challenges. The customer might change his or her mind frequently or ask for additional features.

Even when customers tell you where they want their new deck built, they are often really asking for your professional input. This is when it is important to share what you know and make a good impression. You can help the customer get the deck he or she wants and at the same time make sure it meets the local and/or state building codes. By sharing what you know you can sell yourself and the job.

Site considerations and limitations

The customer might know what type of deck he or she wants but might not know exactly where a deck can be built. You, on the other hand, know that you have to follow the requirements of the zoning and/or building departments in your municipality. Knowing these requirements can give you a competitive edge. It also gives you the opportunity to devise an alternative plan for the customer, yourself, and any government agencies involved. Depending on what the customer wants and the terrain where the deck will be built, you might be required to use a structural engineer in order to secure a building permit. Keep abreast of requirements that involve setbacks and utility easements. I recommend that you visit the local zoning department and learn these requirements.

The work you perform must comply with the codes established and enforced by your local building and zoning departments. This includes building, electrical, plumbing, and zoning, which includes setbacks and easements. Electrical permits and inspections sometimes fall under state jurisdiction depending on your state and whether the project is in the city or county.

Your local building department might follow one of the three widely accepted model codes—International Conference of Building Officials (ICBO) *Uniform Building Code*, Building Officials and Code Administrators (BOCA) *National Building Code*, and Southern Building Code Congress International (SBCCI) *Standard Building Code*—or it might follow its own adopted codes. All new work should meet the codes in force for your area, but allowances can be made depending on the project and/or structure. The staff at the building department is aware that sometimes situations arise, particularly on remodeling projects, when it is difficult to meet the building codes. They do have some latitude and can help you solve a problem in a way that will both comply with the codes and satisfy you and your customer. It would be in your best interests to keep an open mind, work with the department(s) involved, be willing to compromise, and encourage your customer to do the same. Work with the building department. You will get along better with inspectors if they know what you are going to do beforehand.

Tom Craig, Certified Plan Examiner for the City of Spokane, has a suggestion that can help you understand building requirements and simultaneously help your customer. He suggests that you create a couple of master templates (i.e., generic graphic plot plans): one with a house placed on an interior lot and the other for a corner lot with a side street. On the templates, show the following:

- Required minimum front setback
- Required minimum rear setback
- Required minimum side setback

You might need different sets of templates for use within the city, within the county, and possibly for different cities within your county. These handy little tools will help you to answer any questions potential customers might have regarding deck placement (Figs. 5-1 and 5-2).

Other considerations should be noted as well, including:

- Utilities (water, telephone, gas, and electric): Do you know where the easements are?
- Are the utilities underground or overhead?
- Are water, gas, and/or electricity planned for this project?
- Is there a septic tank? If so, where is it, and where is its accompanying drain field?
- What are the soil conditions?
- What is the terrain like?
- Are you planning to build on flat ground or on the side of a hill?
- Are you building a single-level deck at ground level, a single level off the ground, a double level, or a deck with a roof?

- Are there trees that you must build around? Do you know where the main roots are?
- Are you planning to incorporate trees into the deck? (If so, know the type of tree, the time it will take to achieve its maximum diameter, and what that maximum diameter will be. Incorporate a couple of rows of octagons around the tree; as the tree grows, the rows can be removed one at a time, as shown in Fig. 5-3.)
- Are there existing sprinkler lines?
- Where are the property lines?

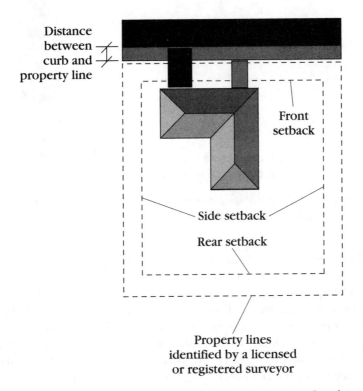

5-1 *A plot plan for an interior lot. Template created with 3-D Landscape software from Books That Work.* C.R.S., Inc.

Concerns such as these affect where the deck can be built, its size, and how deep the footings will be placed. They might also require adherence to stricter building codes or impact the cost of the deck. They can certainly affect the potential customer's ultimate satisfaction with the eventual location of the deck.

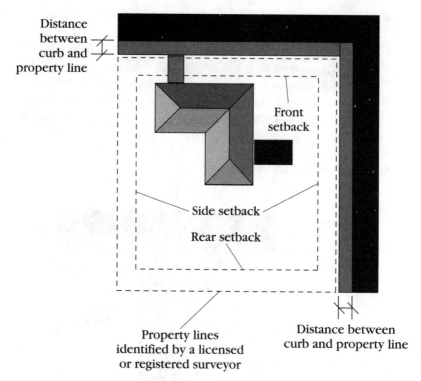

Distance
between
curb and
property line

Front
setback

Side setback

Rear setback

Property lines
identified by a licensed
or registered surveyor

Distance between
curb and property line

5-2 *A plot plan for a corner lot. Template created with 3-D Landscape software from Books That Work.* C.R.S., Inc.

Both the terrain and the deck's height off the ground can determine whether or not a guardrail must be installed. In residential areas, the UBC requires that decks more than 30" off the ground have a 36"-high (minimum) guardrail. Four or more risers require a handrail that can be gripped 34" to 38" high. Apartments and condominiums, depending on their specific code requirements, might need handrails for two or more risers that can be gripped at 34" to 38" and guardrails at 42". Check with your building department for the specific requirements in your area.

It's a good idea to ask the customer if the property has been surveyed; possibly the markers are still there. Depending on the size of the deck you are planning to build, the survey report can help you determine the setback requirements. If the customers are not sure, have them check with the office of the county auditor/recorder.

The survey might also show any restrictions or easements associated with the property. Entrance points and paths of underground services might have to be determined by the individual utility com-

5-3 *The deck boards around the tree can be removed as the tree grows larger.* George B. Sagatov, Inc.

panies involved. Check in your local phone book under "utility companies." Sometimes they have special service numbers for locating underground utilities.

If you are working in a development, there could be covenant restrictions. Check with the association for any guidelines. Also, a subdivision should have been surveyed as part of the subdivision process. Depending upon the date of subdivision, the corner monuments (markers) might still be at the corners.

Climate and weather

Climate and weather should be a consideration when you plan a deck with a customer. Most of us build decks in the summer when plants (especially trees) are fully developed. It is easy in this situation to forget what the sun's rays will do in the winter and how much of the sun's warmth will be captured on the deck during that time period.

The sun crosses the sky in an arc that changes slightly every day, becoming lower throughout autumn as winter approaches and higher throughout spring as summer approaches. If deciduous trees are nearby, the summer shade that helps to protect the deck from the sun's harmful rays will turn to winter sunlight. Another factor is that sunny areas in the summer might fall within the shadow of the house during autumn and winter months. In time, the sun will bleach the surface of the wood to a soft gray color, which some customers prefer.

Theoretically, if a house faces the south, the east side will receive only the morning sun, the south-facing side will stay warm from sunrise to sunset, the west side will absorb the full force of the sun's midafternoon rays, and the north side will normally stay cool because the sun rarely shines on it. If you have lived for some years in the community where you are building the deck, you probably have a fair idea of the surrounding weather conditions. If not, then ask neighbors who are long-time residents. This information could be especially helpful if you are planning to build an overhead structure to shield the deck and its occupants from the sun's rays.

Freezing water is another of nature's most destructive forces; when water freezes, it expands, and expansion can cause irreversible damage. Constant expansion and contraction can cause damage to any deck.

Another consideration is snow load. Snow adds to the weight of a roof and an uncovered deck. This is a real concern, especially if the deck is built high off the ground. Without proper support and bracing, snow load could cause a deck to collapse. If you live in an area with high average snowfall, consult an engineer to ensure adequate and solid construction.

There are plenty of ways to make attractive shade structures, but the only way to protect the deck from the sun's harmful rays or to bring sunshine to those portions where it's wanted is to plan for it:

- Find out if the customers prefer to sit in the sun or the shade.
- In what season(s) and at what time(s) of day do the customers expect to use their deck the most?
- Do the customers anticipate night use? If so, you may want to suggest outdoor lighting and a few ground-fault circuit interrupter-protected electrical outlets.
- What is the direction of the prevailing wind? You might want to suggest some type of buffer such as hedges, trees, etc.
- Are there psychological barriers, such as hedges, trees, or a wall that will bother the customer? Design the deck with a desirable view.
- Is privacy an issue? Suggest louvers, latticework, screens, etc.

It would be a good idea to take the information contained within this chapter and prepare a checklist for potential customers who are undecided about issues like these. This way, they can review their needs and check the boxes on your list. It's better to return for their answers than to sign them immediately and start the job but have unsatisfied customers once the project is completed.

Enlargement

If there is an existing deck, you and the customers should always consider the possibility of enlarging or adding onto it. An existing deck is a great opportunity for you to put your creative skills to work. If you feel that the existing deck structure is sound, there is a good breaking point, or the option is there to interweave new decking boards so the surface looks natural, then by all means suggest it to the customer. It could save them money to go this route.

Your customers might also warm to the suggestion of a "starter" deck: a deck with options that can be added in later years—options that you, the contractor could suggest. The deck could be built so it easily accepts additional phases of deck building. A deck built in stages can help with the budget.

As a professional, you will have to decide whether or not an existing deck is worth adding onto. If you think you will spend a lot of time fixing the existing deck before beginning an add-on, it might not be worthwhile for you or your customer. In the long run, it can cost the customer more than if you built new. You can also suggest that the customer remove the existing deck. This can save your customer some dollars and it frees you to do what you do best, which is building decks!

Perhaps the customer has the classic deck, built on the second story (main floor) when the house was built. As lifestyles change for homeowners, so do their needs. Adding a set of stairs and a new lower deck can meet those needs. This type of deck has a good breaking point so you can add on. In time, you will never be able to tell the deck was constructed in two phases (Figs. 5-4A and B, show "before" and "after").

Figures 5-5A and B show an outstanding remodeling project that added both a second story and a porch. These photos show how you can incorporate a porch into the design, but it is also a major undertaking. What makes this porch unusual is that the surface is made of decking boards and is constructed in the same manner as a standard deck. Your customers will appreciate seeing the "before" photo, especially after the deck is finished.

The deck in Fig. 5-6A doesn't do justice to this beautiful home. It is not only out of place but also weatherbeaten, as you can see in the worn top of the guardrail. The "after" photo in Fig. 5-6B shows what an imaginative deck can do for a home. The new addition, designed by Jan White of Glickman Design/Build, is a beautiful screened porch or sun room with skylights. The deck includes a combination arbor/trellis, which works well for hanging plants or a bench or swing for those romantic summer evenings. Notice the Chippendale design in the guardrail. Designs like these are what the deck business is all about.

A

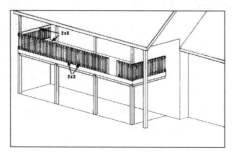

B

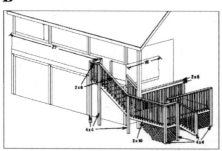

5-4
*A (before) and B (after)
show possibilities for
adding to an existing
deck.* Used with permission of Georgia-
Pacific Corporation

A

5-5 *(before) The beginning of a major undertaking.* George B. Sagatov, Inc.

B

5-5 *(after) A new second story and a porch incorporated into the design.* George B. Sagatov, Inc.

A

5-6 *(before) The deck shown is inadequate for the house.* Glickman Design/Build

B

5-6 *(after) What a difference!* Glickman Design/Build

The project featured in Fig. 5-7 is a simple one that enhances the front of a home and hides a multitude of sins. A project of this type will fit most customers' budgets and make them feel as though they'd spent far more. Satisfying customers is a satisfying part of the business, no matter how large or small the project.

Design and layout

Every job you survey will be unique. The size of the property, the design of the house, the terrain, existing decking, where the house is located on the property, setbacks, easements, rights-of-way, zoning, and building code requirements all contribute to the design of a deck project. Budget, of course, is another factor.

The few basic designs that you will use for most decks can be altered and customized to meet the tastes and needs of your customers. The following descriptions and illustrations can aid you in designing a deck. The same information within this chapter can be used to give your potential customer ideas to work with. Remember, your customers might have a hard time visualizing a finished product at this stage. Use this book as a sales tool to help you close sales.

A

B

5-7 *A (before) and B (after) show how much even a small project can improve a house.* C.R.S., Inc.

Types of decks

Decks built at ground level are the most common. They can either be built directly on the ground or, depending on the slope of the property (normally the backyard), 4 or 5 feet off the ground. If you are following the UBC, decks built close to the ground must have at least 6" of clearance from the ground to the underside of any wood. In some situations, you might need to grade the property to meet the code. When grading, slope the grade away from the house so water won't drain back toward the house. Rain gutter spouts should continue through the deck surface and drain into a PVC drainpipe to carry rainwater away from the house.

High-rise decks are common on the West Coast and normally provide access to an exit that is high off the ground because of property conditions. Split-entry homes are a good example, as are ranch houses where the back lots start to slope just about where the basement footings are located. Decks such as these require adequate supporting members/columns. You might be required to consult an engineer for the structural part of this project.

Multilevel decks can be designed to fit the lifestyle of any customer. They can accommodate many groups of people during a party or provide access to a view. Figure 5-8 is a good example of a triple-level deck. Stairs located on the other side of the dormer addition provide access to the middle and top levels, and the middle level also can be reached through a door in the dormer. Supports must be engineered for this type of application.

5-8 *This deck configuration was constructed to take advantage of a view of the Atlantic Ocean.* C.R.S., Inc.

Load-bearing decks support unusual weight. Because of terrain and the lava deposits or other rock formations in some parts of the country, it is occasionally necessary to make all parts of a home and yard functional; for example, a carport built over the side of a hill, thereby using normally unusable space. In most cases, excavation costs in this type of situation can be prohibitive, so a load-bearing deck is an easy solution. However, because of the additional load support the columns and beams are required to provide, consult an engineer for professional help. Also, if the deck is to support an auto, it might require a solid noncombustible surface, such as concrete or asphalt. Be sure to check with your building department for surface requirements.

Rooftop decks are another option: When there is no place to build, go up! Rooftop decks present many challenges. Building on a flat roof is easier than dealing with a sloped roof, but the main problem is in creating the proper slope for water runoff. You also need to ensure that the building can support the weight of a deck and any appliances (dead load) as well as people (live load) and snow loads (if applicable).

The surface of the roof platform that will be under the deck must be protected from moisture before deck construction. There are a couple of ways to handle this: Use a two-component batch mix urethane coating application or install an EPDM (ethylene propylene diene monomer) roofing system—a rubber membrane.

Gaco Western Inc. offers many products that might be just right for your particular application. One worth considering is Gacoflex UB-64 base coat. Its two-component (1:1 ratio) urethanes are liquid-applied elastomers. When properly combined and applied, they cure to a tough, high-tensile strength hydrolytic stability and a puncture-resistant synthetic rubber membrane. These coatings expand and contract with the substrate in hot and cold weather. Because they are solvents, you must apply them with a roller that is solvent-resistant.

If the product is going to be used in a traffic flow area, apply granules in the second coat of UB-64, then apply two coats of Gacoflex U-66 as a top coat. The U-66 is available in colors and provides a skid-resistant and UV-resistant coating when combined with organic granules.

Allow each coat to dry until tack-free and sufficiently cured for foot traffic before applying any additional urethane coatings. The time required for drying might be less than two hours or as long as overnight, depending on drying conditions, temperatures, and the product applied.

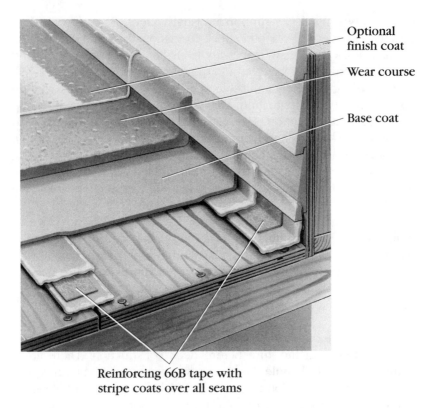

Optional
finish coat

Wear course

Base coat

Reinforcing 66B tape with
stripe coats over all seams

5-9 *Prepping the substrate at all seams is very important.* Gaco Western Inc.

If you opt to apply a membrane, choose a product for which the manufacturer will custom manufacture the membrane to fit. EPDM products are shipped with talc so the rubber doesn't stick to itself, and this makes it difficult to clean the joints in the field to ensure an absolutely solid bond. Membranes also require extra care to prevent punctures. Basically, membranes are not intended for use in areas where there will be foot traffic, and they usually require experienced installers.

One company that can help is Resource Conservation Technology, Inc. Their system uses a black 60-mil sheet of cured EPDM, a synthetic rubber known for its outstanding weathering properties. This product will remain flexible throughout the coldest winters, won't crack or dry out in the hottest summers, and will withstand permanent standing water. It is also fully UV stable and unaffected by air pollution or acid rain; no protection is required even in fully exposed applications. The company can eliminate most installation problems by prefabricating many of the seams and flashings that would normally be done in the field. To learn more, write to them at the address found in Appendix C.

Whether you choose a urethane coating or an EPDM roofing system, it is important not to penetrate the system. Consider building a modular deck in 4' × 4' sections that can be hoisted into place. Decking boards for each section can be altered so they are perpendicular to each other, similar to a parquet design used in hardwood floors. The sections should be built on at least 2" × 6" or 2" × 8" sleepers to help distribute the weight (similar in design to a pallet). Leave off one or two decking boards so you can install bolts. Perimeter sections should include guardrails that can be bolted together for security. Adding a built-in bench to the guardrails can strengthen the entire system. Figure 5-10 shows how to do it.

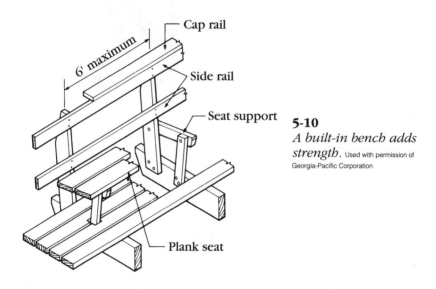

5-10
A built-in bench adds strength. Used with permission of Georgia-Pacific Corporation

Figure 5-11 shows a quick solution using the Dekmate Bench Bracket. Made from polyethylene, a structural foam-injected plastic, it is maintenance-free. Its unique design works well on docks, concrete, and existing decks as well. It also provides an angle back that adds comfort to your bench.

Building in sections also allows your customer to remove sections so areas underneath can be cleaned. The sleepers will be in direct contact with moisture, so be sure they are weather protected (all-weather wood foundation material).

Sample deck shapes

Perhaps you have noticed that decks develop individual shapes determined by such factors as the shape of the house, the terrain, the size of the property, and building and zoning code restrictions. If you

5-11 *A Dekmate Bench Bracket makes constructing built-in benches easy.* Canadian Dekbrands

don't run into restrictions that limit you in design and size, be as creative as you can as you sell to the customer. It just might be your design that convinces the customer to hire you. The deck shapes shown in Fig. 5-12 were furnished by Weyerhaeuser Company (which, incidentally, has treating plants that produce treated lumber). These designs can give you and your customer some basic ideas to work from. The sample deck shapes are shown both freestanding and attached to a house. The direction of the decking boards does not represent the finished product. The same direction is shown to simplify the drawing. You can change the direction of the decking boards to fit the environment and/or the customer's preferences. Of course, you will need to build the deck's framework accordingly.

If you are still not satisfied with your design, then contact Cadd-Con Designs at 800-821-3325 and order their standard plan catalog. All their plans are 24" × 36" blueprints that include materials lists; instructions; plans for footings, posts and beams, framing, decking, handrails, and stairs; and construction details. Their catalog is constantly revised, so it's worth checking to see if they have plans that will meet your needs. Catalog plans can be modified to your require-

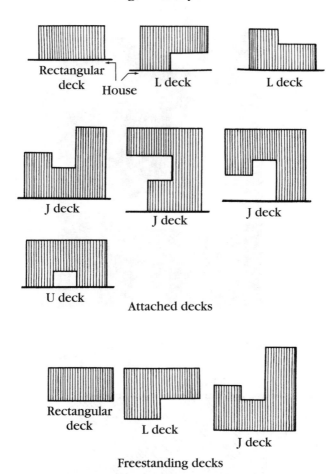

5-12 *Attached and freestanding deck shapes.* Weyerhaeuser Company

ments and custom designs and plans are available for more complex and unique projects. The catalog also includes standard plans for gazebos, screened porches, template plans, handrails, stairs, and deck accessories (Fig. 5-13).

Code requirements

All through this book mention is made of building and zoning requirements. Unless specified otherwise, these references are to the UBC. However, it is possible that the UBC has not been adopted in your area, so be sure to follow whatever code is in force, both for your customer's safety and to protect your own reputation. If you don't know the code requirements, ask! Be a safe-deck contractor and take pride in your work.

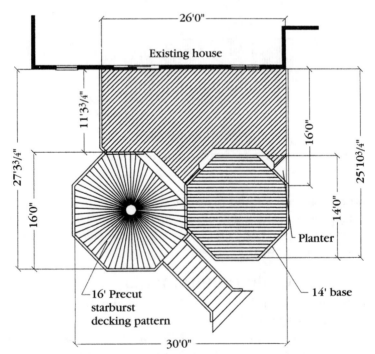

26'0"

Existing house

11'3¾"

16'0"

27'3¾"

16'0"

14'0"

25'10¾"

Planter

16' Precut
starburst
decking pattern

14' base

30'0"

Design Plan

5-13 *A gazebo integrated into a deck design.* CaddCon Designs, Inc.

One other tip worth mentioning is that shortcuts don't pay. Think twice about using shortcuts, either in quality of materials or construction methods—they're just not worth it. Sooner or later someone will get hurt. It could put you out of business as an independent contractor and you might find yourself working for someone else. The bottom line is, don't cheat the customer. Regardless of what the customer is paying for, give a little extra. The customer will appreciate it and you'll be surprised at how fast your name and good reputation will spread.

Don't be afraid to call in an architect for plans and/or an engineer for structural design. It will help you to secure the building permit, and these costs can be added into the bid.

Joists, posts, and beams

As I mentioned earlier, dead weight and live loads play a major role when designing a deck. Both help to determine how far apart joists should be spaced and the sizes of posts and beams that should be used. Building codes are based on minimum requirements, and these are sufficient in most cases, but I have found that in some cases I wished I had exceeded those requirements. This applies to manufacturers' specifications as well. Follow your building experience instincts. Adding an extra joist or an extra support could prevent your being called back at a later date. Besides, the extra materials added into the bid shouldn't cause you to lose the sale. Explain your construction methods and sell them to the customer.

If you install a joist beyond its allowable span, you will get a springy deck. At the same time, spacing the joists too far apart leaves the decking boards springy as well. There are several ways to solve these problems:

- If you planned to use 2" × 6" joists, consider switching to 2" × 8" or 2" × 10" in the same span.
- If increasing joist size is not a possibility because of ground clearances, then use an extra support beam.
- To stop deflection in deck boards, bring the joists closer together; for instance, 24" OC to 16" OC or 16" OC to 12" OC.
- Deflection can also be reduced by the use of stiffeners (2×s attached flat to the underside of the joist) or by the use of solid blocking.

With ¾ wooden decking material, I found that joists spaced at 12" OC helped to eliminate deflection, and 2" × 4" or 2" × 6" worked better with the joists placed at 16" OC rather than 24" OC. Alternative materials with rigid construction (2×) could be placed on joists at 16" OC. However, those that were ¾ in thickness and made in part or whole of recycled and/or reclaimed plastic were better when placed on joists that were 12" OC.

I have corrected many decks where the joists were set at 24" OC. Even though the overall deck was solid and met the building codes, it just didn't feel solid to the customer walking across it. The deflection is real and can give a customer the uncomfortable feeling that the deck wasn't built properly. When a deck is 8' or higher off the ground, inadequate bracing can contribute to a swaying motion that will cause the customer to fear the deck will collapse. I find it easier and better to add an extra joist and/or support right into the bid than to deal with the headaches that will surely follow less-than-solid support.

If you have ever looked in a building code book, you have probably seen tables that deal with the materials used to construct decks, such as allowable spans for floor joists and allowable unit stresses for structural lumber. To help you better understand these charts and the information contained in them, I have explained in detail (with the help of the Western Wood Products Association) the physical property column headings used in the charts.

Lumber strength properties are assigned to six basic properties:
- Fiber stress in bending (F_b) (Fig. 5-14)
- Tension parallel-to-grain (F_t) (Fig. 5-15)
- Horizontal shear (F_v) (Fig. 5-16)
- Compression perpendicular-to-grain ($F_{c\perp}$) (Fig. 5-17)
- Compression parallel-to-grain ($F_{c\,//}$) (Fig. 5-18)
- Modulus of elasticity (E) (Fig. 5-19)

If you know the modulus of elasticity (E factor or MOE), you can find most of the other information you'll need to determine wood

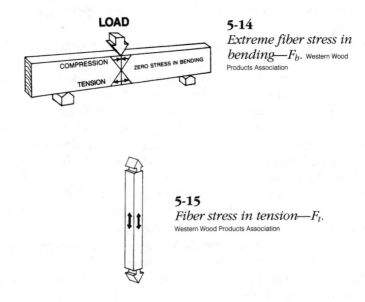

5-14
Extreme fiber stress in bending—F_b. Western Wood Products Association

5-15
Fiber stress in tension—F_t. Western Wood Products Association

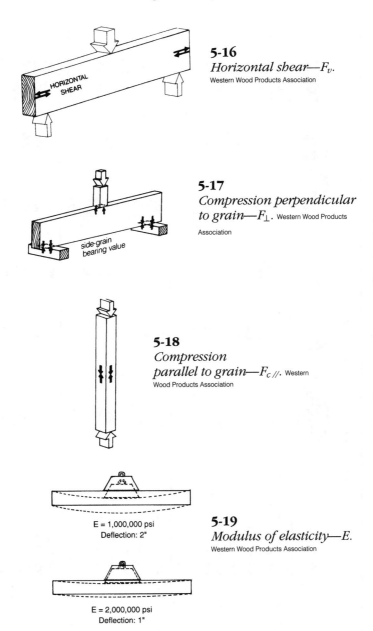

5-16
Horizontal shear—F_v.
Western Wood Products Association

5-17
*Compression perpendicular
to grain—$F_\perp$.* Western Wood Products
Association

5-18
*Compression
parallel to grain—$F_{c\,//}$.* Western
Wood Products Association

E = 1,000,000 psi
Deflection: 2"

5-19
Modulus of elasticity—E.
Western Wood Products Association

E = 2,000,000 psi
Deflection: 1"

strengths. For the wood products currently being produced, be sure
to check the E factor to ensure that you are getting material of sufficient strength to handle the spans. The E factor required is based on
load, span, deflection, and section property; Table 5-1 spells out E
factors for a species or group and its grade.

Table 5-1. Base Values for Western Dimension Lumber*

(Sizes 2" to 4" thick by 2" and wider)

Table 1

Species or Group	Grade	Extreme Fiber Stress in Bending "Fb" Single	Tension Parallel to Grain "Ft"	Horizontal Shear "Fv"	Compression Perpendicular "Fc⊥"	Compression Parallel to Grain "Fc∥"	Modulus of Elasticity "E"
Douglas Fir-Larch	Select Structural	1450	1000	95	625	1700	1,900,000
	No. 1 & Btr.	1150	775	95	625	1500	1,800,000
Douglas Fir	No. 1	1000	675	95	625	1450	1,700,000
Western Larch	No. 2	875	575	95	625	1300	1,600,000
	No. 3	500	325	95	625	750	1,400,000
	Construction	1000	650	95	625	1600	1,500,000
	Standard	550	375	95	625	1350	1,400,000
	Utility	275	175	95	625	875	1,300,000
	Stud	675	450	95	625	825	1,400,000
Douglas Fir-South	Select Structural	1300	875	90	520	1550	1,400,000
	No. 1	900	600	90	520	1400	1,300,000
Douglas Fir South	No. 2	825	525	90	520	1300	1,200,000
	No. 3	475	300	90	520	750	1,100,000
	Construction	925	600	90	520	1550	1,200,000
	Standard	525	350	90	520	1300	1,100,000
	Utility	250	150	90	520	875	1,000,000
	Stud	650	425	90	520	825	1,100,000
Hem-Fir	Select Structural	1400	900	75	405	1500	1,600,000
	No. 1 & Btr.	1050	700	75	405	1350	1,500,000
Western Hemlock	No. 1	950	600	75	405	1300	1,500,000
Noble Fir	No. 2	850	500	75	405	1250	1,300,000
California Red Fir	No. 3	500	300	75	405	725	1,200,000
Grand Fir	Construction	975	575	75	405	1500	1,300,000
Pacific Silver Fir							
White Fir							

Species / Grade						
Standard	550	325	75	405	1300	1,200,000
Utility	250	150	75	405	850	1,100,000
Stud	675	400	75	405	800	1,200,000
Spruce-Pine-Fir (South) *Western Species: Engelmann Spruce, Sitka Spruce, Lodgepole Pine*						
Select Structural	1300	575	70	335	1200	1,300,000
No. 1	850	400	70	335	1050	1,200,000
No. 2	750	325	70	335	975	1,100,000
No. 3	425	200	70	335	550	1,000,000
Construction	850	375	70	335	1200	1,000,000
Standard	475	225	70	335	1000	900,000
Utility	225	100	70	335	650	900,000
Stud	575	250	70	335	600	1,000,000
Western Cedars *Western Red Cedar, Incense Cedar, Port Orford Cedar, Alaska Cedar*						
Select Structural	1000	600	75	425	1000	1,100,000
No. 1	725	425	75	425	825	1,000,000
No. 2	700	425	75	425	650	1,000,000
No. 3	400	250	75	425	375	900,000
Construction	800	475	75	425	850	900,000
Standard	450	275	75	425	650	800,000
Utility	225	125	75	425	425	800,000
Stud	550	325	75	425	400	900,000
Western Woods *Any of the species in the first four species groups above plus any or all of the following: Idaho White Pine, Ponderosa Pine, Sugar Pine, Alpine Fir, Mountain Hemlock*						
Select Structural	875	400	70	335	1050	1,200,000
No. 1	650	300	70	335	925	1,100,000
No. 2	650	275	70	335	875	1,000,000
No. 3	375	175	70	335	500	900,000
Construction	725	325	70	335	1050	1,000,000
Standard	400	175	70	335	900	900,000
Utility	200	75	70	335	600	800,000
Stud	500	225	70	335	550	900,000

Use with appropriate adjustments in Tables A through G (Grades described in *Western Lumber Grading Rules '91*, Sections 40.00, 42.00 & 62.00. Also stress rated boards, see section 30.60.)

*Design values in pounds per square inch. See Sections 100.00 through 170.00 in the *Western Lumber Grading Rules '91* for additional information on these values.

Source: Western Wood Products Association.

Dimension lumber design values for Canadian and Western species are published as base values. Those shown in Table 5-1 are for Western lumber species. Adjustment factors for base values are shown in the smaller tables (A through G) following Table 5-1. Base values must first be adjusted for size (Table A) and then for conditions of use (Tables B through G). The most common condition-of-use adjustments (Repetitive Member, Duration of Load, and Horizontal Shear) are shown with the size adjustment factors. The adjustments for more specific conditions of use (Flat Use, Compression, Perpendicular, Wet Use, and others) are also given.

Table 5-1. Continued

Size Factors (C_F)   Table A
(Apply to Dimension Lumber Base Values)

| Grades | Nominal Width (depth) | F_b | | F_t | $F_{c\parallel}$ | Other Properties |
		2" & 3" thick nominal	4" thick nominal			
Select Structural, No. 1 & Btr., No. 1, No. 2 & No. 3	2", 3" & 4"	1.5	1.5	1.5	1.15	1.0
	5"	1.4	1.4	1.4	1.1	1.0
	6"	1.3	1.3	1.3	1.1	1.0
	8"	1.2	1.3	1.2	1.05	1.0
	10"	1.1	1.2	1.1	1.0	1.0
	12"	1.0	1.1	1.0	1.0	1.0
	14" & wider	0.9	1.0	0.9	0.9	1.0
Construction & Standard	2", 3" & 4"	1.0	1.0	1.0	1.0	1.0
Utility	2" & 3"	0.4	—	0.4	0.6	1.0
	4"	1.0	1.0	1.0	1.0	1.0
Stud	2", 3" & 4"	1.1	1.1	1.1	1.05	1.0
	6" & wider	1.0	1.0	1.0	1.0	1.0

Source: Western Wood Products Association

Repetitive Member Factor (C_r)   Table B
(Apply to Size-Adjusted F_b)

Where 2" to 4" thick lumber is used repetitively, such as for joists, studs, rafters and decking, the pieces side by side share the load and the strength of the entire assembly is enhanced. Therefore, where three or more members are adjacent or are not more than 24" on center and are joined by floor, roof or other load distributing elements, the F_b value can be increased 1.15 for repetitive member use.

REPETITIVE MEMBER USE

$$F_b \times 1.15$$

Source: Western Wood Products Association

Table 5-1. Continued

Duration of Load Adjustment (C_D)   Table C
(Apply to Size-Adjusted Values)

Apply to Size-adjusted Values

Wood has the property of carrying substantially greater maximum loads for short durations than for long durations of loading. Tabulated design values apply to normal load duration. (Factors do not apply to MOE or $F_{c\perp}$).

LOAD DURATION	FACTOR
Permanent	0.9
Ten Years (Normal Load)	1.0
Two Months (Snow Load)	1.15
Seven Day	1.25
One Day	1.33
Ten Minutes (Wind and Earthquake Loads)	1.6
Impact	2.0

Confirm load requirements with local codes. Refer to Model Building Codes or the National Design Specification for high-temperature or fire-retardant treated adjustment factors.

Source: Western Wood Products Association

Horizontal Shear Adjustment (C_H)   Table D
(Apply to F_v Values)

Horizontal shear values published in Tables 1, 3, 4 & 5 are based upon the maximum degree of shake, check or split that might develop in a piece. When the actual size of these characteristics is known, the following adjustments may be taken.

2″ THICK LUMBER

For convenience, the table below may be used to determine horizontal shear values for any grade of 2″ thick lumber in any species when the length of split or check is known and any increase in them is not anticipated:

When length of split on wide face is:	Multiply Tabulated Fv value by:
No split	2.00
1/2 of wide face	1.67
3/4 of wide face	1.50
1 of wide face	1.33
1½ of wide face or more	1.00

3″ and THICKER LUMBER

Horizontal shear values for 3″ and thicker lumber also are established as if a piece were split full length. When specific lengths of splits are known and any increase in them is not anticipated, the following adjustments may be applied.

When length of split on wide face is:	Multiply Tabulated Fv value by:
No split	2.00
1/2 of narrow face	1.67
1 of narrow face	1.33
1½ of narrow or more	1.00

Source: Western Wood Products Association

Table 5-1. Continued

Flat Use Factors (C_fu)   **Table E**
(Apply to Size-Adjusted F_b)

NOMINAL WIDTH	NOMINAL THICKNESS	
	2″ & 3″	4″
2″ & 3″	1.00	—
4″	1.10	1.00
5″	1.10	1.05
6″	1.15	1.05
8″	1.15	1.05
10″ & wider	1.20	1.10

Source: Western Wood Products Association

Adjustments for Compression   Table F
Perpendicular-to-Grain (C_c⊥)
(For Deformation Basis of 0.02″,
Apply to F_c⊥ Values)

Design values for compression perpendicular-to-grain ($F_{c\perp}$) are established in accordance with the procedures set forth in ASTM Standards D 2555 and D 245. ASTM procedures consider deformation under bearing loads as a serviceability limit state comparable to bending deflection because bearing loads rarely cause structural failures. Therefore, ASTM procedures for determining compression perpendicular-to-grain values are based on a deformation of 0.04″ and are considered adequate for most classes of structures. Where more stringent measures need to be taken in design, the following formula permits the designer to adjust design values to a more conservative deformation basis of 0.02″:

$$Y_{02} = 0.73\ Y_{04} + 5.60$$

EXAMPLE: Douglas Fir-Larch: $Y_{04} = 625$ psi
$Y_{02} = 0.73\ (625) + 5.60 = 462$ psi

Source: Western Wood Products Association

Wet Use Factors (C_M)   Table G
(Apply to Size-Adjusted Values)

The design values shown in the accompanying tables are for routine construction applications where the moisture content of the wood does not exceed 19%. When use conditions are such that the moisture content of dimension lumber will exceed 19%, the Wet Use Adjustment Factors below are recommended:

	PROPERTY	ADJUSTMENT FACTOR
F_b	Extreme Fiber Stress in Bending	0.85*
F_t	Tension Parallel-to-Grain	1.0
F_c	Compression Parallel-to-Grain	0.8**
F_v	Horizontal Shear	0.97
$F_{c\perp}$	Compression Perpendicular-to-Grain	0.67
E	Modulus of Elasticity	0.9

*Wet Use Factor 1.0 for size-adjusted F_b not exceeding 1150 psi.
**Wet Use Factor 1.0 for size-adjusted F_c not exceeding 750 psi.

Source: Western Wood Products Association

Table 5-2 provides a quick reference to all of the adjustments applicable to dimension lumber base values. Once all appropriate adjustments are taken, the adjusted number becomes the design value for a specific piece in its application. The formula is shown at the top of Table 5-2. Base value format for Canadian and Western species were published by certified grader agencies in the fall of 1991. When using base values it is important to remember, prior to engineering/design, to adjust the numbers for size and condition for use.

Machine Stress-Rated (MSR) lumber has been evaluated by mechanical stress-rating equipment. The stress-rating equipment measures the stiffness of the material and sorts it according to the modulus of elasticity (E). This lumber is marked with a grade stamp that indicates strength and stiffness values, F_b and E. You can order MSR lumber for your particular job. Just specify the strength value (F_b) and corresponding modulus of elasticity (E) values, nominal sizes, and lengths required (Table 5-3).

If you have not already purchased code books, I highly recommend that you do. The information contained in these books can answer questions you might have after the building department has closed for the day or the weekend. Some of the information and tables contained in this book are similar to those found in the codes.

The Beams and Stringers Design Values (Table 5-4) and Posts & Timbers Design Values (Table 5-5) indicate design values associated with species or groups. (Use Table 5-5A in conjunction with these tables.) When working with beams, the rule of thumb in my area (yours might be different) is that the length of the span should be double the nominal dimension of members. For example, 12' = two 2" × 12". Posts that are 4" × 4" and reach 8' in length (maximum) should be braced for lateral support or go to the next nominal di-

Table 5-2. Adjustments for Dimension Lumber

The boxes in the checklist below indicate when and how to apply adjustments (Table A–G to the Base Values in Table 5-1.)

BASE VALUES	X	ADJUSTMENT FACTORS				X	SPECIAL USE FACTORS			=	DESIGN VALUES	
		Size C_F	Repetitive Member C_r	Duration of Load C_D	Shear C_H		Flat Use C_{fu}	Compression Perpendicular $C_{c\perp}$	Other: Wet Use Temperature Fire-Retardent C_M, C_t, C_R	=	Design Value	
F_b		☐	☐	☐			☐		☐		F'_b	Bending
F_t		☐		☐					☐		F'_t	Tension
F_v				☐	☐				☐		F'_v	Shear
$F_{c\perp}$								(See Table F)	☐		$F'_{c\perp}$	Compression Perpendicular
$F_{c\parallel}$		☐		☐					☐		$F'_{c\parallel}$	Compression Parallel
E									☐		E'	Stiffness
Table 1		Table A	Table B	Table C	Table D		Table E	Table F	Table G & NDS			

Source: Western Wood Products Association

Table 5-3. MSR Lumber Design Values*

(2" and less in thickness, 2" and wider)

Grade Designation [1]	Extreme Fiber Stress in Bending "F_b" [2] Single	Modulus of Elasticity "E"	Tension Parallel-to-Grain "F_t"	Compression Parallel-to-Grain "F_c //"
2850 Fb-2.3E	2850	2,300,000	2300	2150
2700 Fb-2.2E	2700	2,200,000	2150	2100
2550 Fb-2.1E	2550	2,100,000	2050	2025
2400 Fb-2.0E	2400	2,000,000	1925	1975
2250 Fb-1.9E	2250	1,900,000	1750	1925
2100 Fb-1.8E	2100	1,800,000	1575	1875
1950 Fb-1.7E	1950	1,700,000	1375	1800
1800 Fb-1.6E	1800	1,600,000	1175	1750
1650 Fb-1.5E	1650	1,500,000	1020	1700
1500 Fb-1.4E	1500	1,400,000	900	1650
1450 Fb-1.3E	1450	1,300,000	800	1625
1350 Fb-1.3E	1350	1,300,000	750	1600
1200 Fb-1.2E	1200	1,200,000	600	1400

*Design values in pounds per square inch. Design values for compression perpendicular-to-grain ($F_{c\perp}$) and horizontal shear (F_v) are the same as assigned visually graded lumber of the appropriate species, unless indicated on grade stamp.

[1] For any given value of F_b, the average modulus of elasticity (E) and tension value (F_t) may vary depending upon the species, timber source and other variables. The E and F_t values included in the F_b-E grade designations in the table are those usually associated with each F_b level. Grade stamps may show higher or lower values if machine rating indicates the assignment is appropriate. If the F_t value is different for the MSR grade than that shown in the table for the same F_b level, the assigned F_t value shall be included on the gradestamp. When an E or F_t value varies from the designated F_b level in the table, the tabulated F_c //, $F_{c\perp}$, and F_v values associated with the designated F_b value are applicable.

[2] The tabulated F_b values are applicable to lumber loaded on edge. When loaded flatwise, refer to Table E.

Grades described in Section 52.00 of *Western Lumber Grading Rules.*
Source: Western Wood Products Association

Adjustments for MSR Lumber

☐ Repetitive Member Use Factor (C_r)   Table B
☐ Duration of Load (C_D)   Table C
☐ Horizontal Shear (C_H)   Table D
☐ Flat Use Factor (C_{fu})   Table E
☐ Compression Perpendicular ($C_{c\perp}$)   Table F
☐ Wet Use Factor (C_M)   Table G
  (only when appropriate)
Source: Western Wood Products Association

Table 5-4. Beams and Stringers Design Values*

(5" and thicker, width more than 2" greater than thickness**)

Species or Group	Grade	Extreme Fiber Stress in Bending "Fb"***	Tension Parallel-to-Grain "Ft"	Horizontal Shear "Fv"	Compression Perpen-dicular "Fc⊥"	Compression Parallel-to-Grain "Fc∥"	Modulus of Elasticity "E"
Douglas Fir-	Dense Select Structural	1850	1100	85	730	1300	1,700,000
Larch	Dense No. 1	1550	775	85	730	1100	1,700,000
	Dense No. 2	1000	500	85	730	700	1,400,000
	Select Structural	1600	950	85	625	1100	1,600,000
	No. 1	1350	675	85	625	925	1,600,000
	No. 2	875	425	85	625	600	1,300,000
Douglas Fir-	Select Structural	1550	900	85	520	1000	1,200,000
South	No. 1	1300	625	85	520	850	1,200,000
	No. 2	825	425	85	520	525	1,000,000
Hem-Fir	Select Structural	1250	725	70	405	925	1,300,000
	No. 1	1050	525	70	405	775	1,300,000
	No. 2	675	325	70	405	475	1,100,000
Spruce-Pine-Fir	Select Structural	1050	625	65	335	675	1,200,000
(South)	No. 1	900	450	65	335	575	1,200,000
	No. 2	575	300	65	335	350	1,000,000
Western Cedars	Select Structural	1150	700	70	425	875	1,000,000
	No. 1	975	475	70	425	725	1,000,000
	No. 2	625	325	70	425	475	800,000
Western Woods	Select Structural	1050	625	65	335	675	1,100,000
	No. 1	900	450	65	335	575	1,100,000
	No. 2	575	300	65	335	350	900,000

*Design values in pounds per square inch. See Sections 100.00 through 170.00 in the *Western Lumber Grading Rules* for additional information on these values.
**When the depth of a rectangular sawn lumber bending member exceeds 12 inches, the design value for extreme fiber in bending, Fb, shall be multiplied by the size factor in Table J.

Grades described in Sections 53.00 and 70.00 of *Western Lumber Grading Rules*.
Source: Western Wood Products Association

Table 5-5. Posts and Timbers Design Values*

(5" × 5" and larger, width not more than 2" greater than thickness**)

Species or Group	Grade	Extreme Fiber Stress in Bending "Fb"***	Tension Parallel-to-Grain "Ft"	Horizontal Shear "Fv"	Compression Perpen-dicular "Fc⊥"	Compression Parallel-to-Grain "Fc∥"	Modulus of Elasticity "E"
Douglas Fir-	Dense Select Structural	1750	1150	85	730	1350	1,700,000
Larch	Dense No. 1	1400	950	85	730	1200	1,700,000
	Dense No. 2	800	550	85	730	550	1,400,000
	Select Structural	1500	1000	85	625	1150	1,600,000
	No. 1	1200	825	85	625	1000	1,600,000
	No. 2	700	475	85	625	475	1,300,000
Douglas Fir-	Select Structural	1400	950	85	520	1050	1,200,000
South	No. 1	1150	775	85	520	925	1,200,000
	No. 2	650	400	85	520	425	1,000,000
Hem-Fir	Select Structural	1200	800	70	405	975	1,300,000
	No. 1	950	650	70	405	850	1,300,000
	No. 2	525	350	70	405	375	1,100,000
Spruce-Pine-Fir	Select Structural	1000	675	65	335	700	1,200,000
(South)	No. 1	800	550	65	335	625	1,200,000
	No. 2	350	225	65	335	225	1,000,000
Western Cedars	Select Structural	1100	720	70	425	925	1,000,000
	No. 1	875	600	70	425	800	1,000,000
	No. 2	500	350	70	425	375	800,000
Western Woods	Select Structural	1000	675	65	335	700	1,100,000
	No. 1	800	550	65	335	625	1,100,000
	No. 2	350	225	65	335	225	900,000

*Design values in pounds per square inch. See Sections 100.00 through 170.00 in the *Western Lumber Grading Rules* for additional information on these values.
**When the depth on a rectangular sawn lumber bending member exceeds 12 inches, the design value for extreme fiber in bending, Fb, shall be multiplied by the size factor in Table J.

Grades described in Sections 53.00 and 80.00 of *Western Lumber Grading Rules*
Source: Western Wood Products Association

Table 5-5A.

Timbers

Grades/End Uses - "Timbers" is both a general classification for the larger sizes of structural framing lumber and the
name of a specific grade and size. There are two basic grade
groups within this "Timbers" classification:
- Beams and Stringers - 5″ and thicker, width more than 2″
  greater than thickness (6x10, 8x12, etc.)
- Post and Timbers - 5x5 and larger, width not more than 2″
  greater than thickness (6x6, 6x8, etc.)

Design values assigned to each grade and species group
are shown in Tables 4 and 5, page 11. End uses include heavy
framing applications in both conventional and pre-engineered
systems. This classification of grades requires its own Wet Use
Adjustment, Table I and Size/Depth Effect Adjustment, Table J
(see below).

Wet Use Factor (C_M)   **Table I**
**Apply to Beams and Stringers/
Posts and Timbers**
(5" and thicker lumber)

5" and thicker lumber

When lumber 5″ and thicker is designed for exposed uses where the moisture
content will exceed 19% for an extended period of time, the design values shown
in Tables 4 and 5 should be multiplied by the following adjustment factors:

F_b	F_t	F_v	$F_{c\perp}$	F_c	E
1.00	1.00	1.00	0.67	0.91	1.00

Source: Western Wood Products Association

Table 5-5A. Continued

Size/Depth Effect Adjustment (C$_F$)   **Table J**
Apply to Beams and Stringers/
Posts and Timbers
(5" and thicker lumber)

When the depth of a rectangular sawn lumber bending member exceeds 12 inches, the design value for extreme fiber stress in bending (F$_b$) shall be multiplied by the size factor C$_F$, as determined by this formula:	$C_F = \left(\dfrac{12}{d}\right)^{1/9}$

Note: The following adjustment factors are derived from the formula above.

Nominal Depth	Net Surfaced Depth (d)	Depth Adjustment Factor (C$_F$)
14	13.5	0.987
16	15.5	0.972
18	17.5	0.959
20	19.5	0.947
22	21.5	0.937
24	23.5	0.928
26	25.5	0.920
28	27.5	0.912
30	29.5	0.905

Source: Western Wood Products Association

Adjustments for Beams and Stringers/ Posts and Timbers

☐ Duration of Load (C$_D$)	Table C
☐ Horizontal Shear (C$_H$)	Table D
☐ Compression Perpendicular (C$_{C\perp}$)	Table F
☐ Wet Use Adjustment (C$_M$)	Table I
☐ Depth Effect	Table J

Source: Western Wood Products Association

mension size. Tables are available in deck books already on the market, but remember that these are only guidelines and have not been adopted by the building codes.

To determine how far beams should be spaced from each other, or from the house when you are attaching a deck to a house, the distance between the posts supporting the beams and post sizes based on deck height and square footage should first be determined by an engineer. Depending on the structure, the building department will require this before a permit will be issued.

The Floor Joist Spans shown in Table 5-6 provide reference points to help you determine the span required for a particular project. Keep in mind that hot tubs or spas on decks require additional support. This table is only a guide; consult an engineer and/or the building department in your area.

Table 5-6. Floor Joist Spans
(40# Live Load)
(10# Live Load)

Design Criteria: *Strength:* 10 lbs. per sq. ft. dead load plus 40 lbs. per sq. ft. live load.
Deflection: Limited in span in inches divided by 360 for live load only.

Species or Group	Grade*	Span (feet and inches)											
		2 x 6			2 x 8			2 x 10			2 x 12		
		12" oc	16" oc	24" oc	12" oc	16" oc	24" oc	12" oc	16" oc	24" oc	12" oc	16" oc	24" oc
Douglas Fir-Larch	1 & Btr	11-2	10-2	8-10	14-8	13-4	11-8	18-9	17-0	14-5	22-10	20-5	16-8
	1	10-11	9-11	8-8	14-5	13-1	11-0	18-5	16-5	13-5	22-0	19-1	15-7
	2	10-9	9-9	8-1	14-2	12-7	10-3	17-9	15-5	12-7	20-7	17-10	14-7
	3	8-8	7-6	6-2	11-0	9-6	7-9	13-5	11-8	9-6	15-7	13-6	11-0
Douglas Fir-South	1	10-0	9-1	7-11	13-2	12-0	10-5	16-10	15-3	12-9	20-6	18-1	14-9
	2	9-9	8-10	7-9	12-10	11-8	10-0	16-5	14-11	12-2	19-11	17-4	14-2
	3	8-6	7-4	6-0	10-9	9-3	7-7	13-1	11-4	9-3	15-2	13-2	10-9
Hem-Fir	1 & Btr	10-6	9-6	8-3	13-10	12-7	11-0	17-8	16-0	13-9	21-6	19-6	16-0
	1	10-6	9-6	8-3	13-10	12-7	10-9	17-8	16-0	13-1	21-6	18-7	15-2
	2	10-0	9-1	7-11	13-2	12-0	10-2	16-10	15-2	12-5	20-4	17-7	14-4
	3	8-8	7-6	6-2	11-0	9-6	7-9	13-5	11-8	9-6	15-7	13-6	11-0
Spruce-Pine-Fir (South)	1	9-9	8-10	7-8	12-10	11-8	10-2	16-5	14-11	12-5	19-11	17-7	14-4
	2	9-6	8-7	7-6	12-6	11-4	9-6	15-11	14-3	11-8	19-1	16-6	13-6
	3	8-0	6-11	5-8	10-2	8-9	7-2	12-5	10-9	8-9	14-4	12-5	10-2
Western Woods	1	9-6	8-7	7-0	12-6	10-10	8-10	15-4	13-3	10-10	17-9	15-5	12-7
	2	9-2	8-4	7-0	12-1	10-10	8-10	15-4	13-3	10-10	17-9	15-5	12-7
	3	7-6	6-6	5-4	9-6	8-3	6-9	11-8	10-1	8-3	13-6	11-8	9-6

*Spans were computed for commonly marketed grades and species. Spans for other grades and Western Cedars can be computed using the WWPA *Span Computer*.

Source: Western Wood Products Association

The Western Wood Products Association has created a slide rule, the WWPA Western Lumber "Span Computer." This device is intended to assist architects, engineers, code officials, and builders like yourself in determining grade, species, size, and spacing and span requirements.

New base values for Western Lumber, resulting from the In-Grade Testing Program, are incorporated into this span computer. The "Joist and Rafter Computer" has the size and repetitive use adjustments for Base Values built into the calculations. The "Beam Computer" has the size adjustment built in.

The WWPA "Span Computer" is suitable for designing uniformly loaded beams, joists, and rafters for fiber stress in bending (F_b) and modulus of elasticity (E). It is the designer's responsibility to check horizontal shear and compression perpendicular to grain.

Joist, rafter, and beam spans are limited by expected loads and the amount of deflection that might occur. Among the factors involved are dead load, live load, load duration, stiffness, and strength.

The computer is used most often with the loading requirements that appear on the front flap. However, it can also be used for a greater range of loads, spans, and deflections not usually covered by span tables such as odd numbered loads (25 psf snow), higher snow loads (50 psf and greater), and so forth. The joist and rafter loading scales make provisions for abnormal loadings up to 80 psf for deflection and 100 psf for strength. The beam loading scales provide for loading up to 400 lb/ft for both deflection and strength.

To get your Span Computer ($3.50), write to:

Western Wood Products Association
Yeon Building
522 SW Fifth Avenue
Portland, OR 97204-2122

Whenever possible, I prefer to use solid beams in the deck framework because it saves time. If you need to span a large area, consider using a laminated beam. Make sure the beam is fabricated with waterproof glue; I recommend sealing the beam before its installation. If you are considering using a micro-lam beam, be sure it will be used in an area protected by the weather because the manufacturer does not guarantee it for outside use. Again, if you choose to use this product, be sure to seal it as well.

If you are building your own beams at the job site, you are probably using two nominal dimension pieces with ½" plywood between them, a common way to build beams. Because plywood can delaminate, consider substituting a ½" pressure-treated material or solid wood. If you need to increase your span and you are building using this method, then consider tripling your nominal dimension piece. Fasten the lumber together without spaces and use screws.

Another element to consider is cantilever. Ninety-five percent of all the decks I have built were cantilevered. The largest overhang I have allowed is 2'. The rule of thumb for cantilevering that I have always followed is that the cantilever should be no more than one quarter the total span of the joist. For example, to calculate the maximum cantilever for a 16' joist: multiply 16' by 0.25 to get 4'. However, the UBC requires that a cantilever involving a load at the end not exceed the nominal depth of its member. The example I gave would require an engineer's services, whether or not it will be a load-bearing cantilever. If you are designing a deck involving a cantilever, check first with your local building department and, if they consider it necessary, consult a structural engineer.

I firmly believe that the framework is the most important part of a deck, so more time should be spent putting this system together. Increasing the depth of a joist (2" × 8", 10", or 12") can eliminate a lot of the deflection; employing more beams and posts can help when using joists that are smaller (2" × 4", 2" × 6", or 2" × 8").

Subcontractors

Finding talented and reliable subcontractors can be an exhausting trial-and-error process, especially with more than 40 different types of specialty contractors or subcontractors in the industry. You alone must decide on subcontractors for specific jobs, and building and maintaining relationships with subcontractors (once you have found ones you are comfortable working with) can be a very difficult but also rewarding experience.

Whatever your reasons for hiring subcontractors, keep in mind that they are professionals with individual personalities trying to run and manage successful companies. Like many general contractors, they rely on a support network of quality subcontractors to produce much of their work. Your judicious use of subcontractors can make or break a project and can work to your overall advantage. Subcontractors can help you meet state licensing requirements (when appropriate) and can speed production.

To get the best out of your relationships with subcontractors, follow these guidelines:

- Hire and work with the same subcontractors.
- Give subcontractors the opportunity to bid their part of the project.
- Don't let a subcontractor's price cause you to shop for a lower-priced subcontractor.
- Communicate with subcontractors, asking for their opinion and/or input.
- Give adequate notice of scheduled work or delays and immediately advise subcontractors of any changes.
- Provide accurate plans for subcontractors to work from.
- Arrange for materials you are supplying to arrive on time for subcontractors' work.
- Provide good working conditions on the job site.
- Offer general direction (to meet job specifications) as needed, but let the subcontractors do their own work.
- Arrange for a qualified worker (not the customer) to be on hand to answer subcontractors' questions or to tackle any problems that should arise.
- Pay your subcontractors promptly.

Quality

To assure you receive the quality work your customers deserve, build and strengthen your relationships with subcontractors. Quality work requires fewer callbacks; quality relationships produce respect and performance.

Giving subcontractors the opportunity to bid their portion of the work allows them to look over the job and anticipate any potential problems that might not otherwise be discovered and that could affect your bid. Nothing is more embarrassing than to approach a customer with a mistake and then ask for additional funds to cover it. Depending on how the general conditions of your contract are written, such problems are usually yours, not the customer's.

When subcontractors participate in the bidding process, they reaffirm that the job will run smoothly and profitably. Working with the same subcontractors for about 20 years, I have developed relationships with them that help to overcome customers' budget constraints. These relationships have permitted us to rebid jobs, coming up with alternative plans of action that both won the customers' approval and met their budgets. While this didn't happen often, it was reassuring to feel that I could go to subcontractors and be confident they would work with me. When a job was underbid, our give-and-take relationship helped us to work out compromises we could both accept.

Loyalty

In return for their loyalty, you need to support your subcontractors; they, in turn, will support you. Most subcontractors work for other general contractors as well as their own customers, so their schedule could be as tight as yours. Even when you have a strong working relationship, you might not always be able to hire a particular subcontractor for a particular job. Since you might have to hire another subcontractor, it doesn't hurt to establish working relationships with more than one of the same trade.

Your preferred subcontractor could recommend an equally qualified subcontractor for your particular job. Remember, a job could arise when you will need both subcontractors, and their previous relationship could be a big help.

Finally, your payment track record can reinforce the subcontractor's loyalty to you, especially during a busy construction season.

Good neighbor policy

Treat subcontractors as you would like to be treated and work to build personal relationships with them. Keep in mind that they can be a good source of leads. Don't be afraid to ask them to send business your way, and be sure to do the same for them.

It might be helpful to attend meetings or join an association for subcontractors. This can provide an informal opportunity to meet and get to know other subcontractors in your area. You need them as much as they need you. By working as a team, you'll produce the highest quality work possible, ensure the customer's happiness (which means repeat business), keep your overall production costs down, and increase your profits.

Costs

Stay informed about the costs of products that you purchase from your suppliers. If you have a computer, update this information on a monthly basis. Before you pay your invoices, check them over and enter any changes. If you do not have a computer, make up a materials list for each supplier and review the prices on a regular basis.

This process allows you to keep current; if you run into a time crunch, at least you will have the prices at your fingertips for quick bid calculations. It always helps to know your prices. Many suppliers give 1000-board-feet prices instead of linear feet. They will make the conversion for you, but it's a good idea to know the formula. Table 5-7 helps solve such conversion problems.

If you are required to obtain a permit by your municipality, they will ask for drawings of what you plan to build. The drawings or plans should include a site plan (a drawing of the entire property). The site plan should show how the new project relates to the house and other structures as well as to the property. When decks are high off the ground, you might be required to have plans that show elevations or side views. You might also need to provide framing plans that include the foundation, posts, beams, joists, decking, railing, stairs, and the sizes and spacing of members. These plans should probably be done by an architect and might have to include a seal of approval from an engineer for supporting members (depending on the overall deck height and whether you are building over the side of a hill).

If such detailed plans are required, be sure to include their cost in your bid. Before actually hiring architectural or engineering services, have a signed contract for the project first. Keep in mind that when customers sign contracts on their own property, they have the right to cancel that contract within three working days. If the contract is signed at your place of business, you are relatively safe. In any case, I would wait a good four to five days before beginning the project.

You can make simple plan view drawings (looking down from above) on your own. These help when selling a project to a potential customer and give you a worksheet to use when compiling your bid. Additionally, they provide the information you need to pass on to an architect or engineer, should their services be required.

Table 5-7. Conversions from Lineal Feet to Board Feet in Standard Sizes of Western Lumber

Board Measure Equivalents

This table, based on Standard Nominal Sizes (from 1 x 2 to 8 x 24) has been developed by Western Wood Products Association as an aid to:
a. determine lineal (linear) feet per 1000 board feet, and
b. find the equivalents between lineal and board feet.

The common lengths between 6' and 16' are tabulated in the table; a formula is provided for calculating other lengths.

The table can be used when dollar amounts are added, as the basis of converting:
a. cost per 1000 board feet to cost per lineal foot, or
b. cost per piece.

Refer to the other side of this sheet for additional information and examples of how to use the table to solve problems.

Actual dressed (surfaced), green and dry sizes are included for reference; however, **nominal sizes are always used for board footage calculations.**

When using this table start with the NOMINAL SIZES column. Read to the left for lineal foot information. Read to the right for board foot information.

For lengths, other than those tabulated, the formula for converting lineal feet to board feet is:

$$\frac{T \times W \times L}{12} = \text{Board Feet}$$

	Lineal Feet per 1000 Board Feet	Lineal Feet per Board Foot	Green Surfaced Size for more than 19% moist. content	NOMINAL SIZE	Dry Surfaced Size for 19% or less moisture content	Board Feet per Lineal Foot	6'	8'	10'	12'	14'	16'	
BOARDS	6000'	6.0000'	Surfaced Dry Only	1 x 2	¾ x 1½"	0.1667	1	1.33	1.67	2	2.33	2.67	
	4000	4.0000		1 x 3	¾ x 2½	0.2500	1.50	2	2.50	3	3.50	4	
	3000	3.0000		1 x 4	¾ x 3½	0.3333	2	2.67	3.33	4	4.67	5.33	
	2000	2.0000		1 x 6	¾ x 5½	0.5000	3	4	5	6	7	8	
	1500	1.5000		1 x 8	¾ x 7¼	0.6667	4	5.33	6.67	8	9.33	10.67	
	1200	1.2000		1 x 10	¾ x 9¼	0.8333	5	6.67	8.33	10	11.67	13.33	
	1000	1.0000		1 x 12	¾ x 11¼	1.0000	6	8	10	12	14	16	
	857	0.8571		1 x 14	¾ x 13¼	1.1667	7	9.33	11.67	14	16.33	18.67	
DIMENSION LUMBER	3000	3.0000	1 9/16 x 1 9/16"	2 x 2	1½ x 1½	0.3333	2	2.67	3.33	4	4.67	5.33	**BOARD FEET**
	2000	2.0000	1 9/16 x 2 9/16	2 x 3	1½ x 2½	0.5000	3	4	5	6	7	8	
	1500	1.5000	1 9/16 x 3 9/16	2 x 4	1½ x 3½	0.6667	4	5.33	6.67	8	9.33	10.67	
	1000	1.0000	1 9/16 x 5⅝	2 x 6	1½ x 5½	1.0000	6	8	10	12	14	16	
	750	0.7500	1 9/16 x 7½	2 x 8	1½ x 7¼	1.3333	8	10.67	13.33	16	18.67	21.33	
	600	0.6000	1 9/16 x 9½	2 x 10	1½ x 9¼	1.6667	10	13.33	16.67	20	23.33	26.67	
	500	0.5000	1 9/16 x 11½	2 x 12	1½ x 11¼	2.0000	12	16	20	24	28	32	
	429	0.4286	1 9/16 x 13½	2 x 14	1½ x 13¼	2.3333	14	18.67	23.33	28	32.67	37.33	
	1333	1.3333	2 9/16 x 2 9/16	3 x 3	2½ x 2½	0.7500	4.50	6	7.50	9	10.50	12	
	1000	1.0000	2 9/16 x 3 9/16	3 x 4	2½ x 3½	1.0000	6	8	10	12	14	16	
	667	0.6667	2 9/16 x 5⅝	3 x 6	2½ x 5½	1.5000	9	12	15	18	21	24	
	500	0.5000	2 9/16 x 7½	3 x 8	2½ x 7¼	2.0000	12	16	20	24	28	32	
	400	0.4000	2 9/16 x 9½	3 x 10	2½ x 9¼	2.5000	15	20	25	30	35	40	
	333	0.3333	2 9/16 x 11½	3 x 12	2½ x 11¼	3.0000	18	24	30	36	42	48	
	286	0.2857	2 9/16 x 13½	3 x 14	2½ x 13¼	3.5000	21	28	35	42	49	56	
	250	0.2500	2 9/16 x 15½	3 x 16	2½ x 15¼	4.0000	24	32	40	48	56	64	
	750	0.7500	3 9/16 x 3 9/16	4 x 4	Surfaced Green Only	1.3333	8	10.67	13.33	16	18.67	21.33	
	500	0.5000	3 9/16 x 5⅝	4 x 6		2.0000	12	16	20	24	28	32	
	375	0.3750	3 9/16 x 7½	4 x 8		2.6667	16	21.33	26.67	32	37.33	42.67	
	300	0.3000	3 9/16 x 9½	4 x 10		3.3333	20	26.67	33.33	40	46.67	53.33	
	250	0.2500	3 9/16 x 11½	4 x 12		4.0000	24	32	40	48	56	64	
	214	0.2143	3 9/16 x 13½	4 x 14		4.6667	28	37.33	46.67	56	65.33	74.67	
	188	0.1875	3 9/16 x 15½	4 x 16		5.3333	32	42.67	53.33	64	74.67	85.33	
HEAVY TIMBERS	333	0.3333	5½ x 5½	6 x 6		3.0000	18	24	30	36	42	48	
	250	0.2500	5½ x 7½	6 x 8		4.0000	24	32	40	48	56	64	
	200	0.2080	5½ x 9½	6 x 10	Surfaced Green Only	5.0000	30	40	50	60	70	80	
	167	0.1667	5½ x 11½	6 x 12		6.0000	36	48	60	72	84	96	
	143	0.1429	5½ x 13½	6 x 14		7.0000	42	56	70	84	98	112	
	125	0.1250	5½ x 15½	6 x 16		8.0000	48	64	80	96	112	128	
	111	0.1111	5½ x 17½	6 x 18		9.0000	54	72	90	108	126	144	
	100	0.1000	5½ x 19½	6 x 20		10.0000	60	80	100	120	140	160	
	188	0.1875	7½ x 7½	8 x 8		5.3333	32	42.67	53.33	64	74.67	85.33	
	150	0.1500	7½ x 9½	8 x 10		6.6667	40	53.33	66.67	80	99.33	106.67	
	125	0.1250	7½ x 11½	8 x 12		8.0000	48	64	80	96	112	128	
	107	0.1071	7½ x 13½	8 x 14	Surfaced Green Only	9.3333	56	74.67	93.33	112	130.67	149.33	
	94	0.0938	7½ x 15½	8 x 16		10.6667	64	85.33	106.67	128	149.33	170.67	
	83	0.0833	7½ x 17½	8 x 18		12.0000	72	96	120	144	168	192	
	75	0.0750	7½ x 19½	8 x 20		13.3333	80	106.67	133.33	160	186.67	213.33	
	68	0.0682	7½ x 21½	8 x 22		14.6667	88	117.33	146.67	176	205.33	234.67	
	63	0.0625	7½ x 23½	8 x 24		16.0000	96	128	160	192	224	256	

Note: Columns 6'–16' are headed BOARD FEET (rounded to the nearest 100th), LENGTHS.

Source: Western Wood Products Association

Table 5-7. Continued

ADDITIONAL INFORMATION

Three basic units of measure are used for lumber:

1. **Board Measure** — is the term to indicate that **board foot** is the unit of measurement for most lumber items.

   A board foot is defined as a piece one inch thick (nominal) by one foot wide (nominal) by one foot long (actual) or its equivalent. For instance, a 2x6 also equals one board foot for each foot of length.

   Board footage is calculated by multiplying the nominal thickness in inches (T) by the nominal width in inches (W) by the actual length in feet (L) and dividing by 12. The formula is:

$$\frac{T \times W \times L}{12} = \textbf{Board Feet}$$

   Where: **T** = nominal thickness in inches
              W = nominal width in inches
              L = length in feet

2. **Surface Measure** — is the square feet on the surface of a piece of lumber. Surface measure is calculated without regard to thickness of the piece, i.e. a 2x12 board, one foot long equals **one square foot.** The formula is:

$$\frac{W \times L}{12} = \textbf{Surface Measure}$$

3. **Lineal Measure** — is the total **length** in feet of a board, regardless of its thickness or width, i.e. a 2x14 one foot long is one lineal foot.

To calculate the board footage for sizes and lengths other than those given in the table:

1. To calculate the **board feet per lineal foot** of an uncommon size:

$$\frac{T \times W}{12} = \textbf{Board Feet per Lineal Foot}$$

   Example: A lineal foot of 3x5 = 1.25bf

2. To calculate the **total board feet in an uncommon length** of a particular size:

   a. use the board footage formula, or
   b. use the board feet per lineal foot (either from your calculation, i.e. 1.25 bf for a 3x5, or from column ⑥ in the table times the length).

   Examples: 17' of 3x5 = 1.25bfx17 = 21.25bf
              17' of 3x6 = 1.5bfx17 = 25.5bf

   Note: For multiple pieces; multiply the board feet in one piece times the number of pieces (as in Problem 2 opposite).

Western Wood Products Association
Yeon Building, 522 SW Fifth Avenue
Portland, OR 97204-2122
503/224-3930
           1711/A-10/3-93/15M

USING THE TABLE
Explanation of Table Headings

Lineal Feet per 1000 Board Feet	Lineal Feet per Board Foot	Green Surfaced Size for more than 19% most. content	NOMINAL SIZE	Dry Surfaced Size for 19% or less moisture content	Board Feet per Lineal Foot	BOARD FEET (rounded to the nearest 100th) LENGTHS					
						6'	8'	10'	12'	14'	16'
⑤	④	②	①	③	⑥			⑦			

① **NOMINAL SIZE** — is the standard size designation for lumber, used for convenience.

② **Green Surfaced Size for more than 19% moisture content** — this is the actual (surfaced) size of unseasoned lumber which, by definition, has a moisture content in excess of 19%.

③ **Dry Surfaced Size for 19% or less moisture content** — this is the actual (surfaced) size of air- or kiln-dried, seasoned lumber which, by definition, has a moisture content of 19% or less.

④ **Lineal Feet per Board Foot** — the lineal feet, in a given size piece, needed to equal one board foot.

⑤ **Lineal Feet per 1000 Board Feet** — lineal feet, in given size pieces, needed to equal 1000 board feet.

⑥ **Board Feet per Lineal Foot** — the number of board feet per one foot of length, in a given size.

⑦ **Board Feet** — the columns in this section give board footages for corresponding lengths and sizes. Lengths are given from 6' to 16', in 2' increments. Sizes are read from the **NOMINAL SIZES** column in the middle of the table.

Sample Problems

1. How to use the **tabulated values for lengths** given in the table.

        Problem: How many board feet (bf) in 8, 2x4s, 12' long?
        Solution: Find 2x4 nominal size on chart. Read across the column, under the 12' heading and find 8 bf.
                      8 bf x 8 pieces = 64 bf

2. How to find the **total board footage for multiples of uncommon lengths** of standard sizes.

        Problem: How many bf are in 10, 4x8s, 20' long?
        Solution: Find the board feet per lineal foot (column ⑥) for 4x8; it's 2.6667. Multiply times 20' in length, times 10 pieces.
                   2.6667 x 20 x 10 = 533.34 bf

3. How to **convert price per 1000 bf** to **price per lineal foot.**

        Example: $225.00/1000 bf for 2x8s
        Problem: What is the price per lineal foot?
        Solution: Find lineal feet per 1000 bf for 2x8s in the far left column of the table; it's 750.
                   $225 ÷ 750 = 30¢ per lineal foot

4. How to **convert price per 1000 bf** to **price per piece.**

        Example: $255.00/1000 bf for 2x12s
        Problem: What is the price for 10' of 2x12s?
        Solution: Find bf for 10' of 2x12 in the table; it's 20 bf.
                   $255 ÷ 1000 bf = .255
            20 bf x .255 = $5.10 (price for 10' of 2x12)

WWPA positions 13 professional field representatives throughout the country. Employee training seminars for retailers are one of the many services offered by the Association. Call the Field Services department in the home office (Portland, OR 503/224-3930) for additional information.

Source: Western Wood Products Association

Figure 5-20 shows a simple plan view of the extension of a deck on an existing structure. It shows a set of stairs leading down to a patio set with pavers. This deck was high off the ground, and in my city (Spokane, Washington), an elevation drawing was required. This con-

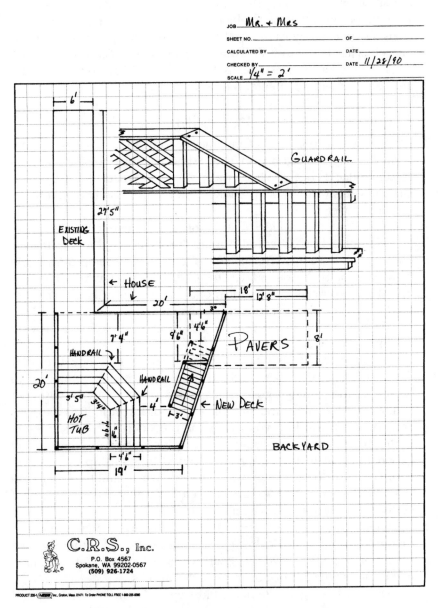

5-20 *This drawing shows a good example of a detailed guardrail.*
C.R.S., Inc.

tract was not granted, however, because the customer did not want handrails added to an existing hot tub. Code required that the four steps leading to the hot tub have two sets of handrails as shown on the drawing. Even though the building department already knew of the situation concerning this job, the customer chose not to work with me because I chose to abide by the building department's decisions. I'm not sure what the final outcome was. My point is that sometimes it is just better to walk away from a situation. Customers will do what they want to please themselves and sometimes building codes and regulations do not enter the picture.

Itemizing

I firmly believe (because of my track record) that itemized bids are easier to sell to a customer than an estimate. An itemized bid helps a customer decide because it shows in black and white where their dollars and cents will be spent. An itemized bid can also help you negotiate a contract.

If the customer decides that the bid is too high, you will be able to curb that bid by either redesigning the project or downscaling the quality of the product. This means, of course, that compromises will be needed on both sides. Maybe the customer can downsize the project. Maybe you can lower your profit margin and/or labor. This can be done easily with itemized bid sheets.

If you get the job, the itemized bid sheets can serve as a material list and a worksheet.

Some professionals would rather not show how they arrived at the bottom line price, but I feel the customer hiring me has a right to see where the money is going. If you are worried about the customer taking your bid sheet and shopping around, forget it. This happens and you can't stop it. If you follow the procedures I have suggested to this point, you don't need to worry. Just sell that job. I know from experience that giving customers itemized bids can tip the scale in your favor. Customers today want to know where and how their dollars will be spent. They want details. Quite frankly, this is the type of customer you want to work for.

Should you estimate? Since an estimate is only an educated guess, I wouldn't. If you feel a customer is shopping around, either over the phone or in person, give a ballpark verbal estimate. You will know immediately whether or not you can do business.

Do you have good itemized bid sheets? Figures 5-21, 5-22, and 5-23 are the itemized bid sheets I used to bid the project shown in Fig. 5-20. Itemized bid sheets clearly spell out the many materials and

CONTRACTOR'S ITEMIZED BID SHEET

CUSTOMER'S NAME Mr + Mrs BILLING ADDRESS Same

JOB ADDRESS 0000 – CHENEY, WA 00000 JOB DESCRIPTION 20'x19' Deck, Doors, Pavers

WORK PHONE 000-0000 RESIDENT PHONE 000-0000

ARCHITECT ADDRESS PHONE

ESTIMATOR LEON A. FRECHETTE APPOINTMENT DATE 11/27/90 BID DATE 11/28/90

MATERIAL LIST

Lumber

Item	Description	@	$
1 x 2			
1 x 4			
1 x 6			
2 x 2			
2 x 4	6/16'	4.08	16.32
2 x 6			
2 x 8			
2 x 10	23/20'	10.73	246.79
2 x 12	3/16', 4/12'	8.80/6.87	46.86
4 x 4	8/10'	2.75	22.00
4 x 6			
4 x 8			
MISC.	Lam Beam 20' 24'	7.05'	310.20
MISC.			
MISC.			
MISC.	Lattice 4x8x1 - 2	28.20	56.40

Treated

Item	Description	@	$
2 x 4			
2 x 6			
2 x 8			
MISC.			
MISC.			

Cedar

Item	Description	@	$
1 x 2	60'	.08	4.80
1 x 3			
1 x 4			
1 x 6			
1 x 8			
1 x 10	Kickers 78'	.55	42.90
1 x 12	80'	.78	62.40
2 x 2	317/4' Redwood C	1.14	361.38
2 x 4	10/20' 6/16' RW,CH	1.10'	325.60
2 x 6	167' 91' RW 42/20'	.77	845.46
2 x 8	2X6 RWC 80'	1.68	134.40
2 x 10			
2 x 12			
MISC.	4X4 12/10' RW	6.80	81.60
MISC.			

Painting

Item	Description	@	$
PAINT	1 gal		14.98
PRIMER	1 gal		12.90
STAIN	1 qt.		7.59
MISC.	1 gal		14.50
MISC.	THINNER		12.00

Drywall

Item	Description	@	$
MUD JOINT/TOPPING			
½" SHEET ROCK	1		4.54
½" WP SHEET ROCK			
⅝" TYPE X SHEET ROCK			
CORNER BEADS			
MISC.	MUD		6.00
MISC.	TEXTURE		7.50

Plywood/Siding

Item	Description	@	$
⅜" SOFFIT MATERIAL			
½" CDX			
⅝" T-1-11			
¾" CDX			
¼" P BOARD UNDERLAYMENT			
¼" AC PLYWOOD EXTERIOR			
¾" TG PLYWD UNDERLAYMENT			
PANELING			
TREAD MATERIAL			
LAP SIDING			
SHAKES (GROOVED)			
MISC.			
MISC.			
MISC.			

Insulation

Item	Description	@	$
3½" - R-11			
6" - R-19			
SILL			
MISC.			
MISC.			

Hardware

Item	Description	@	$
NAIL, SCREW, STUDSHOTS			120.00
SHIMS, STAPLES, PLASTIC	HEAVY		64.00
HINGES/BALL BEARING			
DOOR CLOSURES			
HANDLES	Lock – EXTERIOR	Allowance	21.50
HANDLES			
THRESHOLD			
PIPE/DUCTWORK			
JOIST HANGERS	20/ 2X10'	.45	9.00
BOLTS/WASHERS			
MISC.	Spikes 35	.20	7.00
MISC.	8 - 4X4 BRACKETS	2.79	22.32
MISC.	4- ENDS 4- CENTERS	.79	12.64
MISC.			

Adhesive

Item	Description	@	$
CONTACT CEMENT			
ADHESIVE			
CAULKING	LATEX/Silicone	2.78/7.59	10.37
MISC.			
MISC.			

Doors

Item	Description	@	$
WOOD			
METAL	SELF-S STORM DOOR		116.88
	F 400 KEY LOCK		10.00
BI-FOLD			
POCKET DOOR			
SCREEN DOOR			
PRE-HUNG			
	3° Fiberglass		
	THERMA-TRU		328.00
MISC.			
MISC.			

Frames

Item	Description	@	$
POCKET DOOR			
WOOD			
METAL			
MISC.			
MISC.			

Closed Parts

Item	Description	@	$
SHELF			
RODS			
POLE END			
SHELF SUPPORT			
MISC.			
MISC.			

Molding

Item	Description	@	$
CASING	Mahg. 5/8' 1/10'	.133	23.76
JAMBS			
BASE			
MISC.			
MISC.			

Creative Remodeling Services, Inc. © 1986 Leon A. Frechette

5-21 *Contractor's itemized bid sheet (part 1).* C.R.S., Inc.

CONTRACTOR'S ITEMIZED BID SHEET   **PAGE 2**

Bathroom Parts

Item	@	$
MIRROR	@	$
MEDICINE CABINETS	@	$
SHOWER DOOR	@	$
SHOWER ENCLOSURE	@	$
TOWEL BAR/RING	@	$
TISSUE HANGER/CLAMP	@	$
MISC.	@	$
MISC.	@	$
MISC.	@	$

Concrete

Item		@	$	
CONCRETE	1.5 PER. YD.	@ 47.55	$ 71	33
CONCRETE FOOTINGS	PER. YD.	@	$	
REINFORCING STEEL		@	$	
FILL	SAND PER. YD.	@ 9.00	$ 9	00
PETE GRAVEL 1-5/8	PER. YD.	@ 10"/40B	$ 50	00
EXPANSION STRIPS	Tubes 4/4'8"	@ 3.13'	$ 50	08
QUICK POUR		@	$	
CONCRETE BLOCKS	EDGE PAVER 80	@ .40	$ 32	00
BRICKS	PAVERS - 144'-750	@ .28	$ 210	00
MORTAR	EDGE - 15' - 4	@ 21.00	$ 84	00
MISC.	Delivery	@ 72/55	$ 127	00

Roofing

Item		@	$
ASPHALT CEMENT		@	$
FLASHING		@	$
FELT PAPER		@	$
KRAFT PAPER		@	$
3-TAB	PER. SQ.	@	$
CEDAR SHAKES	PER. SQ.	@	$
DRIP EDGE		@	$
TRUSSES		@	$
MISC.		@	$
MISC.		@	$
MISC.		@	$
MISC.		@	$

Vents

Item	@	$
SOFFIT	@	$
GABLE	@	$
ROOF	@	$
JOIST/WALL	@	$
MISC.	@	$
MISC.	@	$

Tile

Item		@	$
CERAMIC	PER. SQ. FT.	@	$
QUARRY	PER. SQ. FT.	@	$
GLUE		@	$
GROUT		@	$
MISC.		@	$
MISC.		@	$

Flooring

Item		@	$
HARDWOOD	PER. SQ. FT.	@	$
FLOOR COVERING	PER. YD.	@	$
FLOOR TREAD		@	$
SEAMING KIT		@	$
CARPET	PER. YD.	@	$
PAD	PER YD.	@	$
METAL		@	$
RUBBER BASE	PER. FT.	@	$
MISC.		@	$
MISC.		@	$

Counter Material

Item		@	$
PB COUNTER TOP		@	$
BELVCO EDGE		@	$
PRE-MADE LAMINATE TOP	LIN FT	@	$
OAK EDGE LAMINATE TOP	LIN. FT.	@	$
LAMINATE	SQ. FT.	@	$
MISC.		@	$
MISC.		@	$

Glazing

Item	@	$
TAPE	@	$
MOLDINGS	@	$
GLASS	@	$
MISC.	@	$
MISC.	@	$

Windows/Accessories

Item		@	$	
WINDOW WELL METAL		@	$	
WINDOW WELL CONCRETE		@	$	
TRIM		@	$	
WINDOWS	Pella	@	$	
126B W.C. SHADES, BTINT		@	$ 265	35
4 1/2 weeks		@	$	
OXO 26 SLIDER - SHADES		@	$ 1635	26
AF 24 TFD SCREEN -		@	$	
SHADES - 2 weeks		@	$ 1300	41
		@	$	
		@	$	
		@	$	
MISC.		@	$	
MISC.		@	$	

Fireplace

Item	@	$
MANTELS	@	$
FIREPLACE	@	$
CHIMNEYS	@	$
PIPE	@	$
PIPE	@	$
MISC.	@	$
MISC.	@	$

Ironworks

Item	@	$
HANDRAIL	@	$
MISC.	@	$
MISC.	@	$

Rental

Item		@	$	
TOOLS	Tub Tile Saw	@	$ 78	00
MISC.	Elec. Jack Hammer	@	$ 174	00
MISC.	Plate Jack	@	$ 140	00
MISC.	Hopper	@	$ 36	00
MISC.		@	$	

Appliances

Item	@	$
MISC.	@	$
MISC.	@	$
MISC.	@	$
MISC.	@	$
MISC.	@	$

Cabinets

Item	@	$
TRIM	@	$
CABINETS	@	$
	@	$
	@	$
	@	$
	@	$
	@	$
	@	$
	@	$
	@	$
	@	$
	@	$
	@	$
	@	$
	@	$
	@	$
	@	$
	@	$
	@	$
MISC.	@	$
MISC.	@	$

Extras or Misc. Items

Item		$	
THE FIBER - CLASSIC		$	
FINISH Kit		$ 18	00
EXTERIOR Polyurethane	qt	$ 6	95
		$	

SUB-TOTALS

Item	$	
CARPET	$	
WINDOWS	$ 3,655	90
APPLIANCES	$	
REMAINING MATERIALS	$ 4,014	07

Creative Remodeling Services, Inc. © 1986 Leon A. Frechette

5-22 *Contractor's itemized bid sheet (part 2).* C.R.S., Inc.

SUB-CONTRACTOR'S ITEMIZED BID SHEET   PAGE 3
THE FOLLOWING LABOR CHARGES MAY OR MAY NOT INCLUDE MATERIALS

Excavating
EXCAVATE ___ $ ___
GRADING & FILLING ___ $ ___
MISC. ___ $ ___
Concrete
CURBS ___ $ ___
DRIVEWAYS ___ $ ___
FLOORS/FLATWORK ___ $ ___
FORMS ___ $ ___
LIGHTWEIGHT ___ $ ___
STEPS ___ $ ___
WALKS ___ $ ___
PUMP ___ $ ___
MISC. ___ $ ___
Masonary
CHIMNEYS & FIREPLACE ___ $ ___
COMMON BRICK ___ $ ___
CONCRETE BLOCK ___ $ ___
FACE BRICK ___ $ ___
TILE ___ $ ___
MANTELS ___ $ ___
STONEWORK ___ $ ___
MISC. ___ $ ___
Sanitation
SEWER ___ $ ___
PLUMBING ___ $ ___
MISC. ___ $ ___
Electrical
WIRING ___ $ ___
MISC. ___ $ ___
Air Conditioning
DUCTS/MECHANICAL ___ $ ___
EQUIPMENT ___ $ ___
MISC. ___ $ ___
Heating
GAS/ELECTRIC ___ $ ___
MISC. ___ $ ___
Lath & Plastering
DRY WALL ___ $ ___
EXTERIOR ___ $ ___
INTERIOR ___ $ ___
MISC. ___ $ ___
Ceiling
ACOUSTIC ___ $ ___
MISC. ___ $ ___
Glazing
MIRRORS ___ $ ___
MISC. GLASS ___ $ ___
PLATE GLASS ___ $ ___
MISC. ___ $ ___
Mill Work
CABINETS ___ $ ___
COUNTER TOPS ___ $ ___
DOORS ___ $ ___
MISC. ___ $ ___
Doors
CUSTOM ___ $ ___

COMMERCIAL ___ $ ___
RESIDENTIAL ___ $ ___
GARAGE OPENERS ___ $ ___
MISC. ___ $ ___
TILE
CERAMIC TILE ___ $ ___
QUARRY TILE ___ $ ___
MISC. ___ $ ___
Floors
CARPET ___ $ ___
FLOOR COVERING ___ $ ___
HARDWOOD ___ $ ___
MISC. ___ $ ___
Painting & Decorating
PAINTER/STAINER ___ $ ___
WALL PAPER ___ $ ___
MISC. ___ $ ___
Roof
COMPOSITION ___ $ ___
HOT ROOF ___ $ ___
TILE ___ $ ___
TRUSSES ___ $ ___
MISC. ___ $ ___
Metal Work
ORNAMENTAL IRON ___ $ ___
SHEET METAL ___ $ ___
STRUCTURAL STEEL ___ $ ___
MISC. ___ $ ___
Miscellaneous
AWNINGS ___ $ ___
CLEANING WINDOW, ETC. ___ $ ___
INSULATION/SOUNDPROOFING ___ $ ___
MOVERS ___ $ ___
REFRIGERATION/FREEZERS ___ $ ___
REMOVING DEBRIS ___ $ ___
WINDOW SHADES ___ $ ___
MISC. ___ $ ___
Fire Prevention
FIRE EXTINGUISHERS ___ $ ___
FIRE SPRINKLERS ___ $ ___
MISC. ___ $ ___
Landscaping
FENCE ___ $ ___
LAWN ___ $ ___
SHRUBBERY ___ $ ___
SPRINKLER SYSTEM ___ $ ___
MISC. ___ $ ___
Extras
___ $ ___
___ $ ___
___ $ ___
SUB-TOTAL ___ $ ___
*CONTRACTORS ___% ___ $ ___
SUB-CONTRACTORS TOTAL ___ $ ___

*The percentage we place on the sub-contractors is for contracting and guaranteeing their work.

If this bid is not within your budget, please call and we will re-evaluate your needs, and work out a compromising bid. Thank You.

ESTIMATE: an approximate bid, which reflects only educated guesses. The total price the consumer pays can be hundreds over that quote.

ITEMIZED BID: an exact bid, which reflects all material costs, labor, taxes and permits. This is the total price.

THIS IS AN ITEMIZED BID, AND YOU CAN HAVE CONFIDENCE IN THE PRICES WE QUOTE.

The House Doctor, D.M., Inc.
E. 1024 - 40th
Spokane, Washington 99203
(509) 747-3323

GENERAL CONDITIONS ON THE REVERSE SIDE.

PROFIT MARGINS
CARPET ___ @ ___% $ ___
WINDOWS _3,655.90_ @ _15_% $ _4,204_ _29_
APPLIANCES ___ @ ___% $ ___
MATERIALS _4,014.07_ @ _30_% $ _5,218_ _29_
LABOR ___ $ _4,000_ _00_
SUB-CONTRACTORS ___ $ ___
DEBRIS ___ $ _300_ _00_
SUB-TOTAL ___ $ _13,722_ _58_
BLDG. PERMIT _EXTRA_ $ _EXTRA_
PLAN CHECK ___ $ ___
ENGINEERING FEE _EXTRA_ $ _EXTRA_
ARCHITECT _EXTRA_ $ _EXTRA_
SURVEY ___ $ ___
2nd SUB-TOTAL ___ $ _13,722_ _58_
TAX _.078_% ___ $ _1,070_ _36_
COMPLETE BID ___ $ _14,792_ _94_

Creative Remodeling Services, Inc. © 1986 Leon A. Frechette

5-23 *Contractor's itemized bid sheet (part 3).* C.R.S., Inc.

products you will use on your projects. These sheets will help you to organize your thoughts as you itemize the requirements of the job and calculate expenses. If you would like to obtain these forms for your own use, an order form for the Helping Hands Packet can be found in Appendix D.

If you are like me, you don't want to spring expensive surprises on a customer just because you estimated a job too low. Try using the itemized method.

Markup

The purpose of using an itemized bid is that it helps you determine the direct job costs related to a particular project. Many contractors go out of business because they don't know the five basic direct job costs:

- Labor
- Materials
- Subcontractors
- Debris
- Plans and permits

Once you have determined your direct job costs, you need to apply an adequate markup to the bid and/or proposal. There is no easy solution to determining the proper markup, but the markup you determine helps set your goal for a comfortable net profit. Unfortunately, the competition can sometimes dictate your markup. However, if you are a creative salesperson, you will sell that contract over a low bidder.

Many contractors work with a 70 percent markup. Multiplying your overall hard costs by 1.70 will yield the general contract price you'll present to the customer. You might want to include taxes in the hard costs, but consult your accountant regarding the legality involved in this practice before applying your markup to taxes. There are also some ethical considerations. Not all jobs need or require a huge markup, but some do. How you determine your markup depends on what the market will bear and your track record for closing sales.

A 70 percent markup could put you right out of the running, so you need to find the correct markup for the market in your area. First, you need to distinguish between markup and gross profit margin. We have already established that a markup is the percentage applied to the overall hard costs to arrive at a total dollar figure (contract price). That same dollar figure divided by the dollar amount of the markup will give you the gross profit margin. Out of the gross profit margin you will pay your overhead, and what is left over is your net profit, so it is important to keep your overhead down in order to yield a higher net profit. Overhead consists of such expenses as:

- Advertising
- Tools and equipment
- Rent
- Vehicles
- Administration
- Sales force

Rick Parish of DECKS APPEAL maintains that 5 percent of their gross sales is devoted to showroom costs, which is only part of their total overhead. I would recommend setting aside at least 20 to 25 percent or more of the gross volume to cover the total cost of your overhead. Be aware that as your company increases, so will your overhead costs; it's a continuous upward spiral.

Assume it will take 22 percent to cover DECKS APPEAL's overhead costs, and they are maintaining a 30 percent gross profit margin. Subtracting 22 from 30 leaves an 8 percent net profit.

To make it a little clearer, here are a couple of examples of different markups and gross profit margins using the same job costs:

Example 1:

$7500 (hard costs)
+$3000 (40% markup)
$10,500 (contract price)

$3000/$10,500 = 29% (markup divided by contract price = gross profit margin)
Gross profit margin (29) less percent overhead cost (22) equals net profit percent (7)

Example 2:

$7500 (hard costs)
+ 5,250 (70% markup)
$12,750 (contract price)

$5250/$12,750 = 41% (markup divided by contract price = gross profit margin)
Gross profit margin (41) less percent overhead cost (22) equals percent of net profit (19).

Keep in mind that if you underestimate the job, make a mistake, have an accident, or if more labor and materials are required or the unexpected occurs, these and any other contributing factors relating to the job can and will eat into your profits. Be sure to spell out in black and white on your contract exactly what you are going to do.

Leave no room for misunderstanding or misinterpretation. Use itemized bid sheets to eliminate errors during the bidding process, and
don't be afraid to add into the bid a contingency figure to cover the
unexpected. Cover all your bases.

6

Construction methods

The saying, "A project is only as good as the materials you choose to use," is only partially true. You also need to consider construction methods. High-quality materials combined with proper construction techniques will determine how long a structure can withstand the natural elements.

You can continue to build with nails or you can select screws that hold the materials more securely. You can frame joists at 24" OC or add an extra support by framing them at 16" OC. You can use brackets and add a brace here and there to stop the deck from swaying side to side. In other words, the construction methods you choose help to guarantee that your structure is solid and will last a long time. Even if you are already using good construction techniques on the projects you build now, there are probably ideas in this chapter that you could incorporate into your next project.

Disposal considerations

Many new products on the market and a wide selection of existing products contain chemicals. You need to know how to dispose properly of waste from these products. Protection of the environment is a major issue, and disposal laws are being added to the books and enforced. These regulations might impact your material selections because proper disposal affects costs and therefore your bid to the customer. In this case, it is far better to know before bidding the job than after the fact. As an old Nigerian proverb says, "Not to know is bad; not to wish to know is worse."

Correct waste disposal is important. To be both a people-oriented professional and one with values, you should value the environment. It is our responsibility as professionals to set a good example and cooperate with governing agencies to help protect our environment.

Tear-out

Before starting any project, evaluate the tear-out situation. This necessary step could help to prevent mistakes that reduce profits. Some specific areas to watch out for include tear-out, site preparation, protection of the property where you are working as well as any adjacent properties, and knowing utility locations.

Ask yourself the following questions as you look over your next project. Keep in mind that realistic answers can affect how you tackle the project as well as how you bid it.

- How much has to be torn out?
- What will I find once this area has been removed?
- Is it necessary to tear any of the structure apart?
- Can products be used that will allow construction right over the existing structure?
- What necessary steps will I have to take to prepare the site for construction?
- What is the soil like in this area?
- Will something special need to be done for footings and/or embedding columns or posts?
- Will heavy machinery be required for this project?
- Will this heavy machinery have to work in the backyard?
- Do I have full access to the backyard?
- Will I have to remove a fence?
- Will I have any access to the property from the neighbors?
- Is the ground soft and wet?
- Will the machinery leave impressions in the lawn?
- Will I need to cover the lawn with plywood in order to move heavy machinery across it?
- Will any trees need to be removed altogether or moved to another location?
- Will the project interfere with the main root of any trees that need to remain?
- Where are utility lines located?
- Will I need to have utility lines moved?

A word of caution: Never assume that utility lines are exactly where the utility (or locator service) has marked them to be. Be extremely careful when working in these marked areas. Here's a case in point:

A few years ago I was installing a deck on the front of a house in the country. When I arrived at the job site, I noticed that the customer had two meters about 40' from the house. Those meters fed two 200-volt main service panels located in the basement on the same wall where I was to install the new deck. The utility company locating service marked the lawn in orange right up to the cement stairs that were about 6' off the ground, which were slated for removal.

After checking the location of the panel boxes in the basement, I knew approximately where everything was in relation to the steps. The utility company had also marked the landing so I knew where the line was running through the cement.

The only thing they couldn't tell me was the depth of the lines. I cautiously started with the jackhammer and within about 10 minutes the tip of the hammer went into the conduit of the first main line. Before I knew it, 2" of the tip was missing, sparks were flying, and flames were shooting from the service panel box in the house. What a mess! Thankfully, I was wearing excellent work boots and leather gloves because I didn't feel a thing.

Apparently, when the house was built, the service panel boxes were mounted high on the wall, so the contractor kept the lines high as well. In this particular case, the main lines were only buried 4" into the concrete. Along with everyone else involved in this project, I assumed the lines to be 18" deep, the code requirement.

The point of this story is that you can never be too careful. Exercise extreme caution when working around utilities, whether overhead or underground.

Basic layout of decking area

I'm sure that we each have a preferred way of laying out the deck area for footing placement, whether we are using construction tubes or post installation. The best way is to use wooden stakes and mason's line or heavy twine. You can lock the corner together with a cross member to create a sturdy frame to tie the mason's line to. The cross members should be a good 12" to 18" long. This way you have room to adjust the mason's line so that the corners are at a true 90° angle to the baseline (Fig. 6-1). Of course, you can always use the 3'-4'-5' method to check this. Measure up from the baseline (B) and make a mark at 3'. Then measure along the other line (C) out from the intersection (A) a distance of 4' and mark the twine. Finally, measure the diagonal distance between these two points (3' and 4'). It should be 5' even. If not, adjust the stakes until that distance measures 5'. I recommend checking each corner in this fashion.

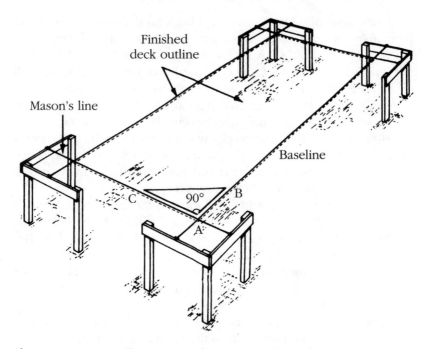

Finished
deck outline

Mason's line

Baseline

C   90°   B

A

6-1 *A simple but effective way of laying out the deck area.* Weyerhaeuser Company

I find it easy to install the ledger board first, followed by all the joist hangers. Next I temporarily install a joist at each end and a couple in between. Once the joists are squared with the proper slope and temporarily held in place, I attach a mason's line to the underside to mark the placement of the construction tubes. This is the fastest way to lay out a deck area and footing placement all at the same time.

Whatever method works best for you is the one you should use. Once you have selected a system, perfect it!

Ledgers

Attaching a ledger board to the wall of a home provides opportunities for water to seep into the house or areas that will not dry out once they get soaked by rain or accumulated snow and ice. It is important to protect these areas from decay and provide airspace so the wood can dry after it gets wet. As I mentioned in Chapter 3, there are products to help minimize moisture problems or you can use the following methods on new or retrofit projects.

New construction ledger

If you are adding a deck to new construction, first install a protective layer of bituminous eave flashing (a black, rubbery membrane) over the sheathing. This membrane seals around any nails that pass through it, forming a tough barrier against unwanted water, unlike metal flashing or tar paper. Then attach the ledger board several inches below the interior floor level, bolting or lagging it through the rim joist. Site-bend metal flashing and slip it behind the building paper as shown in Fig. 6-2. Notice that the first decking board has notches (½" deep × 1¾" wide) on the underside to allow water to drain off the top of the ledger. When fastening this first board, keep the fasteners in the joists rather than the ledger board to avoid puncturing the metal flashing. Be sure the metal flashing covers the top of the ledger.

To learn more about bituminous eave flashing, contact:

Bird Roofing Division
1077 Pleasant Street
Norwood, MA 02062

or call (800) 247-3462, and ask for the "Bird Ice & Water Barrier."

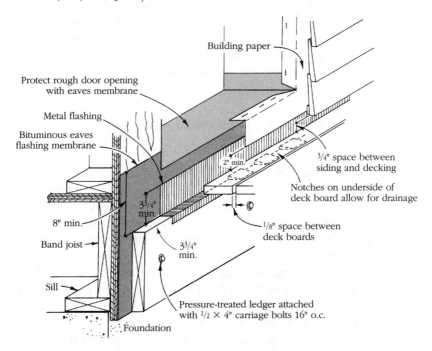

6-2 *When attaching a new ledger, consider using copper, zinc, or aluminum for the flashing, depending on the customer's budget.* The Journal of Light Construction

Retrofit ledger over skirtboard or siding

A common question you will ask yourself as a deck builder is whether you should tear off the skirtboard or siding in order to install a ledger board. As you can clearly see in Fig. 6-3, it is not always necessary. For retrofit ledgers, use PVC spacers to create a drainage gap behind the ledger. Cut the spacers square when installing them flat against a finish skirtboard (Fig. 6-3). Over siding (Fig. 6-3), cut one side on an angle to match the angle of the siding.

Retrofit ledger over skirtboard   Retrofit ledger over siding

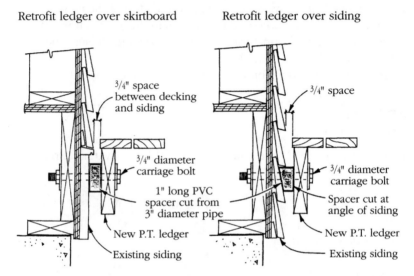

6-3 *PVC spacers create a drainage gap behind the ledger.* The Journal of Light Construction

When using lags, try to install them directly into the end of an existing joist if joist ends are on the side of the house where the ledger board will be mounted. Otherwise use bolts, providing you have both access and a second body. I have found that lag screws work well.

As an extra precaution, use silicone or exterior caulk in the pilot hole and behind the washer of the lag screw or bolt. Alternatively, you could countersink the bolt into the ledger and seal both the hole and the head of the bolt with silicone. Then cover the top of the ledger with flashing, including down the side to either the full width of the 2× or down far enough to cover the bolt hole. You might also want to consider a secondary flashing placed behind the ledger and extended down below the ledger and over the existing siding. This will sheet water away from the house on the underside of the deck.

Another idea to consider when installing a new deck is to lower the entire deck 2" to 4" below the threshold of the door. This will help keep water away from around the door area. Check with your local building department to see if there are any code requirements for such a riser (i.e., the height of the doorstep above the deck). If so you might have to have a minimum 4" riser, in which case you could lower the deck from 4" to 8" from the threshold. Be sure to check with the customers to see what is comfortable for them. The shorter the transition (the smaller the riser) between the threshold and deck surface, the easier it is for the customer to stumble. This is an area that needs attention.

In Fig. 6-4, the ledger board is fastened directly against the siding. Unfortunately, no precautions have been taken to make sure the ledger board, even though it is treated lumber, could dry out if it does get soaked. The use of the 2" × 4" (ledger) and notching the joists can eliminate the use of joist hangers. It's a good construction method, but it creates a lot of areas where water can get trapped. If this were a fully covered deck, porch, or sunscreen porch, this method of framing would be acceptable, but if the customer ever washed the surface, it is possible that water could penetrate this area. It is important to consider the methods you use, especially if you do not want to be called back for warranty work.

6-4 *Brackets that hold the ledger board out away from the wall or flashing should be installed to help protect this area from moisture. Here, the 2" × 4" should be removed and replaced with joist hangers for proper drainage.* Used with permission of Georgia-Pacific Corporation

Water-protected deck or porch structure

The style of beam you construct could create a potential water trap. If you are using a post-and-beam method, you'll have little problem with water absorption (Fig. 6-5), but if you use a double or triple 2× material sandwiched together (girder), then water can be trapped between the 2× material. Consider using bituminous eave flashing membrane to cover the top of the girder. In fact, cover any sandwich constructions or areas that exceed 1½" in thickness. If you have a height restriction and to meet the codes you have to place the girder directly on top of the concrete piers, then slope the top of the piers on both sides of the girder. This will help keep water from creeping under the girder (Fig. 6-6). If the concrete edges are not sloped, then use an elevated metal post base or an aluminum post standoff to raise the wood off the concrete so the wood cannot rest in standing water.

6-5 *Good example of post-and-beam method.* C.R.S., Inc.

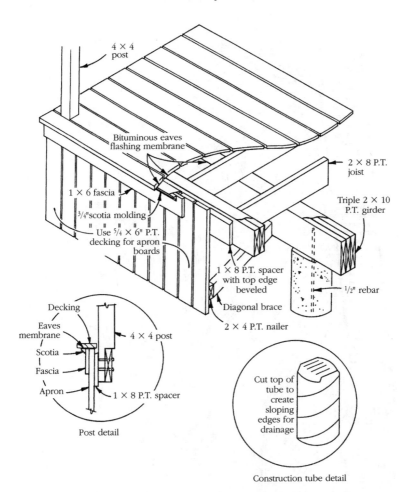

4 × 4 post

Bituminous eaves flashing membrane

2 × 8 P.T. joist

1 × 6 fascia

3/4"scotia molding

Use 5/4 × 6" P.T. decking for apron boards

Triple 2 × 10 P.T. girder

1 × 8 P.T. spacer with top edge beveled

1/2" rebar

Decking

Eaves membrane

Scotia

Fascia

Apron

4 × 4 post

1 × 8 P.T. spacer

Diagonal brace

2 × 4 P.T. nailer

Post detail

Cut top of tube to create sloping edges for drainage

Construction tube detail

6-6 *A beveled 1× spacer directs water through the spaces between the vertical apron boards. Even the construction tube is fashioned to create a water-shedding surface at the top.* The Journal of Light Construction

The anatomy of a deck

The layout of the deck in Fig. 6-7 might provide some ideas on how you can improve your next deck. More important, it will help your potential customer get an overview of what it takes to put a deck together, and this could help close the sale. The call-outs (numbers 1 through 6) refer to the chapter headings that follow throughout the remainder of this chapter.

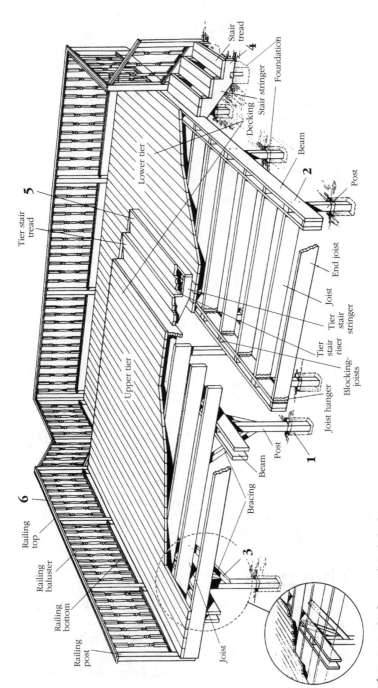

6-7 *Detail of completed deck.* Weyerhaeuser Company

1. Foundation options

A well-structured deck always starts with the foundation (Fig. 6-8). This is not a place to cut corners; the foundation must meet the building codes for the area in which you are building. Consult with your building department to determine the requirements for setting posts, specifically:

- How deep should the hole be to be below the frost line?
- How wide does the hole need to be?
- How far out of the ground does the concrete need to be?
- What are the restrictions when using precast piers?
- What are the restrictions regarding embedding posts?

Construction tubes are convenient. The supply house will cut them to the length you need, saving you time. If you run into a situation where a patio or driveway is in your way, call a concrete cut-

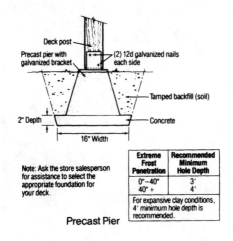

Note: Ask the store salesperson for assistance to select the appropriate foundation for your deck.

Extreme Frost Penetration	Recommended Minimum Hole Depth
0″–40″	3′
40″ +	4′

For expansive clay conditions, 4′ minimum hole depth is recommended.

Precast Pier

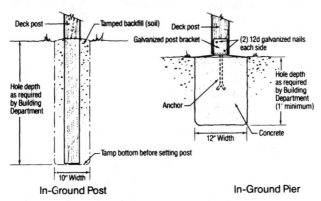

In-Ground Post

In-Ground Pier

6-8 *Detail of several foundations.* Weyerhaeuser Company

ting firm. They can cut into the concrete just the diameter you need for the tube, and you won't be able to tell that any cuts were made. The installation will look as though it has always been there, very clean and tidy. This is one subcontractor well worth the cost.

As you can see in Fig. 6-9, the top of the pier has been tapered to shed water. Also, the bracket has been lifted off the concrete so water won't get trapped between the post and bracket. While this is the proper size tube to use for this particular project, the overall job does not reflect a good finished appearance because all the concrete piers are visible. The framework should have been constructed to allow the lattice to drop in front of the piers within 6" off the ground. Then, standing back and viewing the overall project, you wouldn't notice the piers. An alternative would be to plant shrubs in front of the piers.

6-9 *The only thing left to do is remove the tube and install the trim.* C.R.S., Inc.

2. Connections: Post and beam
and joists over beam(s)

If you choose to use the post-and-beam method instead of the girder method (two or three 2×s sandwiched together), follow the bolt schedule in Fig. 6-10 and use bolts that won't rust. Also check with your local building department for code requirements for the size of 2×s to be used as the beam. Joists should be spaced at 16" OC rather than 24" OC. Complaints from past customers who felt the decking boards were giving way underfoot should have had 24" OC decking.

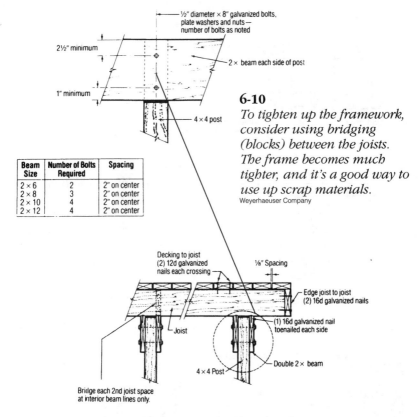

½" diameter × 8" galvanized bolts, plate washers and nuts — number of bolts as noted

2½" minimum

1" minimum

2 × beam each side of post

6-10

To tighten up the framework, consider using bridging (blocks) between the joists. The frame becomes much tighter, and it's a good way to use up scrap materials.
Weyerhaeuser Company

4 × 4 post

Beam Size	Number of Bolts Required	Spacing
2 × 6	2	2" on center
2 × 8	3	2" on center
2 × 10	4	2" on center
2 × 12	4	2" on center

Decking to joist (2) 12d galvanized nails each crossing

⅛" Spacing

Edge joist to joist (2) 16d galvanized nails

(1) 16d galvanized nail toenailed each side

Joist

Double 2 × beam

4 × 4 Post

Bridge each 2nd joist space at interior beam lines only.

Typical connections: joists at same level as beams

It can happen: you just don't have enough room and a code requirement dictates that you can't get too close to the ground. Certainly you could hire an excavator and grade the area but it would add costs to the bid and it's not worth it. Another alternative is to lower the joists to the same level as the beam. Figure 6-11 provides a good bird's-eye view of options. While these illustrations are post-and-beam installations, they apply just as well when using girders.

Beam and joist splice connections

The time will also come when the material you are using for beams will not be long enough to do the layout in one piece. The length of your stock might determine where the post will be located. This can happen with joists as well. With a girder or solid beam, the splice should be located directly in the center of the post. Joists can run past each other on the beam and you can install screws into the joists at this point to secure them together. When it is time to fasten the decking surface, be aware of these transition points, otherwise you will be attempting to drive screws into thin air. The joists will be off by 1½" of each other at this point. Figure 6-12 gives good examples of beam

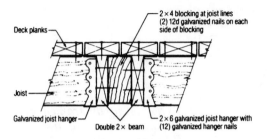

2 × 4 blocking at joist lines
(2) 12d galvanized nails on each
side of blocking

Deck planks

Joist

Galvanized joist hanger

Double 2 × beam

2 × 6 galvanized joist hanger with
(12) galvanized hanger nails

Joist To Beam Connection

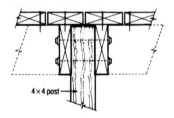

4 × 4 post

Beam To Post Connection

6-11
Joists at same level as beams.
Weyerhaeuser Company

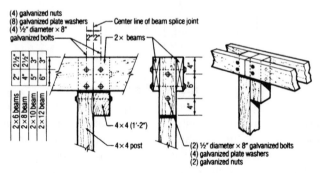

(4) galvanized nuts
(8) galvanized plate washers
(4) ½" diameter × 8"
galvanized bolts

Center line of beam splice joint

2 × beams

2" 2"

2" 2½"
4" 2½"
5" 3"
6" 3"

2 × 6 beams
2 × 8 beam
2 × 10 beam
2 × 12 beam

4 × 4 (1'-2")

4 × 4 post

4"

6"

4"

(2) ½" diameter × 8" galvanized bolts
(4) galvanized plate washers
(2) galvanized nuts

Beam Splice

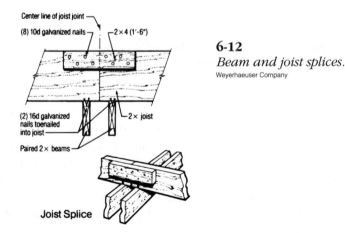

Center line of joist joint

(8) 10d galvanized nails

2 × 4 (1'-6")

(2) 16d galvanized
nails toenailed
into joist

2 × joist

Paired 2 × beams

Joist Splice

6-12
Beam and joist splices.
Weyerhaeuser Company

and joist splices. Wherever splices are required, use screws (not dry-wall screws) to provide better holding power. Even though the illustration recommends the use of galvanized nails, I still recommend using screws. Also, when splicing a beam to a post, use bolts to secure the system rather than screws because screws will shear with weight.

3. Knee brace

A simple brace from a post to a joist or from a post to a beam can determine whether or not a deck will sway. Bracing is absolutely necessary when the deck is 8' or more off the ground, especially when building on the side of a hill. However, I have seen many decks built (especially on new homes) where the bracing was insufficient for the size of the deck. To get a completely sway-free deck, install two braces from the same post: one to the joist or cross beam (a 2× between two joists) and one to the beam. Figure 6-13 shows a couple of ways to attach braces.

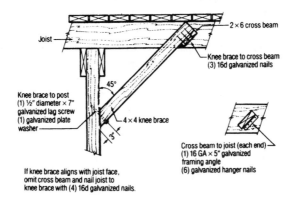

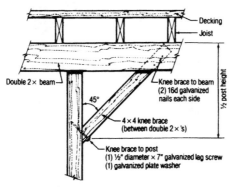

6-13 *Attaching knee braces.* Weyerhaeuser Company

4. Stairs to ground

Over the years I have built some beautiful stairs, but I confess that stairs are not my strong suit. Stairs can be time-consuming and they require mathematical thinking to correctly calculate measurements for risers (height) and treads (width).

To simplify the stair-design process for you, I have included some tools, charts, and diagrams. Before considering these, however, there are some basics to review that help in calculating the risers and treads.

Remember to cut off the bottom of the stringer by the thickness of the tread material. Otherwise, the first riser increases (possibly to a height exceeding the codes) by the thickness of this material (Fig. 6-14A). At the same time, lowering the stringer by the thickness of the tread material requires that you increase the top riser height by the same thickness, since the tread thickness will shorten the top riser by this amount. Remember that the top step is part of the finish floor— not another tread.

There is always one tread less than the number of risers.

When laying out the stringer, allow enough stock to tie in the top end of the stringer to supports. Be sure to maintain the same tread measurement at the top step. Also, consider how the stairs will be incorporated into the design of the deck as well as how they match up with the directions of the decking boards. The top riser can be formed by some part of the finished deck or landing framework. Make sure that this riser is the same measurement as the rest of the risers (Fig. 6-14B).

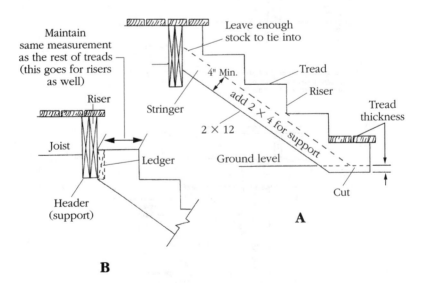

6-14A, B *Stair-to-ground basics.* C.R.S., Inc.

Basic stairway layout
The following information should prove helpful before you lay out your stringers.

- The sum of all unit runs (tread less nosing) = total run.
- The sum of all unit risers = total rise. This is measured from the surface of the finished deck to a level point on the ground (existing slab or poured pad). To find a level point on the ground from which to measure, place one end of a level about where the stringers will land. Point the other end toward the place where the stringer will attach to the deck. If your level is not long enough, use a straight 2" × 4" with a level on top of it.
- As the angle of a stringer changes, so does the riser-tread ratio. There are three general rules for riser-tread ratio (excluding tread nosing; I recommend the nosing extend beyond the riser from 1" to 1⅛"):
  ~Rise plus tread width = 17" to 18"
  ~Rise times tread width = 72" to 76"
  ~Sum of two risers plus tread width = 24" to 25".
- An "ideal" ratio for wooden steps is a 7" rise with a 10" to 11½" tread; the "ideal" ratio for concrete steps is a 6" to 6½" rise with a 12" to 13" tread. Be sure to consult your building codes for the requirements that apply in your area.
- In residential construction, avoid risers more than 8" and treads less than 9". Commercial stairs have a maximum 7" rise and a minimum 11" tread.
- Try to keep the angle to the ground 34° to 37°.
- Maintain the same height for risers as well as treads. A ⅜" difference is allowed between the largest and smallest risers and treads.
- Treads should slope forward about ⅛" for drainage.
- Maintain a stairway at least 36" wide.
- Consider using a 2" × 12" for a stringer. This would give about 11½" tread widths. The use of three stringers instead of two for a stairway system stops the springy or spongy feeling on treads as they span the distance between two stringers.
- Make sure at least 4" of the stringer remains once the risers and treads have been cut out. For extra support, add a 2" × 4" on the inside of each stringer. If you have a middle stringer, attach a 2" × 4" to each side with screws. Do not hammer because you could break off the tread on the stringer (Fig. 6-14A).

- When stairs are going to end at ground level, be sure they land on a concrete pad. Finish the outside edges and broom the pad for traction. The landing should extend beyond the stairs a distance equal to the width of the stairs (36") (Fig. 6-15). Also hold the stringer, including the kicker plate, off the concrete pad by using an aluminum post standoff or PVC spacers. This will prevent the material from soaking up water. Otherwise, make sure that the kicker plate is treated wood that can hold the stringer up and off the concrete pad.

6-15 *Finished concrete pad.* C.R.S., Inc.

Stairway construction tables

You will find the following tables handy when working on stairway layouts.

Table 6-1. Stairway Layout

Approximate angle to floor line (degree)	Rise (inches)	Tread run (inches)
30½	6½	11
32	6¾	10¾
33¾	7	10½
35¼	7¼	10¼
37	7½	10
38½	7¾	9¾
40	8	9½

Adapted from: *Blue Book*, Swanson Tool Co., Inc.

Table 6-2. Decimal Equivalents of 8ths, 16ths, 32nds, and 64ths

Inches	Decimal equivalent	Inches	Decimal equivalent	Inches	Decimal equivalent
$\frac{1}{64}$	0.015625	$\frac{11}{32}$	0.34375	$\frac{43}{64}$	0.671875
$\frac{1}{32}$	0.03125	$\frac{23}{64}$	0.359375	$\frac{11}{16}$	0.6875
$\frac{3}{64}$	0.046875	$\frac{3}{8}$	0.375	$\frac{45}{64}$	0.703125
$\frac{1}{16}$	0.0625	$\frac{25}{64}$	0.390625	$\frac{23}{32}$	0.71875
$\frac{5}{64}$	0.078125	$\frac{13}{32}$	0.40625	$\frac{47}{64}$	0.734375
$\frac{3}{32}$	0.09375	$\frac{27}{64}$	0.421875	$\frac{3}{4}$	0.750
$\frac{7}{64}$	0.109375	$\frac{7}{16}$	0.4375	$\frac{49}{64}$	0.765625
$\frac{1}{8}$	0.125	$\frac{29}{64}$	0.453125	$\frac{25}{32}$	0.78125
$\frac{9}{64}$	0.140625	$\frac{15}{32}$	0.46875	$\frac{51}{64}$	0.796875
$\frac{5}{32}$	0.15625	$\frac{31}{64}$	0.484375	$\frac{13}{16}$	0.8125
$\frac{11}{64}$	0.171875	$\frac{1}{2}$	0.500	$\frac{53}{64}$	0.828125
$\frac{3}{16}$	0.1875	$\frac{33}{64}$	0.515625	$\frac{27}{32}$	0.84375
$\frac{13}{64}$	0.203125	$\frac{17}{32}$	0.53125	$\frac{55}{64}$	0.859375
$\frac{7}{32}$	0.21875	$\frac{35}{64}$	0.546875	$\frac{7}{8}$	0.875
$\frac{15}{64}$	0.234375	$\frac{9}{16}$	0.5625	$\frac{57}{64}$	0.890625
$\frac{1}{4}$	0.250	$\frac{37}{64}$	0.578125	$\frac{29}{32}$	0.90625
$\frac{17}{64}$	0.265625	$\frac{19}{32}$	0.59375	$\frac{59}{64}$	0.921875
$\frac{9}{32}$	0.28125	$\frac{39}{64}$	0.609375	$\frac{15}{16}$	0.9375
$\frac{19}{64}$	0.296875	$\frac{5}{8}$	0.625	$\frac{61}{64}$	0.953125
$\frac{5}{16}$	0.3125	$\frac{41}{64}$	0.640625	$\frac{31}{32}$	0.96875
$\frac{21}{64}$	0.328125	$\frac{21}{32}$	0.65625	$\frac{63}{64}$	0.984375

Adapted from: *Blue Book*, Swanson Tool Co., Inc.

Table 6-3. Decimal Equivalents of 12ths

12th	Decimal equivalent
1	0.083333
2	0.166666
3	0.25
4	0.333333
5	0.416666
6	0.5
7	0.583333
8	0.666666
9	0.75
10	0.833333
11	0.916666

Adapted from: *Blue Book*, Swanson Tool Co., Inc.

Calculating risers

Just for practice, assume you are working on a deck that is 6'3" off the ground (Fig. 6-16).

1 The total rise of this deck is 6'3" or 75". You want a 7" rise per step, staying close to the 35° angle (see Table 6-1).

2 To determine the number of risers, divide 75" by 7 which equals 10.714 risers.

3 Since 0.714 is over one-half of a riser, round 10.714 to 11 and divide 75" by 11, which equals 6.818".

4 Refer to Table 6-2. The closest you can get to 0.818 is 0.8125, which is ¹³⁄₁₆". Your figure now becomes 6.8125, or 6¹³⁄₁₆".

5 To recheck the total rise, multiply 6.8125 by 11, which equals 74.9375.

6 Since 0.9375 = ¹⁵⁄₁₆", you will be short by ¹⁄₁₆" of your total rise of 75". Rather than trying to divide 0.625 evenly between the 11 risers (adding 0.005 to each riser), just add ¹⁄₁₆" to the bottom riser to reach the total rise of 75". My experience is that if the bottom riser is within ⅛" of other riser heights, you won't notice the difference when walking the stairs and neither will your customer.

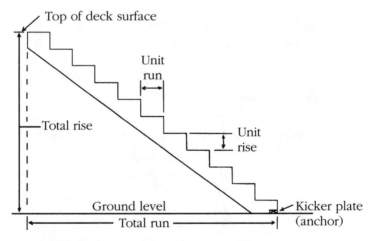

6-16 *When attaching a kicker plate to the concrete pad, use a PVC or ABS spacer on the plate so it is not directly in contact with the concrete; this allows water to drain from under the plate.* C.R.S., Inc.

Calculating treads

Now that you have established 11 risers at 6¹³⁄₁₆", you need to calculate the 10 treads (remember, there is always one less tread than riser). Applying the three general rules, we have:

1 6¹³⁄₁₆" (rise) + 11" (calculated run) = 17¹³⁄₁₆" (17" to 18" is ideal).
2 6.8125 (6¹³⁄₁₆ riser height) × 11 = 74.9375, or 74¹⁵⁄₁₆ (72" to 76" is ideal).
3 6.8125 + 6.8125 (sum of two risers) + 11 = 24.625, or 24⅝ (24" to 25" is ideal). Therefore, we have 10 treads × 11" = 110" (9.166, see Table 6-3) for a total run of 9'2".

Calculating stringer length

1 Rise of 75": 75 × 75 = 5,625
2 Run of 110": 110 × 110 = 12,100
3 5,625 + 12,100 = 17,725
4 The square root of 17,725 = 133.13526 (divided by 12 = 11.094 or 11'1⁷⁄₆₄". Add 12" to 24" to this figure for waste. In this particular case, the question is whether you can cut the stringer from a 12' 2×. Depending on how lucky you feel, you might want to use a 14' piece to be safe.

There is now a calculator that can solve hundreds of building problems at the touch of a button. The Construction Master III (Calculated Industries Inc.), shown in Fig. 6-17, can solve riser and tread calculations in a matter of minutes. The stair key instantly finds the number of risers and treads, riser height, tread width, and any amounts over or under what is required.

6-17
The Construction Master III.
Calculated Industries, Inc.

This calculator can also add, subtract, multiply, and divide in feet-inch fractions, decimal feet (tenths, hundredths), inches and fractions, decimal inches, yards, meters, centimeters, millimeters, board feet, and square and cubic dimensions. Besides stair solutions, it also has rafter solutions for commons, jacks, and hips and valleys (even irregular hips). If you don't have one, you should. Contact Calculated Industries, Inc. at 800-854-8075.

Another tool that can help with the layout of risers and treads on the stringers is Swanson's "Big-12" Square. This is a compact tool incorporating a rafter/framing square, stairway layout gauge, protractor, tri- and miter-square, and layout scribes with easy-to-read numbers (Fig. 6-18).

6-18 *The Big-12 Square.* Swanson Tool Co., Inc.

The Swanson Speed Square comes with an illustrated Blue Book for roof and stairway layouts. This 62-page, pocket-sized manual gives complete instructions on basic roof construction with all rafter length tables as well as complete stairway building instructions including figuring proper tread width and rise, stairwell opening sizes, overhead clearance, stringer layout, and so on. Some of the information contained in this chapter is from the Blue Book. If you don't already have one, I would strongly recommend you add it to your collection and put it to good use. You might have to purchase the tool in order to get the Blue Book, but you will find the tool a valuable addition to your collection.

5. Stairs between deck tiers

Stairs between deck tiers require the same methods and techniques you would use to construct stairs to the ground. Normally, it is easier to get a total rise measurement because you are working on an already finished (flat) surface. Be sure to consider the following:

- The proximity of any stairs to the entrance to an exterior house door.
- Maintaining the same riser and tread measurements as the primary set of stairs or with as many sets of stairs as you have incorporated into the deck.

- For four or more risers, you are required to install a handrail at 34" to 38" high. Decide where and how you will install the handrail(s) and how many are required. The need for handrail supports will affect how you frame this area.

In situations like the one shown in Fig. 6-19, stairs do not have many risers, which makes them simple to build. You can also build the stringers as one unit (Fig. 6-20).

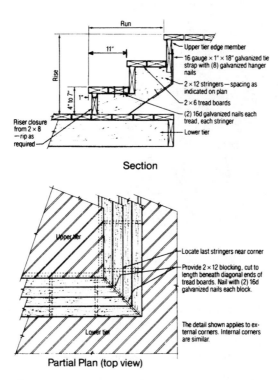

Section

Partial Plan (top view)

6-19 *Good example of a cross section and top view of stair installation.* Weyerhaeuser Company

You might want to consider adding metal spiral stairs to a deck that has two or three levels. Spiral stairs can add square footage to the deck because the stairs can be mounted on the exterior side of the deck. In addition, you can either purchase a kit or have them manufactured as small as 3'6" in diameter, which takes up less space than conventional stairs. If space is limited, this might be worth considering. Spiral stairs don't have to be mounted in a spiral design only. You could incorporate a one-half spiral turn, a combination stair, or floating straight stairs. A creative approach could really enhance the deck project. Before you order a kit or have a spiral staircase manufac-

6-20
One-unit stair stringers. C.R.S., Inc.

tured, be sure to consult your local building department for any specific code requirements.

Ramps are a related concern. Is someone in the household confined to a wheelchair or in a position where stairs are difficult to use? This is an important issue that should be settled before you bid the job. Know exactly what it will entail to incorporate a ramp into the deck design. The general construction requirements are the same as for decks:

- Span distance
- Setting of posts
- Live and snow loads

I recommend you work closely with your local building department on this issue for your state's accessibility regulations. I also recommend that you contact the U.S. Department of Justice Office on the Americans with Disabilities Act (800-514-0301) to obtain a copy of the Americans with Disabilities (ADA) Handbook or ask for Federal Register Part III (28 CFR, Part 36, Vol. 56, No. 144, Order No. 1513-91), which gives ramp design specifications and dimensions.

In general, consider the following points.

- Ramp width: Single-family residences have no dimensional requirements but I recommend a minimum 36" clear (consider 48" clear). Commercial work requires 44" clear.

- Level landings are needed at both the top and the bottom of the ramp. In addition, a 60" landing the same width as the ramp or greater is needed after every 30" elevation change. If the ramp changes direction at a landing, the minimum landing size is 60" × 60".
- Guardrails need to be mounted along both sides of the ramp and handrails are to be mounted to the inside.
- The top of the handrail (gripping surface) must be between 34" and 38" from the ramp surface. Consider installing a second handrail about 20" from the ramp surface.
- A clear space of 1½" should be between the handrail and the surface to which it is mounted.
- Use 2" × 6" decking boards and install the short way (36") to provide better traction for wheelchair tires; install a nonslip surface.
- The maximum slope of a ramp in new construction is 1:12, but a slope of 1:16 or 1:20 may be easier for a wheelchair user to navigate (see Fig. 6-21). Find out what slope (within code limits) your customer prefers.

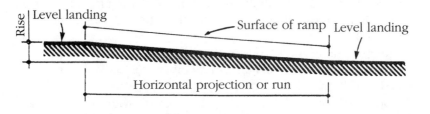

	Maximum rise		Maximum horizontal projection	
Slope	in	mm	ft	m
1:12 to < 1:16	30	760	30	9
1:16 to < 1:120	30	760	40	12

6-21 *Components of a single ramp run and sample ramp dimensions.*
Americans with Disabilities Act Accessibility Guidelines (ADAAG), 7/26/91, as published in the Federal Register

There are other areas of concern regarding ramps. The transition at the point where a concrete walk or drive meets the ramp should be smooth and level with the landing. The landing should be at least as wide as the ramp, and the length should be a minimum of 60" (72" according to the UBC).

On an exterior door (door swings to the interior) and/or slider, the landing immediately outside should be level and clear of any obstacles. Depending on how a wheelchair approaches the door, the landing requires a maneuvering clearance in front and/or to the side of the entrance. The entrance itself requires a minimum net opening (width) of 32" for the wheelchair to pass through. This 32" net measurement starts from the doorstop to the door face when the door is in a 90° open position or, the case of a slider, when the door is fully opened. A wheelchair can approach a door or slider straight on, from the hinge and/or slider side, or from the latch side. Each of the approaches requires a minimum landing size as follows:

Straight-on approaches Both door and slider require a minimum 32" width net opening by a minimum 42" in depth (measuring out from the exterior wall).

Hinge and/or slide side approach Both doors require a 54" minimum width (with the measurement starting from the latch side and measuring back toward the hinge/slide side) by a minimum depth of 42".

Latch side approach Both doors require a minimum 32" width net opening plus 24" (with the measurement starting from the hinge/slide side and measuring back toward the latch side) by a minimum depth of 42".

Keep in mind the barrier of the threshold for the exterior slider should not exceed ¾" in height. For all other types of doors, it should not exceed ½" in height.

Door hardware should be easy to grasp with one hand and should not require tight grasping and pinching or twisting of the wrist to operate. Use a U-shaped, lever-operated, or push-type handle. The operating hardware should be exposed and usable from both sides on a slider when the door is fully open. Mount the hardware no higher than 48" above the finished floor.

When installing a handrail, there should be a clear space of 1½" between the wall and the handrail. The diameter or width of the gripping surface should be between 1¼" and 1½". If you prefer to design the handrail so it is located in a recessed area, the recess should be a maximum of 3" deep with 1½" between the handrail and the adjacent wall. The recess should extend 18" above the handrail.

The ramp shown in Fig. 6-22 could have been made wider to incorporate the handrails on the inside of the ramp. The transition also needs some work, but the overall design should give you an idea of how to integrate a ramp into a deck project.

6-22 *A wheelchair ramp.* C.R.S., Inc.

6. Railing options

Before you install the decking boards, remember that you have to consider posts and how they will be attached. There are many ways to attach a post. At this point, the type of post and railings you are going to use should have been decided upon.

The design of the railing system and the proper installation of its component parts can make or break the appearance of a deck. Be sure to incorporate the right design. One other issue I feel strongly about is that this is one stage where you can't skimp on the quality of the material. In fact, this is where quality is most important for appearance's sake. The material should be clear (especially if it is not being painted) for all handrails, guardrails, posts, balusters, and bottom rails. It is possible that the bottom rail could use a lesser quality, but it's hardly worthwhile to bother with such minimal amounts.

Posts

There are a couple of ways to attach a post. The first is to incorporate the post into the deck's framework as shown in Fig. 6-23. Add an extra framing member and blocks fastened with screws to create a completely secure system.

You can also bolt the post on. I recommend, when using a 4" × 4", that it be notched to add strength once it is bolted (not lagged) into place. Leave at least 1½" or more of stock for the bolts to run

6-23
Starting newel posts. C.R.S., Inc.

through. As you can see in Fig. 6-24, because of the framework one post had to be fastened with a lag screw and the other was bolted into place with a carriage bolt.

Top and bottom rails

Top rails can be finished in different widths as well as styles. Personally, I like a 2" × 6" for a top rail, but when tied into a handrail for the steps, I incorporate a 2" × 4" for easier handling. Check with your local building department to see whether you have to install a handrail on the inside. A space could be dadoed for the handrail so it fits easily into the area and provides comfortable, easy gripping. Have a clear space of 1½" between the handrail and the surface to which it will be mounted.

Top guardrails should be placed at a minimum height of 36" when a deck is 30" or more off the ground. Four or more risers require a handrail at least 34" to 38" high (UBC).

Bottom rails are part of the system and are not for standing on. It is important, however, that you support the bottom rail when spanning certain distances, either by attaching blocks under the rails or by bringing the posts closer together. Personally, I keep the spans between 5' and 6'. Keep the bottom rail not more than 4" from the deck to meet building codes. This clearance also allows snow and any other debris to be swept under the rail and off the deck.

6-24
A 4"× 4" redwood post.
C.R.S., Inc.

Balusters should be placed so that a 4" sphere will not pass between them. In some areas, this requirement might still be 6", so be sure to check with your local building department. If there are small children in the household, you will want to place those balusters at 4" even if the code allows 6" spacing.

When using a 4" × 4" post, dado so it can accept a 2" × 4" from the inside of the deck as shown in Fig. 6-25. When using a 2" × 4" as a post, also keep the 2" × 4" to the inside but do not dado. Fasten it so the 4" width of the 2" × 4" is directly attached to the vertical 2" × 4". When installing decorated top and bottom rails, use galvanized finish nails and predrill. Fill using exterior filler. If you are gluing, use exterior glue (Fig. 6-26).

Railing designs
A distinctive railing design gives the deck a touch of class, a personality that your customers will enjoy. Many options are available; it is up to you and your customer to decide which design to use, depending on the customer's budget.

Pay close attention to the view. How will the railing design affect the customer's view as seen from a chair on the deck? Maybe corrections could be made by lowering a portion of the deck or leaving a 4" space between the cap and top rail, or installing ³⁄₁₆" tempered glass panels in wooden frames.

6-25
Be sure the dados are precise. C.R.S., Inc.

6-26 *Use a block under the bottom rail when fastening.* C.R.S., Inc.

The traditional look of most railings involves simple, straight lines and right angles for shape and definition. Consider adding curves into the deck and railing to match the personality of the house to the landscaping that surrounds it. Too many curves can be confusing and might look out of place, so don't overdo it.

If you feel uncomfortable trying curves, then hire a professional who specializes in laminated and curved rails. Alternatively, you might want to check out laminated products that can be incorporated into the design. One such firm is Carrousel Wood Products, Ltd. (800-962-7235). They have all kinds of interesting products, and some may fit into your next project.

If you decide to try this on your own, you might find working in a 7' radius (or greater) easier. You will have fewer problems with splitting or popping the grain loose. Consider using clear vertical grain green redwood. Purchase the material ahead of the schedule and sticker it. This will help keep joints from opening up later when the wood dries completely.

A planer is handy for reducing overall thickness so you can get the material to bend. Also check out ⅜" bender boards. They could serve as a subfascia covering the ends of joists. If the deck has a radius, cantilever the joists at least 2' to 3' beyond the support beam to allow for cutting the radius. The same is true for decking boards: Hang them over the fascia about 1", then draw the radius and trim. Finally, apply the fascia board.

When working with a radius, make sure that everything you cut, sand, and block (between joists) is perfectly plumb and level. This helps prevent the fascia board from wandering away from level when you push the board into the belly of the curve.

I recommend that you build your 4" × 4" post within the structure and make sure it's blocked and bolted. Top and bottom rails can be cut with a band saw, sanded, and then routed. For seams, use a 45° lap joint or a biscuit cutter and waterproof glue.

Curves are expensive. They use expensive materials, produce lots of waste, and consume a lot of your time and your helpers' time. Be sure to bid accordingly. Creating a curve could add three or more extra days, depending on the size of the radius and what you are putting the radius on (deck, guardrail, or built-in seat). Have a carefully constructed plan in mind and plenty of confidence before walking into a project such as this.

Some potential customers have a hard time visualizing a finished product. It is also possible that a customer doesn't need a new deck but would like the railing rebuilt with a new design. Figures 6-27 to 6-40 will help both you and your customers zero in on the right design for their railing system.

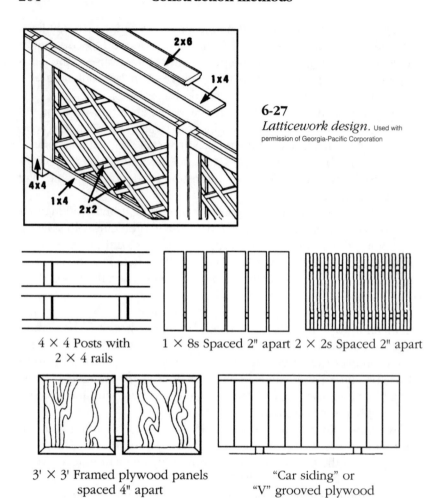

6-27
Latticework design. Used with permission of Georgia-Pacific Corporation

4 × 4 Posts with
2 × 4 rails

1 × 8s Spaced 2" apart

2 × 2s Spaced 2" apart

3' × 3' Framed plywood panels
spaced 4" apart

"Car siding" or
"V" grooved plywood

6-28 *The 4"× 4" posts with 2"× 4" rails (upper left corner) are purely decorative and can be used when the deck is less than 30" off the ground.* Used with permission of Georgia-Pacific Corporation

Additional products

As shown in Figs. 6-30, 6-31, and 6-34, using a cap design and/or post top can bring new life to a post and add personality to the overall design of the deck. Figure 6-41 features some interesting post tops that can dress up any post. This variety is by Waddell Manufacturing Company. They are made of pine and treated. The large ball, contemporary, and small plate are available in redwood. Show your customer what is available.

6-29 *Before: Standard 2" × 2" After: Starburst.* CaddConn Designs

The design you select for the balusters can change the appearance and personality of the deck. A good share of existing decks use 2" × 2" for balusters, which is pretty standard. This next product moves from the standard to an idea that's both creative and unusual.

6-30
*Traditional with crisp
detail.* Courtesy of Louisiana-Pacific

6-31
*Traditional using small ball
post tops.* Western Red Cedar Lumber
Association

6-32
*Contemporary—use round
balusters (ABS, PVC, metal,
or wood) mounted vertically
or horizontally.* Courtesy of Louisiana-
Pacific

6-33 *Privacy screen incorporating lattice.* Courtesy of Louisiana-Pacific

6-34 *The colonial look. Remember when installing a turned (decorative) baluster, a 4" sphere cannot pass through the widest points between two balusters.* C.R.S., Inc.

Cable·Rail (Feeney Wire Rope) consists of ⅛" stainless steel cables that can enhance any railing system and are a perfect solution for customers who require a view. The system combines two special fittings to attach and stretch each cable. The "threaded terminal" is fitted at the factory to one end of each cable. The cable

6-35 *Standard 2" × 2" railing design.* C.R.S., Inc.

6-36 *Lattice incorporated with 2" × 2".* C.R.S., Inc.

comes in 5' to 80' lengths (with custom lengths available). The terminal is inserted through holes in the end post and secured with a washer and hex nuts. Cable tension is adjusted by tightening or loosening the nuts.

6-37 *Diagonal design.* C.R.S., Inc.

6-38 *Inner and outer radii.* Carrousel Wood Products, Ltd.

6-39 *Outside radius.* Design by Ell Sutton with HBM. California Redwood Association

6-40 *Louvers.* Design by Christopher & Westbrook Klos. California Redwood Association

The other end of the cable uses a "Quick Connect" fitting. It has a special one-way wedge design that allows the cable to slide easily through the fitting in one direction. Once the cable has been released, the wedge grabs and locks onto the cable. Excess cable can then be cut off.

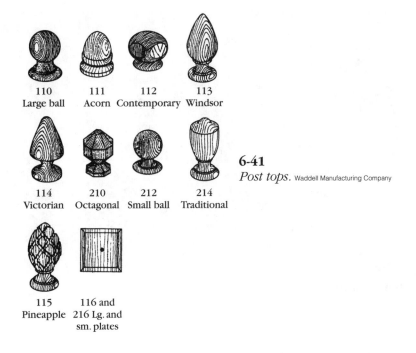

110
Large ball

111
Acorn

112
Contemporary

113
Windsor

114
Victorian

210
Octagonal

212
Small ball

214
Traditional

6-41

Post tops. Waddell Manufacturing Company

115
Pineapple

116 and
216 Lg. and
sm. plates

The cable cannot pass continuously through a single corner post. You will have to offset the cables at least ½" to allow clearance for the fittings. Personally, I think using two posts, which allows the cable to pass continuously around the corner, gives a more attractive look. Also, if the end of the post that has the threaded terminal is exposed, I would recess the nuts and cap the exposed end with a 1×. Again, consult with your building department for proper spacing requirements (Fig. 6-42).

Decking boards

The majority of decks are built with decking boards placed either parallel or perpendicular to the house. Of course, this is the most economical way to go. If finances are not a problem, then be creative and sell the customer on an interesting pattern and design that could give a deck personality and distinction, and make it come to life.

When bidding a deck with an unusual design, remember that the framework has to be built accordingly. Creative decking board patterns require more materials and labor, so adjust your bid to reflect these changes. Figures 6-43 through 6-48 should give you and your customers some ideas for appealing designs.

6-42 *For that invisible railing.* Feeney Wire Rope

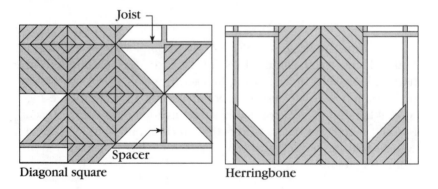

Diagonal square

Herringbone

Parquet

6-43
*Diagonal square,
herringbone, parquet.*
Southern Forest Products Association

6-44 *Diagonal on primary deck. The upper deck is octagon shaped with a Starburst design.* CaddCon Designs

6-45 *Parallel to the house. Note the two different styles of radius stairs. Designer/Builder Greg Dowdy.* California Redwood Association

6-46 *Parallel, perpendicular, and diagonal, including an interesting radius. What a masterpiece!* DECKS APPEAL

6-47 *Unusual design: One 2" × 6" followed by two 2" × 2" and then bordered with five 2" × 4s".* DECKS APPEAL

6-48 *Diagonal boards (45° pattern or herringbone design) meeting at a 2" × 2" incorporated into a sunburst with an outside radius bench and guardrail combination.* Glickman Design/Build

7

Additional construction concerns

Good framework along with regular and correct maintenance contribute to the longevity of a deck. Planning for what your customers want now and in the future helps to eliminate costly mistakes for both you and the customers. Take the time to determine as accurately as possible what your customers want. Perhaps they are not sure, haven't thought about it, or because of budget constraints they cannot predict what will meet their future needs. You can still help them reach some general decisions by making appropriate suggestions. Bring to their attention items such as lighting, hot tubs, water gardens, and so on. While it is possible they can't afford such items now, they might someday be able to afford them; you can help them make sensible choices that will save their money and your time in the future.

For instance, you could install the electrical system up to a point which will make it easy to tap into later on, or you could pour a concrete pad and design the framework to accept a hot tub at some point in the future. Plans like this contribute to the customer's satisfaction and make it more likely you will be called back when they are ready for the next phase of the project. Preplan, work with the customer, and help them meet the future.

Electrical systems

The deck you complete might be beautiful and enjoyable during the day, but is it useful after nightfall? Lighting plays a major role in how the customers are able to use their deck at night. Lighting is more than merely functional; it brings out the beauty of the deck.

Any deck accessories your customer chooses will probably require electricity. Some of these might include:

• Radio or stereo equipment
• "Bug zapper"
• Hot tub
• Lighting (spot or floodlights)
• Rotisserie for the barbecue
• Timer

These items might be hard-wired or require receptacles, so plan to run 120 volt, 240 volt, or both to the deck. Include enough receptacles to cover these items without the use of an extension cord. Also include a switch to activate some of the receptacles, e.g., for the bug zapper. Once your customers decide on their needs, you can incorporate appropriate wiring and receptacles during the design stage so wires can be concealed in the framing with conduits (PVC or metal) or buried using underground fused (UF) cable at least 1' underground. Be sure to check the local electrical codes concerning electrical installation.

Receptacles should be placed in watertight outlet boxes approved for outdoor use. Not only should the outlet box covers have gaskets, but the receptacles themselves should be ground fault circuit interrupters (GFCIs) with spring-loaded covers that have a gasket or a weatherproof outlet cover as shown in Fig. 7-1. I firmly believe an electrician should be hired for this part of the job. Besides, your state might require a licensed electrician.

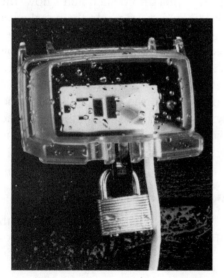

7-1
Horizontal application.
A good example of a
see-through weatherproof
outlet cover featuring a
lockable hasp for added
security. Intermatic, Inc.

If push comes to shove and you need to begin installation of the decking boards, then you can always bury the cable or install the conduit for the electrician. It will be up to the electrician, then, to run the wires, hook up the wires to the service panel, and wire the receptacles, hardwire, and inspect the work you have already done. In cases like this, consult with your electrician. He should supply you with the materials you need to complete this phase of the project. That way you'll be working with the correct materials and have good advice in complying with the National Electrical Code (NEC) and your local or state electrical codes. Whatever you do, do not hook anything up or tie the new system back into the service box unless, besides being a deck builder, you are a licensed electrician.

Low-voltage lighting

To enhance the natural beauty of the home, driveway, sidewalks, gardens, and finished deck, consider using low-voltage outdoor lighting. In fact, this is something your customers could do on their own. Of course, you could also do it or help your customers to plan for it.

You can help them get started by obtaining a copy of *Light Up Your Life* by Intermatic Malibu, a company that specializes in low-voltage systems. This 52-page booklet covers the selection of lights, the installation and maintenance of low-voltage lighting systems, and an understanding of how low-voltage lighting works. It's available for $1.75 to cover postage and handling. Consider stocking this booklet and handing them out to your customers. It could help you as well. Write to:

Lighting Book
Intermatic Malibu
Intermatic Plaza
Spring Grove, IL 60081

The heart of a low-voltage system is the transformer which reduces regular household current (120 volts) to a safe 12 volts. Transformers range in size from a small unit (powering a single entrance light) to large models that can safely operate 25 or more lights. They are available with several control options. The customer can choose among options such as an automatic timer, photo control, photo control with timer, and manual control to fit their particular needs. It is important to use the proper transformer to handle the number of lights you plan to install as well as the correct gauge cable for the length of the run.

To determine which transformer will best suit the job, add up the wattage of all the lamps you plan to install and then select a transformer that most closely matches the total normal wattage (TNW) of these lights. For example, to power seven 11-watt lamps, you'll need a transformer that has an output of at least 77 TNW. Table 7-1 spells out transformer size and correct cable gauges.

Table 7-1. Transformer Selection Chart

Total nominal wattage of transformer	150-Watt, 16-gauge cable		200-Watt, 14-gauge cable		250-Watt, 12-gauge cable	
	Maximum watts	Maximum length	Maximum watts	Maximum length	Maximum watts	Maximum length
25	25	100	25	125	25	150
44	44	100	44	125	44	150
88	88	100	88	125	88	150
121	121	100	121	125	121	150
196	150	100	196	125	196	150
300	150	100	200	150	250	200

Source: Intermatic Malibu

The "rule of thumb" is that the total load wattage of the lamps should not be less than half of the transformer's TNW, nor should it exceed the transformer's maximum capacity. If the TNW rating of the lamps is too high, divide the electrical load between two transformers or use a more powerful transformer.

For most installations, 16-gauge cable is just right. However, for runs longer than 100 feet or less than 150 total lamp watts, there could be insufficient light output. Again, see Table 7-1: 14-gauge is recommended for up to 150 feet, and the larger 12-gauge is recommended for up to 200 feet.

Another way to reduce voltage drop is to divide the cable into shorter lengths. Figure 7-2 shows five of the most common wiring layouts and provides you with alternative wiring opportunities besides the common series installation (one light after another).

The alternatives include:

- **A Split the load**: Run up to the recommended maximum distance in two or more directions from the transformer (Fig. 7-2A).
- **B The tee method**: Distribute power more evenly to the center of a run or to a run some distance away (e.g., across a driveway). Heavier gauge cable (10- or 12-gauge) or a double run of cable should be used to make the tee (Fig. 7-2B). All connections should be soldered (see Fig. 7-2, insert).

- **C Split tee**: Distribute power more uniformly to both legs, i.e., to both sides of the yard (Fig. 7-2C). Otherwise, the layout is the same as B.
- **D Complete loop around yard**: Distribute power in a loop, allowing for relatively uniform light output. (Polarity note: Be careful to connect the same wire ends to the proper transformer terminals by noting the ridge on one side of the cable.)

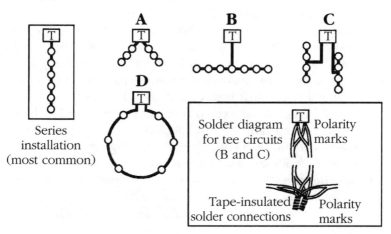

7-2 *Cable layout options.* Intermatic Malibu

A low-voltage outdoor lighting system can make a dramatic impact on a home's appearance. According to Phil L. Kinzer, Marketing Manager for Intermatic Malibu, setting the proper "lightscaping mood" isn't as difficult as one might think. Kinzer recommends that you (or the customer) select one or two focal points to highlight, such as a tree, pathway, flower bed, etc. Then he suggests using a variety of lighting techniques, such as downlighting, uplighting, and cross lighting to achieve special effects. Here are some other general recommendations:

- **Try to conceal the light source,** unless the lights themselves are to be a focal point.
- **Don't overlight;** a little light goes a long way.
- **Strive for a natural look.** Lighting should imitate moonlight or filtered light without glare.
- **Consider illuminating steps, paths, and changes in the sidewalk level,** or any potential obstacles that could cause injury.

- **Situate lights so they don't shine into a neighbor's window or** cause unpleasant glare when viewed from neighboring homes and yards.
- **Keep color in mind.** Colored lenses are available for most floodlights. In addition, some companies now offer silicone-colored bulb sleeves to change the color of tier lights, deck lights, walkway lights, and entrance lights.
- **Consider the ease of servicing the lights.** Make sure they are easy to reach so that changing lamps and cleaning lenses is as simple as possible for your customer.

It's a good idea to incorporate lights into the deck's design before actual construction begins. Many styles of deck lights are available. Some lights can be mounted either horizontally or vertically and are great for steps, benches, and railings. Choose the correct light to give unique lighting effects that your customers will enjoy.

Some of the lighting effects to consider incorporating include:

- **Path lighting** (Fig. 7-3): Install along walkways or any place where careful footing is required. Such lighting makes the walkway both safe and eye-pleasing.
- **Spotlighting** (Fig. 7-4): A sequence of spotlights can create an intriguing mosaic of colors and textures. After dark, unusual textures on garden walls can create attractive focal points.
- **Uplighting** (Fig. 7-5): Uplighting is great for interesting objects such as statues, fountains, or tree foliage canopies. Be sure to direct any glare away from the viewer. Concealing fixtures behind shrubbery affords the most natural appearance.
- **Crosslighting** (Fig. 7-6): In this type of application, the unusual interaction of beams of light can yield as much visual artistry as the feature being illuminated. Again, direct any glare away from the viewer and conceal fixtures behind shrubbery for the most natural look.
- **Highlighting** (Fig. 7-7): Providing imaginative illumination on a broad surface behind a landscaping feature creates a showplace for that feature. The larger illuminated area also increases safety and security.
- **Floodlighting** (Fig. 7-8): Floodlights are versatile for illuminating a wide range of landscaping features. Garden ponds, gazebos, statues, and prized plant specimens all become more visually impressive when properly lit with low-voltage lighting products.

Figures 7-9 through 7-11 provide some additional low-voltage lighting ideas from Intermatic Malibu.

7-3
Path lighting. Intermatic Malibu

7-4
Spotlighting. Intermatic Malibu

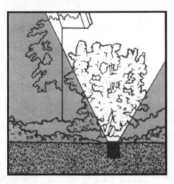

7-5
Uplighting. Intermatic Malibu

7-6
Crosslighting. Intermatic Malibu

7-7
Highlighting. Intermatic Malibu

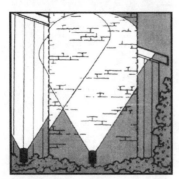

7-8
Floodlighting. Intermatic Malibu

7-9 *Mushroom prismatic tier lights are great for illuminating waterfalls in a rock garden.* Intermatic Malibu

7-10 *Traditional tier lights are used throughout this deck.* Intermatic Malibu

7-11
The decorative mariner/surface deck light provides great lighting around steps. Intermatic Malibu

When creating a lighting plan, take a walk both before and after dark around the yard with the customer. Observe the different lighting effects created by the sun and the moon on the area where the deck will be built and the surrounding landscaping. Remember to use the three basic lighting techniques when recreating these effects:

- **Choose a focal point:** Look for main features of the deck, the home, and the landscaping. Select the main element(s) around which to design the lighting plan. Choose no more than one or two focal points. A good focal point could be a large tree, a main entrance, a front walk, or a landscaped island.
- **Plan for safety and security:** Look for dark spots in corners and behind large bushes. Look for potentially hazardous steps and curbs. Plan to light these areas for both safety and security. Consider adding infrared motion detectors and photo control accessories to turn lights on automatically to scare off would-be intruders.
- **Combine lighting techniques:** For maximum interest and appeal, blend different lighting techniques into one plan. For example, backlight a row of bushes along a wall, or uplight a nearby small tree while downlighting the surrounding low ground cover.

The following list will serve as a handy checklist or for quick reference as you work with the customer or assemble your bid package:

- Light up the deck and patio
- Accent a garden
- Light a pathway
- Create an entryway
- Accent a walkway
- Highlight landscaping
- Border a driveway
- Highlight the home

Other electrical concerns

As stressed throughout this book, preplan for everything, including both current needs and possible future needs. This holds true for electrical matters as well. Nothing looks worse than to see conduit across the face of a home. Sometimes you don't have a choice about where a conduit goes, but you do have a choice about how much of it actually shows. With a deck, conduit can be run on the underside of the framework.

When designing a deck, keep in mind those items used on the deck that require electricity. For example, you could design a 45° bay on the deck to hold a barbecue as shown in Fig. 7-12. Before installing the electrical receptacle, check with the customers to see if they use a rotisserie. If they do, find out what side of the barbecue it is on and locate the receptacle there. A bay not only keeps a hot barbecue out of the traffic flow but also keeps the receptacle and electrical cord out of the way too, helping to prevent accidents.

7-12 *This bay could be a simple addition to any existing deck.* Used with permission of Georgia-Pacific Corporation

The scrap wood (left over from building the deck) can be used to create unique lighting fixtures for use with low-voltage systems. Fixtures can be designed to blend in with the overall design of the deck. Work with your customer and don't be afraid to show your creativity.

Another lighting option is lamp posts. Cast iron units have an old-fashioned look that suggests an aura of days gone by. If these suit the style of the home, they can provide a real nostalgic touch (Fig. 7-13). Mel-Nor manufactures cast aluminum bases that would probably fit your customers' budgets. A variety of shapes, sizes, colors and lighting head styles is also available. Coordinating wall and pier mount fixtures can be purchased as well (Fig. 7-14).

Help your customer discover the beauty, effective sun shading, and glare control qualities of one of the most innovative products on the market today: motorized retractable awnings by Somfy Systems, Inc. These awnings move with the touch of a button or even automatically with the help of a sun and wind control. These awnings are a perfect complement to a deck or patio area, providing shade when the customer wants it. Systems are available in vibrant designer colors of solution-dyed acrylic fabrics that are fade- and mildew-resistant by Sunbrella (Glen Raven Mills, Inc.). They are available in a variety of sizes to match the dimensions of virtually any window, door, patio, deck, or terrace (Figs. 7-15A and B).

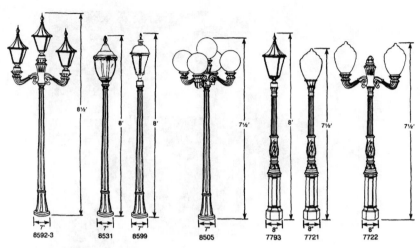

7-13 *Lamp post sizes and styles.* Mel-Nor

For more information on motorized retractable awnings, contact Somfy Systems, Inc. For fabric samples, contact the Custom Fabrics Division of Sunbrella at the addresses provided in Appendix C.

Plumbing

Nothing is more enjoyable than to sit in a hot tub gazing at the stars in the middle of winter. Many customers envision just such an activity once their deck has been built. Will the deck you built support some type of spa? If your preplanning has included a spa, there is no problem. In most cases, a deck will not hold the weight of a spa without additional support.

Building a deck is a major expense for most customers; even though a hot tub is on their minds, it might not become an immediate reality because of the cost. Within a couple of years, however, that hot tub will become a priority. What you can do now is help the customers to achieve this goal without adding extra expense at the time of the hot tub installation.

First, find out where your customers might plan to install a hot tub. Specific installation locations have specific needs; determining this information will help you decide how to construct the framework or where to pour a pad to carry the weight. The whole idea here is to make it cost-efficient for the customer and easier on yourself if you come back to install the tub.

If the tub will be placed on the deck, find out its size and total weight including water and occupants. Then build the framework and

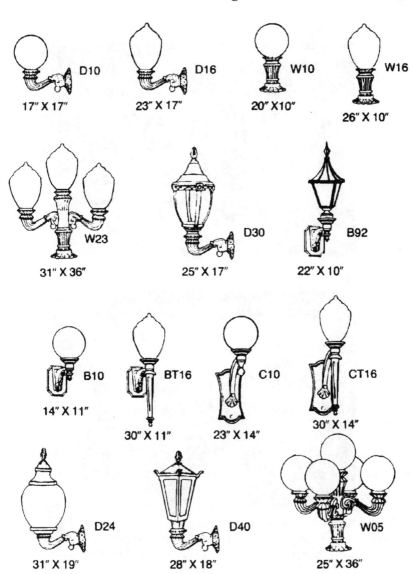

7-14 *Wall and pier mount sizes and styles.* Mel-Nor

supports to carry that weight. Building codes are another area of concern with hot tub installations. If the tub will be situated close to the guardrail, then the guardrail in this area needs to be extended at least double the normal height requirement to prevent children and adults from falling backward when sitting on the edge of the tub. Be sure to check step and railing requirements to protect yourself from a liability suit. Install a step around all open areas of the tub (whether anyone

A

B

7-15A *(Closed)* and **B** *(Open) One advantage of a modern retractable awning is that it does not include unsightly poles as part of a permanent structure.* Somfy Systems, Inc., and Glen Raven Mills, Inc.

would attempt to climb in or out of the tub at that point or not) according to code and install handrails in at least two spots. In case the customer selects someone else to install the hot tub, make sure your original contract states that you "are not responsible for installing the hot tub and/or spa" and that "code requirements such as guardrails, handrails, and steps associated with the hot tub and/or spa will be the responsibility of the homeowner and the firm installing the hot tub and/or spa." Consult your attorney for the proper wording of this text. It's important to protect yourself in this litigious society.

If the spa will be recessed in the deck at a later date, then convince the customer to let you pour a concrete pad and frame the area where the tub will be installed in an appropriate fashion, so that all that has to be done later is to loosen deck screws and remove joist hangers. This makes the joists easy to remove, and the deck boards can be cut in this area.

Basically, you are creating a self-supporting framework around the area where the tub will be recessed. This area can then be filled in with joists that follow the existing joist pattern and hung in place with joist hangers. This inner framework can be easily removed at a later date. Also consider making the outer framework anywhere from 1' to 2' larger just in case the customer later decides to install a larger spa unit. Your customers will save money in the long run because they have preplanned for the hot tub. It is easier and less expensive to do it right the first time than to retrofit the deck to accommodate the tub.

Also make sure that there is an access panel that can be removed in front of the plumbing to provide easy access for regular maintenance and repairs. The access panel should feature a recessed handle and be completely removable (no hinges) when access is required.

If the tub will be installed on the ground at a later date, then there is no problem and the customers can deal with the issue later. One exception would be a situation in which you would only be able to poor concrete before the deck is constructed, due to its location. Under these circumstances, you would want to pour both the pad and deck piers at the same time. Also consider installing the electrical system up to the tub's future location so it can be hooked up easily once the tub is installed.

If the deck has multiple levels, be sure that the primary deck that might have to carry the load of a secondary level as well as a hot tub is adequate to support all the weight. Again, remember to consider the weight of the tub plus the weight of the water and the occupants.

Another area of concern is placing a hot tub in an enclosure, such as a screened porch or an addition where the deck is built around the unit. Be sure to design for adequate ventilation and install a ceiling fan. The question here is whether the tub can be removed if it needs repairs or replacement. This requires careful planning on your part. Here's an idea I used that might come in handy if you find yourself in this type of situation.

Figure 7-16 shows a hot tub addition and a very large tub on the ground, waiting to be installed. The customer specifically wanted to be able to get the tub out for any reason, without having to tear the addition apart to do so.

7-16 *This hot tub made it through the rough open on its side and with the help of four bodies.*
C.R.S., Inc.

Since the addition had sliding doors, I framed the slider on the left beyond the maximum width of the rough opening which, in this case, was by two 2" × 6"s (that would have been the two trimmers normally required). This gave me an extra 3" in width, so the rough opening was increased by 3". I installed the two trimmers using screws. (The trimmers do not support anything; they are just filler pieces for the slider.) Once the slider and the window above it (which was also installed with screws) were removed, then the trimmers (including the crossmember) could be removed. The casing on the outside as well as the inside was wide enough to cover three quarters of the jamb and included the width of the trimmer plus an extra ½" for overlap over the finish wall. The jamb and the casing were also installed with screws. If you have to do something similar to this, don't make the same mistake I made: I cut the header the standard length for the slider, forgetting to add the extra 3". The secondary trimmers became filler pieces for the slider to attach to as well as the finish jamb (Fig. 7-17).

If the opportunity ever arises to create a masterpiece, then the deck shown in Fig. 7-18 should give you some ideas. This redwood

7-17
*View of the inside of the
hot tub room. The decking
is level for easy access.* C.R.S.,
Inc.

7-18 *Notice the built-in benches, which feature rounded backs and
lattice inserts enhancing the design of the pavilion.* California Redwood Association, photo
by Ernest Braun

deck was built by Bryan Hays (Ahwahnee, California). Notice the spa unit; it is an 8' × 12' swim-in-place Jacuzzi-jet pool. I personally like the massive arches on the dome roof of the overhead shade structure with its lattice accents. What a grand pavilion in which to entertain guests!

Water gardens

Plumbing and the electrical system are important components of accessory items used on or around a deck. One such item is a rock garden or water garden that includes a pond and perhaps a fountain spray, as shown in Fig. 7-19. These gardens need both plumbing and electrical service (120 volts and low-voltage). Water gardens require a lot of maintenance from the customer, but can certainly increase the appeal of any deck. They will require careful planning on your part.

7-19 *The bridge gives a final touch to this rock garden.* MacCourt Products, Inc.

It is not necessary to run a plumbing line to a pond. The customer can use a garden hose, though it is certainly inconvenient, and dragging a hose around the pond can damage foliage. A better plan would be to include a water line in a convenient area to fill the pond when water has evaporated to the point that the pond requires refilling.

Water gardens do not have to be expensive to build. There are many products on the market that can simplify the construction process.

You just have to know the products and be able to incorporate them into an eye-appealing design the customer can enjoy from the deck.

There are a few things to keep in mind when designing such a garden. The following information was supplied by MacCourt who sells EPDM flexible liners and preformed HDPE ponds.

Site selection

When discussing with your customers an appropriate location for a water garden, you will want to point out some basics to them. For example, make certain that the site is in full view of the deck and has good drainage. Choose an area that is accessible to both water and electricity; this simplifies some maintenance chores. If the customers want their water garden located under or near a tree, you might want to point out that maintenance will be higher because of fallen leaves, branches, pine needles, and so forth. If the customers plan to use aquatic plants within the pond, then an area that gets at least four to six hours of sun each day is preferable.

Choosing the pond

Ponds can be made of concrete, fiberglass, flexible rubber or PVC, and premolded HDPE. The following are some maintenance considerations for each of these options:

Concrete A friend of mine has a pond, and it seems that every year a new crack appears. A good concrete pond should have walls that are at least 4" to 6" thick and reinforced with steel. Even so, there is no guarantee that a crack won't appear. Concrete ponds are not totally maintenance- or trouble-free. Perhaps my friend should consider filling the cracks and then lining the pond with an EPDM rubber flexible liner. This way, he won't have to worry about the liner cracking or having to paint.

Fiberglass Stress cracks can occur in fiberglass units once they are filled if they are not properly installed. Because of the chemicals used to produce the unit, it could be toxic to plants and fish. Like other fiberglass products, the color is on the surface so scratches, when they occur, will most likely show.

Preformed ponds These units are easy to install. They have a smooth surface, which means no brushing or scrubbing when it comes time to clean. There is no painting required because the color is consistent all the way through the product. There are all kinds of shapes and sizes from which to select (Fig. 7-20).

EPDM rubber flexible liners These pond liners work when larger ponds are not available or if you are designing your own con-

7-20
This connecting pool allows the creation of a waterfall, perfect to connect multiple ponds.
MacCourt Products, Inc.

figuration. MacCourt liners are nontoxic, so they are safe for fish and plants.

Installation

With preformed ponds, installation is easy. Using marking paint, mark the perimeter both at the bottom and top of the pond on the ground where the pond will be installed. Dig the corresponding hole, following the pattern of the pond's contour, slightly larger than what you marked. Make sure that the excavation has a firmly compacted base. Remove any debris, tree roots, and rocks. Line the base of the hole with 2" to 4" of soft sand. I recommend you do a trial run to make sure the pond does not stick out of the ground too high and that the pond is level. While the preformed pond is empty, backfill around it with loose dirt, but do not compact the fill! When the backfill reaches the halfway point of the pond, begin to fill the pond with water. Once you are satisfied with the backfill, then continue filling with water while you backfill, gauging the timing so the filling and backfilling are finished together. This way you neither stretch nor push in the pond as you are backfilling the hole and filling the pond.

If the pond you are installing features shelves to hold plants or statues, make certain that these shelves are properly supported underneath with the backfill.

When installing a flexible liner, you'll find it much easier to work with the liner if it has been spread in the sun. The sun's warmth will make the material more pliable so it will more readily conform to the contours of the hole.

Draining

If the unit does not come with a drain, leave it alone. Achieving a watertight seal can be difficult and the sealant or adhesive you use might bond poorly with the pond material (polyethylene). Even if you could get the drain system to seal, the debris at the bottom of the tub would only clog or restrict the flow. It is easier for the customer to use a recirculating pump to remove the water.

Pumps

The pump is the heart of the system, so make sure to select the correct pump for the size of the pond. The flow can be regulated with most pumps, but you can't increase the flow from too small a pump. The pump provides the water flow required for an ornamental fountain and introduces oxygen into the water for a healthier pond. To determine the size of pump necessary for a waterscape, contact Cal Pump (address given in Appendix C). They have pumps that will work with any product you have in mind. They also feature submersible halogen spotlights, biological filters, fountain spray heads, and accessories.

Once a pond has been in place for a time, it is possible that your customers might phone you with questions. While you do not have to be an expert in pond care, you will want to be able to address their concerns in a professional manner, and the following information, supplied by MacCourt, may help. If you do not know an answer, at least be prepared to steer your customers to someone who does. How you handle this phone conversation will leave a lasting impression; make sure it's a good one.

Algae

Algae are simple microscopic plants that love sunlight, mineral salts, carbon dioxide, and ponds. There are over 100 varieties, but their growth can be controlled. Shade ponds normally have little problem with algae because they lack sunlight, an ingredient necessary to algae growth. For ponds in sunny locations, a commercial dye/colorant or a minuscule amount of artist's carbon black mixed in the water may block sunlight.

Biological filtration can help to control free-floating single-cell algae. Small water fleas (Daphnia) and tadpoles can also bring the problem to a quick end but if you have fish, you will not find the flea treatment effective: they won't last long enough to eat the algae before they become dinner themselves.

The type of algae called blanketweed is recognizable by its long filaments and is associated with crystal clear water. While it generally presents itself in the spring, it can also be found during the fall season. Biological filtration will not work with this variety of algae. To get rid of it, wind the masses around a rough stick and pull the material out.

A solution of permanganate of potash (¼ tsp. for every 200 gallons, dissolved in one-half gallon of water) will combat single-cell algae. Take care not to spill this solution on your skin; the resulting stain will have to wear off over time. Another alternative is to shop for algae-fighting formulations already on the market. The product should be nontoxic to plants and fish and specially formulated for use in water gardens (do not use swimming pool products). Chemical formulations might solve the problem on a temporary basis, but for more effective long-term control, starve the food supply by introducing aquatic plants that will compete for nutrients required by the algae.

Aquatic plants

Aquatic plants are an effective way of starving the food supply of algae. There are four major categories of water plants: lilies, oxygenators, floaters, and marginals (some consider deep marginals to be a fifth category). Ideally, water plants should occupy between 60 and 70 percent of the surface. As their leaves grow, they shade the water's surface and block the sunlight—thus inhibiting algae growth. The plants work together to balance a pond naturally, precluding the use of chemicals.

Lilies These plants bloom in a variety of colors from white and yellow to red and purple. Most bloom during the day, but some varieties bloom at night. Some are more fragrant than others but all are attractive and enjoyable.

Lilies can be classified as either hardy or tropical. If you are constructing a pond in a northern climate, your customers may want to consider the hardy variety for low maintenance. However, tropical lilies can be used provided they are removed before the first frost. Like most aquatic plants (floaters are the exception), lilies remain in pots filled with dirt (not potting soil). The pots should be fairly large, 10" in diameter, and the plants require a layer of gravel or stone over the top to contain the dirt and to protect the plant from the fish. Lilies like to grow at a depth of 18", so their pots should be placed on the bottom of the pond.

Oxygenators These plants are among the least expensive to buy yet contribute the most to the overall ecosystem of the pond. They thrive on mineral salts in the water and can usually eat more per plant than the algae can, causing the algae to starve.

Oxygenators are also extremely important for fish. They meet several needs within the pond by providing both a hiding place and food for baby fish. Oxygenators also have an affinity for the toxic nitrates present in the pond as a result of the conversion of fish wastes from ammonia to nitrates by bacteria. You might want to recommend this plant to your customers who plan to stock their ponds with fish.

These plants should be established in the pond a couple of weeks before fish are added, one bunch per two square feet of water surface. Different plants grow at different depths but all should be planted in pots with gravel on the top.

Floaters These plants help to control algae in two ways: they provide surface shade before the lilies have matured to a point where their leaves will adequately shade the surface and they eat mineral salts which helps to starve the algae. Like lilies, floaters come in two varieties: tropical and hardy. In northern climates, tropical varieties (like water hyacinths) should be planted after the threat of frost. If the plant should be caught by frost, surface damage might not appear but the plant will probably suffer a delayed reaction. As their name implies, these plants float on the surface of the water and therefore require no dirt or pots.

Marginals Grown mainly for their ornamental effect, marginals live in the marshy soil surrounding the pond, helping to provide some surface shade. Common examples are marsh marigolds, iris, ranunculus, forget-me-not, mint, and creeping varieties, such as menyanthes and veronica. Deep marginals actually sit on the pond's bottom.

Fish

Briefly, cold-water fish need food and plenty of room to swim in water with an adequate supply of oxygen. Fish do well in a pond where the pH is between 6.5 and 7.5. Author Stanley Russell (*The Stapeley Book of Water Gardens*, David & Charles, Inc., ISBN #0-7153-8649-2) suggests that a new pond be stocked at the rate of 1" of fish length for each square foot of water surface area. This allows the fish and the ecosystem to acclimate to each other. Once the pond is established, a final stocking guide is 2" of fish length for each square foot of water surface area. Fish will grow in proportion to their surroundings.

Fish are available at pet stores and even bait shops. Koi are colorful and usually expensive fish. They are enjoyable to watch but can also uproot oxygenators and eat plants. The most common fish used to stock garden ponds are goldfish. These hardy fish can live to be 12 years old and weigh up to 4 pounds. Because they are a cold-water fish, goldfish are stressed in water temperatures over 85°F. However, they are quite hardy and can survive in some poor water conditions, reproducing usually twice a year. Left unfed, they will determine the amount of fish the pond can support. Fed, goldfish may overpopulate and require thinning. Underfeeding is preferable to overfeeding because the latter can both kill the fish and make the algae impossible to control. The fish do eat algae, but their waste products cause the algae to grow. A biological filter is highly recommended when fish are involved in a pond. A pet store can provide more complete care instructions.

Landscaping the pond

How to best landscape around ponds is up to you and your customers, based on their lifestyles. Imagination is the only limiting factor. The landscaping selected will depend on both your professional expertise and your customer's personal preferences. Shrubs, flowers, pavers, stones, bricks, wood timbers, connecting logs, fountains, statues, underwater lighting, stepping stones—there are so many options that a pond can be whatever the customer wants and the budget allows.

Ponds for all seasons

Ponds are not maintenance-free. In the spring, they will require a clean-up, and the filter should be turned on once the water temperature has reached 60°F. Any fish will require food once the water is up to 65°F. Plants must be returned to their positions or repotted if they are rootbound.

During summer months, plants will require regular fertilization. Dead leaves must be cleared away. Water in the pond will evaporate so regular refilling will be important. In the fall, dead leaves, pine needles, etc., will need to be removed. You might want to suggest that your customers use a net over the top of the pond if it is located in an area where there are lots of trees.

In the winter, once the temperature has dropped below 55°F, the fish will no longer require feeding but a heater should replace the biological filter. The plants will also require some care before winter comes. The supplier of these plants can provide your customer with the ins and outs of pond plant care.

For a list of addresses of aquatic suppliers that carry plants, copper fountains, waterwheels, waterfalls, pumps and fountains, pond heaters, underwater lighting, algae inhibitors, natural stone statuary, biological filters, and stone, write to:

MacCourt Products, Inc.
111 South Virginia Street
Crystal Lake, IL 60014

Deck care specialists

Just as customers will come back to you with questions concerning the maintenance on their water garden, they will also want some answers regarding the maintenance of their new decks. Maintaining decks can be a full-time profession. Restoring decks to the wood's natural beauty is profitable and rewarding work, especially when you see the amazed expression on your customers' faces.

Most homeowners are unaware that a deck can be restored to its original beauty. One thing is certain: today's two-income families have limited time; spending a precious weekend restoring their deck is not high on their priority lists. This is where you, the professional, come in. Not only can you build decks, you can maintain them as well.

Over the past several years, the deck maintenance industry has grown at an astounding rate. In 1989 when Mark Abbott, John Abbott, and Rick Stearns started Deckshield, Inc., there were no other companies listed in the Washington, D.C., metropolitan yellow pages that specialized in cleaning and watersealing decks. In 1995, there are more than 25 in that area alone. This is truly a growth industry.

According to statistics, one out of every four homes in America today has a wooden deck; in the Washington, D.C., area this translates to almost half a million decks, each one a potential job. How many decks are there in your area? In 1994, Deckshield cleaned and sealed 1,100 decks, the most that any one company in this industry did nationwide. Even if 25 companies were competing in the same market doing the same amount of business as Deckshield, approximately 95 percent of the decks would still remain untouched. Think about all the new homes with decks just now coming onto the market; the potential for growth in this industry is tremendous.

The following information was provided by Mark Abbott, a leader in the deck maintenance industry.

Deck cleaning

The industry was so new when Deckshield began that the best method of cleaning a deck was to use a "deck brightener" and aggressively scrub. Obviously, this method wasn't very appealing for a deck maintenance technician because sheer exhaustion limited the amount of work that could be done. The addition of pressure washing equipment to clean decks greatly increased the amount of work that could be accomplished in a single day. This, of course, translated into more profits.

Pressure washing machines are difficult to use properly and require a significant amount of training and practice prior to starting a business. The machines come with different sizes of engines, pumps, and tips to accommodate the different types of wood or material requiring cleaning. The different cleaning tips are designed to reduce or enhance the direct pressure so as to minimize the risk of damage or maximize the cleaning effect. For example, concrete can be cleaned with a machine that generates water pressure in excess of 2500 psi.

However, this pressure applied to a pressure-treated deck will most certainly damage the surface of the lumber.

Once you have acquired equipment and skills, the results are like magic to your customers. All the gray, green, and black colorations will be removed, leaving the deck looking new. The beauty of this process is that it sells itself. Neighbors frequently approach a technician on the job site in disbelief, which generates even more business (Fig. 7-21).

7-21 *This deck was partially cleaned (right half shows "before," left half shows "after") using Wolman Deck Brightener (no acid or chlorine bleach) and a stiff brush. For larger decks, a power washer is faster and more effective.* Wolman Wood Care

Of course, there is no magic involved. All the natural discoloration on a wooden surface is topical, e.g., algae, mildew, and gray oxidation from the sun. Certain stains, such as grease and the little circles left behind from iron furniture, are difficult to remove without applying a chemical first, but generally water pressure alone is adequate to remove deck discoloration.

The idea that water pressure is, in itself, adequate has fueled debate between Deckshield and various chemical manufacturers. The main ingredient in many of these chemical cleaners is bleach. However, bleach is not only harmful to the surrounding environment, it is also time-consuming and expensive to use. If it is not properly rinsed off a deck, bleach will break down whatever sealant is applied. The idea of using a chemical cleaner first and then pressure washing it off appears to be so logical that one company uses the advertising analogy of a person bathing with or without soap. Abbott maintains that nothing could be further from the truth.

The logic behind chemical usage stems from the idea that the deck cleaning technician must first kill the mold and mildew spores lodged in the surface cells of the wood. Then, after application of a sealant to prevent or retard their recurrence, the deck will live free of mildew growth for a longer period of time. This assumes that algae, mold, and mildew are actually detrimental to the wood. It is Abbott's experience, with over 4,000 decks cleaned, that the reverse is actually true: in some cases, algae acts as somewhat of a preservative. In one case, he cleaned a deck that rarely got sun and was covered with algae. In fact, it had not been cleaned or sealed for about ten years. After cleaning, the deck looked new and the wood surface was tight and free of any splintering or cracking.

Another debate between chemical usage versus plain water has its origin in the pressure washing aspect of cleaning. Most of the prominent chemical cleaning companies say that pressure washing alone, without killing the mold and mildew spores first, actually drives unharmed spores deep into the surface of the wood so even though it looks clean and new, it is actually covered with embedded mold and mildew spores. However, chemical cleaners actually do little, if anything, to retard the recurrence of mold and mildew spores, and by the time the deck cleaning technician returns to the cleaned deck to apply sealer (assuming an interval of a day or two to allow the deck to dry) the surface is covered with new spores.

Most of the prominent sealants on the market contain a mildewcide, and it is this that retards the growth of mildew. In Abbot's experience, a deck cleaned with chemical cleaners will look the same as a deck cleaned with plain water in a year's time, provided a quality sealant was applied.

High-pressure vs. low-pressure cleaning

In response to the potential damage that can occur to a deck with a high-pressure system through operator error (incorrect combination of pressure, wand tip, and distance from tip to surface), low-pressure cleaning is offered as an alternative. The idea behind low-pressure cleaning is that a chemical is applied to the deck and after a few minutes the deck is hosed off. Unfortunately, low-pressure systems only work well if the deck is scrubbed after chemical application and prior to being rinsed off.

It is Abbott's strong recommendation that you first test any low-pressure system you are considering. He has recently come across an organization that claims by using their chemical first, a simple rinsing will achieve the same results on a pressure-treated deck as high-pressure washing. However, their solution is bleach-based and prone to do more damage than good. The lesson here is that if it sounds too good to be true, it probably is.

A valid low-pressure system requires a chemical detergent, preferably non-chlorine-based, to be applied to a dirty deck. This will loosen the algae, dirt, and mildew from the pores of the wood, permitting the technician to use less pressure to clean the deck. In this case, an adequate pressure to maintain is approximately 1200 psi. This system actually requires more time than high-pressure washing but has a very low risk level with regard to damaging the wood.

Cedar and redwood decks and siding are excellent candidates for cleaning at lower pressures given the softness of these woods. If the pressure exceeds approximately 1800 psi, there is a good chance of leaving ridges on the surface of cedar and redwood because the pulp can become compressed while the grain lines remain rigid.

Remember, if the chemical being applied during a low-pressure cleaning contains bleach, it will in fact kill the mold and mildew. However, the dirt still needs to be pressure-washed off, not just rinsed. Too much bleach can kill the homeowner's lawn and landscaping plants, turn the deck white, and perhaps accidentally stain clothing or awnings.

High-pressure systems use pumps requiring three to four gallons per minute that emit water at roughly 2000 to 3000 psi. Four gallons per minute can be obtained by most public water systems, which means that a high-pressure system can be hooked up to the homeowner's outdoor spigot. The other obvious advantage to a high-pressure system is that no chemicals or scrubbing are required, saving both time and energy. A high-pressure wash, if applied with the proper technique and tip, will not damage the wood at all.

Watersealing

You may have heard that prior to watersealing a deck built of pressure treated lumber, you should "let the wood breathe." In fact, the wood used to build the deck has probably spent several months "breathing" prior to arriving at the site. By "breathing," I mean the expansion and contraction that takes place with pressure-treated wood throughout the year given changes in temperature and moisture levels.

When it rains, the surface of a board absorbs water and becomes saturated if the water stands on the board long enough. When the sun comes out, the board can dry so rapidly that cracking and warping result. As this cycle of soaking and drying continues, an unprotected deck can show signs of cracking and warping within just a few months of the time it was built. New lumber is more susceptible to these cycles because the pressure-treating process involves a water-based mixture, and therefore the lumber is saturated when it arrives at the lumber yards. If a sealant is applied when the deck is built, rapid moisture loss will be retarded, maintaining the integrity of the wood for a longer period of time.

Water-based sealants are perfect for new decks. By *water-based*, I mean that water rather than petroleum is used as the carrier of the solvents. It might sound strange to speak of water-based sealants since the term seems contradictory, but they are actually easier to use, absorb more readily, and will not harm any vegetation surrounding the deck, an important consideration given the general interest in preserving the environment.

Oil-based sealants do not moisturize pressure-treated wood. Oil is used as a preservative that protects lumber from wood-boring insects and rot. However, pressure-treated wood has already been preserved against insects and rot with chemicals such as copper chromium arsenate (CCA). Simply stated, pressure-treated lumber needs to be made water repellant to reduce the harmful effects of soaking and drying.

Cedar and redwood are not as susceptible to moisture absorption and loss as pressure-treated lumber, and therefore will not warp, crack, and check as pressure-treated lumber will. These woods (cedar shake roofs, siding, decking) should be sealed with an oil-based sealant in order to preserve the lumber.

Finishing touches

A clean deck looks beautiful, but if the house is not properly rinsed after the deck is cleaned, the most flawless deck can lose its appeal. Thoroughly rinse the house and the areas around the deck, and if the deck is on the second level, the house and patio underneath the deck should also be rinsed.

After a deck has been pressure washed, it is common for the wood grain to be raised. This might appear to be damage caused by the pressure washes but in most cases it can be sanded off with very minor sanding. Abbott recommends that all surfaces which might come in contact with hands be sanded lightly prior to watersealing. Also sand any benches built into the deck. Sanding the decking surface itself is generally unnecessary unless the deck is near a pool where people will be walking barefooted. Pressure-treated lumber breaks down over time and the splintering can be dramatic, so it's best to advise inquiring customers not to walk barefooted over a deck. An adequate amount of sealant can cover some of the minor splintering.

Abbott generally carries a hammer and spends a few minutes pounding down any nails that might have popped up. With pressure-treated lumber, nails are often worked up due to expansion and contraction over the seasons. Customers appreciate this extra step and will remember it when the time comes to have the deck redone.

In conclusion, the deck care industry is growing at an astounding rate which is exciting for deck care professionals. However, there are many pitfalls in this industry and you will want to do your homework before you purchase any equipment or chemicals. Acquire the proper training and take the necessary precautions before venturing into the deck maintenance business. Deckshield's motto is that a job is never just "good enough." It is either done correctly or incorrectly. Abbott recommends that you make a point of never settling for "good enough." The mediocre companies will eventually be weeded out.

If you have any questions about deck maintenance, feel free to contact Mark Abbott at 800-982-7325. He is just a phone call away and will be able to address any concerns you might have regarding this growing industry.

8

Overhead structures

Nothing is more appealing to the eye than a full or partial overhead structure added to a deck. You don't have to look for excuses to include them; they are very decorative and your customers will find them both attractive and an asset to the home environment. Overhead structures provide shade, act as windbreaks, and buffer neighborhood noise.

Overhead structures can also serve many other purposes. If you add screens, your customers can enjoy their deck in bug-free comfort. By installing clear acrylic glazing, the overhead structure can act as a greenhouse, and with the addition of a false ceiling, customers can hang plants. Vertical latticework permits plants to grow up and over the structure. Depending on its style and location, an overhead structure can make a great romantic retreat. Or it can serve as a place to entertain guests or just to have a simple picnic. It can provide privacy or partial shade for a nearby pond or garden. You can design an overhead structure that will tie the new deck into the details of the existing house. Overhead structures also make a great cover for any spa or hot tub.

There are all kinds of overhead structures from which your customers can choose, but the classic option is the gazebo. A gazebo is a polygon structure that is normally based on an octagonal (eight-sided) shape. It is also referred to as a freestanding roofed structure with open sides to command the view. This stand-alone structure can add a striking dimension to a landscape, serve as a romantic garden retreat, and provide shelter from the elements throughout the year.

The most famous and well-known gazebo style is the elaborate Victorian gazebo. You can devise other designs that make quite an impact on any surroundings. Some of these include:

- **Waterside gazebo:** Built near the water, this structure can make a great romantic setting, especially at sunset.
- **Lattice gazebo:** Latticework is incorporated into the sides as well as the roof of this structure.
- **Solid roof gazebo:** Normally covered in cedar shakes, the roof of this structure could be constructed of other roofing materials as well.
- **Twin gazebos:** This matched pair of structures is normally built close together, frequently on a dock over water.
- **Raised gazebo:** A structure normally built on the upper tier of a deck, this gazebo can also be built on a lower tier or on the ground.
- **Corner gazebo:** Normally built into a right angle, this addition works well with built-in seating.
- **Rose-covered gazebo:** With plants growing up and over this structure, its roof is more functional when designed in an A-shape gable and covered with 2" × 2" or 2" × 3" material spaced from 4" to 7" apart.
- **Garden gazebo:** Built in or near the garden with some type of pathway leading to it, this structure makes a great place to relax, especially if you add a porch swing. To add interest to the roof design, build a second small roof above the first. Raise it high enough to add latticework or screens if it is an enclosed structure. This small roof structure is called a cupola. You can also add skylights to the roof.

Gazebos are not easy to build. Because most of the framework is open, details and miter cuts are clearly visible. It is important that every cut you make be precise and fit like a glove. A slide compound miter will definitely help to achieve those cuts; you just have to cut on the mark. When building gazebos, take to heart the old maxim: "Measure twice, cut once." Customers don't intentionally look for mistakes, but since the real purpose of these structures is to provide a place in which to relax and enjoy the view, perhaps while sitting in a swing or lounging in a hammock, customers have the time to look at every detail. They can't help but see mistakes as they gaze through the framework at the stars or enjoy the sunset. In a gazebo, your choice of wood and construction methods are highly visible to your customers and to their friends, so your work must be more than just satisfactory. Shoddy work does not bring in referrals!

A variety of plans for gazebos are on the market. Contact the Western Wood Products Association at the address given in Appendix C and ask for Plan Sheet #28 (75¢).

The most important factor in constructing a gazebo is the layout of the footings. If you install the footings precisely, you ensure that the framework will go up without any difficulties. I caution you to tie the main framing supports to these footings. If a strong wind should come along, it could uproot the gazebo and carry it away like an oversized umbrella. I'm sure your customers don't want to wake up one morning to find their gazebo on its side in the neighbor's yard!

For those of you who have never built a gazebo, understanding three key elements can help move the construction along smoothly: accurately locating the footings, cutting proper angles, and tying the rafters to a center block.

Locating the footings

Use the string and stake method to lay out the gazebo, just as you lay out a deck. For the purpose of illustration in this section, I describe the layout of a gazebo based on a 12' diameter octagon.

Once you have determined the location for the gazebo, drive a perfectly square stake at least 2" in width into the center of the site. (You may have to make your own; you'll use it for other jobs.) Be certain the stake is embedded deeply into the ground and that it is level both horizontally and vertically. Find the center of the stake by marking it with an "X" from corner to corner, and through the center of the "X" make a cross (+) from side to side, thus creating eight equal divisions with eight equal angles.

Hammer a nail dead center into the stake, then tie one end of a string to the nail and the other end 6' out to a can of marking paint. Using the stake as the center, mark a circle on the ground. You should now have a 12' diameter circle. Untie the string from the center stake and remove the nail. Now you are ready to lay out the stakes.

An octagonal gazebo requires eight stakes. Place the first stake roughly 2' outside the circle and in line with one leg of the "X" marked on top of the stake. This will give you enough room to dig holes for the footings on the marked circle. Tie a string on the stake outside the circle, run the string over the "X" marked on the center stake to the opposite side of the circle, and place your second stake, again, roughly 2' outside the painted circle. It is helpful to have a second person watch to make sure that the string exactly matches one leg of the "X" as it passes over the center stake. Basically, you have cut the circle into two equal halves.

Now you need to cut the circle into four equal quarters. Repeat the first step, but this time pass the string over the second leg of the "X". You should now have two strings and four stakes. If you matched the "X" on the stake precisely, the two strings should cross at true right angles. Check that you have 90° angles by measuring from the center out along one string and making a mark at 3'. Then measure out from the center on the second string (at a right angle to the first) and place a mark at 4'. Measure the distance between these two marked points. You should have a diagonal line that is 5' long. If not, adjust the outer stakes until the diagonal measures 5'. Check all four quarters as shown in Fig. 8-1.

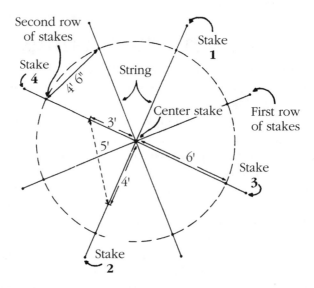

8-1 *Use the stake and string method for laying out the gazebo.* <small>Western Wood Products Association</small>

Now you are ready to divide the circle again, this time into eight equal parts. Use the cross on the center stake for your reference lines. Repeat the same procedure to stake and stretch two more strings, measuring carefully and checking your angles. These four stakes should also be placed 2' outside the marked circle. You should now have four strings stretched between eight stakes.

Each point at which a string intercepts the circle should be 4'6" apart from the next point. Set temporary stakes at each point where a string crosses the circle to check this measurement. Check the second set of strings for a true right angle using the 3'-4'-5' method as done with the first set of strings (Fig. 8-1). The temporary stakes mark the locations where the footings will be dug; remove them as you dig the holes.

Be sure to consult your building department for any requirements on the footings, and don't forget to have them inspected. It is important to make sure your stakes are in place securely and that nothing moves while you dig the holes for the footings. It is okay to remove a string while digging the hole but be sure to put the string back exactly after each hole is dug; the string will help you place the post brackets exactly, which is the next important step.

Set the brackets so their centers will be 6' out from the center stake and the on-center distance between brackets is 4'6". Before the concrete sets, check and recheck those measurements. It will help to have a second person. If you install many gazebos, you might find it faster to set brackets using a couple of wooden sticks cut at 6' and 4'6" rather than a tape measure.

Cutting proper angles

Whether you are using 4" × 4"s, 4" × 6"s, or 2" × 4"s sandwiched between two 2" × 6"s as your main supports, they should be placed according to Fig. 8-2. Your rim joists will be cut at 22½° angles to create the octagon. Remember that whatever distance you choose from the center stake to the post bracket, all eight rim joists must be of equal length in order for the 22½° angles to fit exactly on each quadrant point (refer to Fig. 8-2).

Figure 8-3 features the anatomy of a gazebo. This "exploded" gazebo provides an overall view of all the components required for this structure and the rough order in which they should be installed.

Tying rafters to a center block

The roof you design and the materials you choose can make quite a conversation piece for those who will admire your structure. They can add a touch of personality that will set this gazebo apart as an individual unit while the rest of the structure keeps it in harmony with the deck and house.

Building the roof of any gazebo can be quite a challenge, although it looks harder than it really is. Once the posts are in place, you have a reference point to work from and tie into. One challenging problem common to gazebos is tying in the rafters at the center; perhaps you've had similar problems. The easy solution is to make a decorative center block that will be exposed on the inside of the gazebo.

One way to make this center block is to glue four 2' lengths of 2" × 6" together (or use solid material) to achieve a finished width of 6" × 6". You can make this block longer or shorter depending on the rafter size

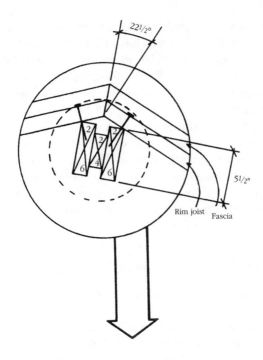

22¹/₂°

2

2
2

6   4   6

5¹/₂"

Rim joist   Fascia

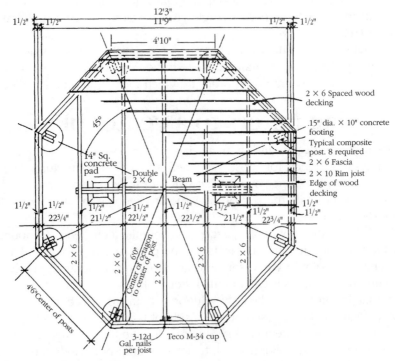

12'3"
1¹/₂"   1¹/₂"   11'9"   1¹/₂"   1¹/₂"

4'10"

2 × 6 Spaced wood
decking

.15" dia. × 10" concrete
footing
Typical composite
post. 8 required
2 × 6 Fascia
2 × 10 Rim joist
Edge of wood
decking

45°

4" Sq.
concrete
pad

Double
2 × 6

Beam

1¹/₂"   1¹/₂"   1¹/₂"   1¹/₂"   1¹/₂"   1¹/₂"   1¹/₂"   1¹/₂"
22³/₄"   21¹/₂"   22¹/₂"   22¹/₂"   21¹/₂"   22³/₄"

2 × 6   2 × 6   Center of octagon   2 × 6   2 × 6
to center of post
60"

46"Center of posts

3-12d   Teco M-34 cup
Gal. nails
per joist

8-2 *Deck framing plan.* Western Wood Products Association

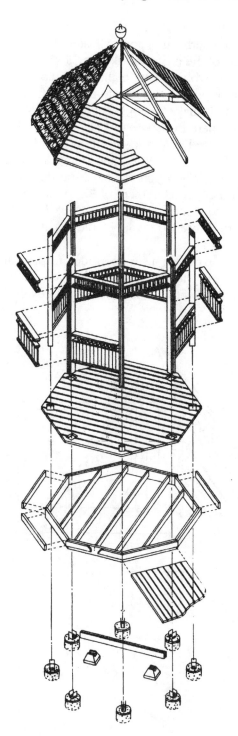

8-3
Anatomy of a gazebo. Western
Wood Products Association

or what the customer prefers. When using 2" × 6" material as your rafters, you will have an exposed overhang of approximately 12".

Rip the four outside corners of the center block using a 45° cut to add four more sides to the center block. The eight-sided block resulting from this process makes it possible for you to tie the rafters in at 90° angles. All you need to do is make an angle cut for the desired roof pitch, which could be anywhere from 4:12 to 12:12.

In order to make all the exposed angles identical on the 6" × 6" center block, measure 1¾" in from each corner, and draw diagonal lines from 1¾" mark to 1¾" mark. When you cut on these diagonal lines, you end up with an exposed measurement of 2½" on all eight sides. The measurement from the center of the block to each angle will be 3". By following this procedure, you will be able to cut every rafter the same length.

Because the center block is exposed, it's a good idea to predrill all holes before installing screws or nails to prevent damage such as cracking to the block. You might want to consider using hardwood for the center block (Fig. 8-4).

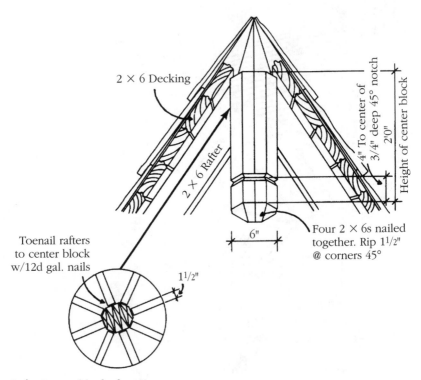

8-4 *Center block elevation.* Western Wood Products Association

Connectors

If the budget is an issue and you need to cut back in order to win the job, there are ways to do so without sacrificing any construction quality. One way to do this is to use special connectors that were specifically designed for building gazebos. Simpson Strong-Tie has created three ties (Fig. 8-5) that allow you to build a six-sided (hexagon) gazebo easier and faster by reducing the number of angle cuts and mitered corner cuts required.

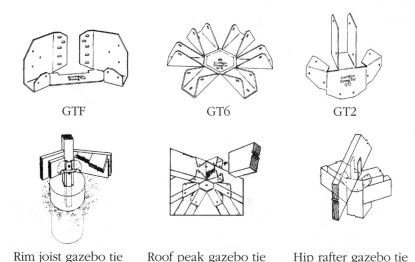

GTF   GT6   GT2

Rim joist gazebo tie   Roof peak gazebo tie   Hip rafter gazebo tie

8-5 *Gazebo connectors.* Simpson Strong-Tie Company, Inc.

- **The Rim Joist (Model GTF)** connects 2× rim joists to the post. The design allows installation over a post base so you can adjust the height of the rim joist.
- **The Roof Peak (Model GT6)** is designed to tie the rafters together at 90°. It is recommended that you use two connectors: one above and one below the rafters. All you need to do is bend the rafter tie to the angle you chose for the pitch of the roof.
- **The Hip Rafter (Model GT2)** adds strength and rigidity to a three-way connection by securing the 2× rafter to the top plate and to the post. Units like these save on materials and labor.

Kits

For those of us whose time is limited, there are always kits. A kit can be assembled in a matter of days once the foundation has been completed. There is nothing wrong with using a kit as long as the quality is up to your standards. It all comes down to what your time is worth to you.

If the excellence of Amish craftsmanship appeals to you, check out the Heritage by Cox Wood Preserving Co. They offer two styles (standard and double-roofed) and three sizes (8', 10', and 12'). Each design includes arched openings, classic turned balusters, cedar shingle roofs, and parquet-style flooring. All components are made from #1 grade Southern pine that has been pressure treated with a special water repellent added for built-in resistance to moisture damage. The wood is dried after the treatment.

The kits contain all the needed materials, most of which are already mounted in factory-assembled panels. All hardware is included and all holes are predrilled (Figs. 8-6A and B). What else could you ask for?

8-6A *Good example of a gazebo kit laid out.* Cox Wood Preserving Co.

8-6B *The unit completely assembled to form an 8' octagon.* Cox Wood Preserving
Co.

Placement

Gazebos allow your creative juices to flow freely. However, take care
not to let your imagination get carried away; it's easy to bid yourself
right out of the project. Also, you do not want to overbuild with too
many gazebos or allow the gazebo structure to overpower or detract
from the design of the new deck or the existing home. You can always add other types of overhead structures (discussed later in this
chapter) to the design. Good planning is essential to make everything
harmonize. Placement of the gazebo or any other overhead structure
in the right location is very important both in the overall design and
in the structure's usefulness to the customer. Things to consider when
planning that placement include:

- Landscaping
- The design of the deck
- Tying the deck into the existing home
- What the existing home offers
- The purpose of the structure
- The type of wood to be used

- The type of finish planned for the structure (left to weather naturally or painted)
- The inclusion of a spa or hot tub in the design
- Code requirements

The deck plan shown in Fig. 8-7 is a prime example of a well-planned deck; I would have liked the opportunity to bid on this one! This particular project was designed and built by Glickman Design/Build of Rockville, MD.

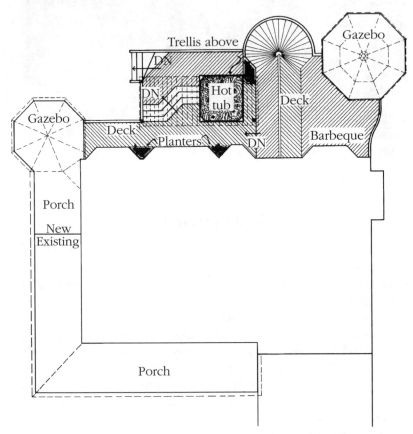

8-7 *A unique design and an ambitious project.* Glickman Design/Build

In this case, the customers wanted a deck added to their new home (eight months old) in order to enjoy the view of the lake from their backyard. They were not looking for a typically designed deck, nor did they want any of the structure to block the view from inside the home. The result was this beautiful, unique $50,000 (early 1990s) two-level structure covering 1,300 square feet. The deck offers six different focal points for entertaining or relaxing:

- Two octagonal gazebos
- Lower landing
- Sunburst-patterned overhang
- Hot tub lounging area
- Barbecue area

The existing home was incorporated into the design to tie the whole project together. Planters were built between the bay areas, and triple 2" × 10" beams were used to support the deck above while spanning across basement windows. The hot tub was built level with the upper deck in order to avoid obstructing any interior views, and the adjacent flow of steps kept the view free of railings.

The wraparound porch was added on to tie in the Victorian-style gazebo; the other corner houses a second gazebo with an upward-curving pagoda-style roofline. The lower decking surface features a diagonal pattern while the upper deck incorporates a herringbone design. The middle of the herringbone pattern leads to a sunburst pattern (Fig. 8-8). This is an excellent project that combines all the elements into one unit while incorporating the home into the design.

Gazebos do not have to be designed to be out at the end of a deck as a free-standing unit. As I mentioned earlier, gazebos come in all shapes and forms depending on what you design and what the customer wants.

8-8 *This radius lookout point of the deck is fitted with a laminate guardrail. Notice the unique railing design.* Glickman Design/Build

A gazebo built into a big porch can significantly enhance the house's appeal and can make a great romantic retreat for your customers, especially at the end of a long day (Fig. 8-9).

8-9 *This beautiful gazebo integrates well with the existing porch.* Used with permission of Georgia-Pacific Corporation

When you add a gazebo to a porch, I think it is important to give it special design treatments. Adding exterior brackets, gables, pediments, spandrels, carved and turned finials, corbels, and designed balustrades can really add personality to the overall project (Fig. 8-10).

Cumberland Woodcraft Co., Inc., is a company that offers just such creative parts. Write to them at the address given in Appendix C and ask for their catalog of parts. I'm sure you'll find their catalog interesting and it will probably be helpful on your next project.

8-10 *Extra design details pay off in gazebo building.* Cumberland Woodcraft Co., Inc., Carlisle, PA.

Trellises and arbors

A gazebo is not the only overhead structure that can enhance a home environment. A combination of trellises and arbors or other overhead structures, such as a single arbor, two-tiered garden roof, poolside pavilion, sun shelter, corner shelter, or cabana, could be added to any project. These structures can also be constructed in conjunction with a gazebo.

Whatever you call your structure, the purpose is to help your customers enjoy the outdoor environment and at the same time protect them from sun, wind, and rain. Part of the appeal of such structures lies in their flexibility; they can reflect a simple design or they can be as complex as you and your customer want.

Roofs on these structures are normally flat with open beams, latticework, or spaced 2× material, either on edge, flat, or louvered. They can be designed to carry massive beams for a sturdy pavilion look. Use of weathered rough-sawn lumber can give a strong rustic air to the design.

Overhead structures make good yard separators because trelliswork can be added for plants to grow up and over. They can provide partial shade for a pond or a garden. To store garden tools, a small storage unit can be built so it blends in with the design of the over-head structure. An arching trellis or an arbor presents a welcoming sight to any entryway. A trellis is a lightweight framework that supports a vine or other climbing or spreading plant. An arbor is a heavier framework that supports trelliswork overhead, which in turn can support climbing plants that provide shade. It is not necessary to use plants for shading because the design of the overhead trellis provides shade.

Beam ends can be detailed so they become attractive conversation pieces, especially if you are planning a Japanese-style pavilion. Rafter tails can be just as decorative—use your imagination here.

Figure 8-11 is a prime example of a massive but simple arbor using boxed beams, turned columns, and latticework to provide privacy and a wind break. Notice that the rafter tails have been cut in a decorative design. In addition, they have been dadoed to accept the cross-members and its tails, in turn, have been cut to match the rafter tails.

8-11 *This arbor blends perfectly with both the home and its newly constructed deck.* George B. Sagatov, Inc.

Figure 8-12 shows how a fence, bench, and latticework can be integrated to make a deck come alive. This combination overhead structure was made of rough-sawn cedar designed in a post-and-beam construction. The beam ends were cut with a decorative pattern while the 2" × 4" crosspieces were installed upright on edge (the 1½" width).

8-12 *This is a simple but functional and attractive design.* Western Red Cedar Lumber Association

Other considerations

Not only is the deck important, but so are all the little extras that go along with it, whether built in or placed on top. These extras can bring the project together. Certainly, the customer can purchase some or all of these items, but building them will keep them tied into the deck's original design. Some of these can be expensive to build, which will add to the final bid price, while others are quite affordable.

A simple addition to a deck is a privacy screen, as shown in Fig. 8-13, which supports hanging flower boxes. It makes an attractive focal point to any deck or walkway as well as providing shade.

Flower boxes can add beauty to any deck. They can be contemporary, rectangular in design, built to fit a niche, or built into the deck. They can be built in multiple levels with a bench spanning between two flower boxes. Alternatively, a seating area can be built around a flower box as shown in Fig. 8-14. This looks great in the center of a deck, and incidentally, the same design can be used around a tree.

8-13
*Some customers can benefit
from attractive privacy
screens.* Courtesy of Louisiana-Pacific.

8-14
*Flower boxes can jazz
up even simple decks.*
Courtesy of Louisiana-Pacific

A built-in fire pit creates a warm, cozy gathering spot. Your customer might want a built-in barbecue as shown in Fig. 8-15. Be sure to check the building code in force in your area for the specifics concerning these types of installations. You might have to install tile around the barbecue or fire pit. If that is the case, recess the tile so it is flush with the top surface of the decking or platform surface. This is especially true at the decking surface level so no one will stub a toe or trip.

8-15 *Built-in barbeques are a simple, convenient amenity.* Courtesy of Louisiana-Pacific

A recessed deck with a wraparound seating area makes a great place for cozy gatherings. Figure 8-16 shows an unusual design with a laminated bench incorporated into the deck design. Because of the rustic environment, this design is a perfect blend. However, the picture also shows a table set that just doesn't seem to fit in with the design. A wooden picnic table might have harmonized just a little better, and you could build it as part of the entire deck package—another sales opportunity.

8-16 *Built-in seating makes good use of space and should always be a consideration.* CaddCon Designs

Figure 8-17 is an example of a picnic table with benches you could build. The design shown in Fig. 8-18 could easily be converted into a picnic table. You could also design your own collection to fit the theme of your next deck project.

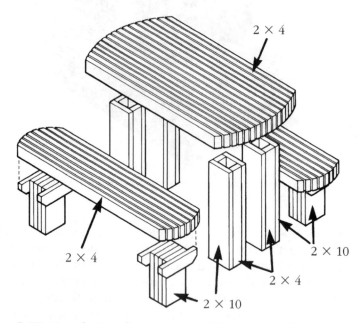

8-17 *Board sizes for a picnic table and benches.* Used with permission of Georgia-Pacific Corporation

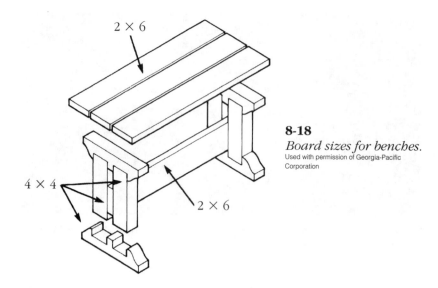

8-18
Board sizes for benches.
Used with permission of Georgia-Pacific Corporation

Accessories

As a professional, you want to make sure that your customers are aware of new products on the market that can enhance their project. Consider incorporating some of these items into your deck designs. If you own a deck showroom, these are the types of items that should be sold right along with a deck package. If you have a storefront, they will make your decks more appealing.

Figure 8-19 features a great idea for integrating a professional grill and man-made rock. The photo shows Model DCS 27BQR with power burner and Model DCS131-S, optional wok ring, commercial wok, drop-on griddle plate, and stainless steel access doors. This system is by Dynamic Cooking Systems, Inc.

8-19 *This system can be purchased in porcelain enamel or stainless steel and can be powered by either natural or LP/propane gas.*
Dynamic Cooking Systems, Inc.

Even in the summertime, it can get chilly in the evenings, but this is still a great time to entertain guests. By incorporating a couple of free-standing or built-in patio heaters, your customers can maximize use of their deck. These heaters can also complement the warmth of a spa or heated pool during evening swims. Figure 8-20 shows Model DCS PH1 (free-standing), also by Dynamic Cooking Systems, Inc. A 40,000-Btu burner system with a built-in configuration for use with natural or LP/propane gas is also available. These units can be ordered in stainless steel or painted. The address for Dynamic Cooking Systems, Inc., is included in Appendix C.

8-20
Heaters can extend deck use into the fall. Dynamic Cooking Systems, Inc.

As mentioned earlier, it takes the right furniture to blend in with the environment and the overall design. The Barlow Tyrie Company manufactures teakwood outdoor leisure furniture that lends itself to any deck theme. Figure 8-21 shows a 51" Balmoral dining table with a 10' Roma circular parasol (umbrella) and Devon dining chairs. Also shown is a 6' Rothesay seat, which looks great at poolside, in a garden, or near a pond.

Everyone entertains, which is one of the major reasons decks or pools are installed. One way your customers can get in the mood to entertain and simplify their hosting duties is by using a Crichton serving trolley by Barlow Tyrie. This unit (Fig. 8-22) features an Italian tile work surface, two removable serving trays, bottle rack, wine glass storage, and cutlery compartment. The wheels are solid teak with rubber tires and the rear wheels are mounted in cast brass casters for easy positioning.

Figure 8-23 shows an easy way to enjoy a favorite tree. Whether on the ground or on a deck, this seat finishes the base of the tree and makes it functional for those romantic evenings. The photo shows Barlow Tyrie's Glenham circular seat, which is also available in a hexagonal shape. They are manufactured in two halves that are held together around the tree with solid brass fittings. Barlow Tyrie's address is given in Appendix C.

8-21 *Choose furniture that accents the environment.* Barlow Tyrie

8-22 *Entertain in style.* Barlow Tyrie

8-23 *You can purchase seating to fit around trees.* Barlow Tyrie

Product knowledge and all the tools you need to promote your-self and "sell" the customer are included in this book. Apply them and they will help you be the best in the industry. Take the time to write to the companies and investigate the new products introduced in this book. Request samples and have an open mind. You never know when a customer will want that specific product incorporated into a deck project. Be prepared, educate yourself, and stay on top of the market.

A

American softwood lumber standard

The commercial names listed in the following table are intended to provide a correlation between commercial names for lumber and the botanical names of the species from which the lumber is to be manufactured. The information is compiled by the American Lumber Standard Committee, Voluntary Product Standard PS 20-94.

In some instances, more than one species is associated with a single commercial name. For stress-graded lumber, the species to be associated with a commercial name will be determined in accordance with 6.3.2.1.[2]. These commercial names are to be used in grading rule descriptions and in specifications (see 2.15[3]).

Commercial Names of Principal Softwood Species[1]

Commercial Species or Species Group Names[4]	Official common Tree Names[5]	Botanical names
Cedar		
Alaska Cedar	Alaska-cedar	Chamaecyparis nootkatensis
Incense Cedar	incense-cedar	Libocedrus decurrens
Port Orford Cedar	Port-Orford-cedar	Chamaecyparis lawsoniana
Eastern Red Cedar	Eastern Red Cedar Southern Red Cedar	Juniperus virginiana J. siliciocola
Western Red Cedar	Western Red Cedar	Thuja plicata

Commercial Species or Species Group Names[4]	Official common Tree Names[5]	Botanical names
Cedar		
Northern White Cedar	Northern white-cedar	T. occidentalis
Southern White Cedar	Atlantic white-cedar	Chamaecyparis thyoides
Cypress[6]		
Baldcypress	baldcypress	Taxodium distichum
Pond cypress	pondcypress	T. distichum var. nutans
Fir		
Balsam Fir[7]	balsam fir	Abies balsamea
	Fraser fir	A. fraseri
Douglas Fir[8]	Douglas-fir	Pseudotsuga menziesii
Noble Fir	noble fir	Abies procera
White Fir	subalpine fir	A. lasiocarpa
	California red fir	A. magnifica
	grand fir	A. grandis
	noble fir	A. procera
	Pacific silver fir	A. amabilis
	white fir	A. concolor
Hemlock		
Eastern Hemlock	Carolina hemlock	Tsuga caroliniana
	Eastern hemlock	T. canadensis
Mountain Hemlock	mountain hemlock	T. mertensiana
West Coast Hemlock	Western hemlock	T. heterophylla
Juniper		
Western Juniper	alligator juniper	Juniperus deppeana
	Rocky Mountain juniper	J. scopulorum
	Utah juniper	J. osteosperma
	Western juniper	J. occidentalis
Larch		
Western Larch	Western larch	Larix occidentalis
Pine		
Jack Pine	jack pine	Pinus banksiana
Limber Pine	limber pine	P. flexilis
Lodgepole Pine	lodgepole pine	P. contorta
Norway Pine	red pine	P. resinosa

Commercial Species or Species Group Names[4]	Official common Tree Names[5]	Botanical names
Pitch Pine	pitch pine	P. rigida
Ponderosa Pine	ponderosa pine	P. ponderosa
Radiata/Monterey Pine	Monterey pine	P. radiata
Sugar Pine	sugar pine	P. lambertiana
Whitebark Pine	whitebark pine	P. albicaulis
Idaho White Pine	Western white pine	P. monticola
Northern White Pine	Eastern white pine	P. strobus
Longleaf Pine[9]	longleaf pine	P. palustris
	slash pine	P. elliottii
Southern Pine (Major)	loblolly pine	P. taeda
	longleaf pine	P. palustris
	shortleaf pine	P. echinata
	slash pine	P. elliottii
Southern Pine (Minor)	pond pine	P. serotina
	Virginia pine	P. virginiana
	sand pine	P. clausa
	spruce pine	P. glabra

Redwood

Redwood	redwood	Sequoia sempervirens

Spruce

Eastern Spruce	black spruce	Picea mariana
	red spruce	P. rubens
	white spruce	P. glauca
Engelmann Spruce	blue spruce	P. pungens
	Engelmann spruce	P. engelmannii
Sitka Spruce	Sitka spruce	P. sitchensis

Tamarack

Tamarack	tamarack	Larix laricina

Yew

Pacific Yew	Pacific Yew	Taxus brevifolia

[1]The information contained herein was obtained from ASTM (American Society for Testing and Materials) Standard D 1165-80, *Standard Nomenclature of Domestic Hardwoods and Softwoods*, which was reapproved by ASTM in 1987.

[2]Development of design values—Design values contained in grading rules shall be developed in accordance with appropriate ASTM standards and other technically sound criteria. The National Institute of Standards and Technology, with the advice and counsel of the U.S. Forest Products Laboratory, shall be the final authority as to the appropriateness of such standards or criteria. The Board shall seek the assistance of the U.S. Forest Products Laboratory in reviewing design values set forth in grading rules and,

in the case of each set of grading rules submitted for certification, the Board shall obtain a report from the Laboratory to verify that the procedures used in developing the claimed values are in accordance with the standards and criteria described herein. Rules-writing agencies shall make available upon request an explanation of the means by which the claimed values were derived. When more than one rules-writing agency has responsibility for writing grading rules for a given species, a group of species, or a geographical subdivision of a species or of a group of species, a common set of strength and stiffness values shall be used by the agencies involved for that species, subdivision, or group of species in the interest of uniformity and standardization.

[3]Species—The commercial names contained in Appendix A for lumber cut from the principal botanical species of softwoods that shall be used in the formulation of lumber grading rules and in the terms of purchase and sale of ALS lumber.

[4]The commercial names for species represent those commonly accepted. Some grading rules certified by the Board provide for the inclusion of additional species under the established names.

[5]The official common tree names conform to the *Checklist of United States Trees (Native and Naturalized)*, Agriculture Handbook No. 541 (1979), and are sometimes used as names for lumber. In addition to the official common names for a species, the Handbook lists other names by which the species and the lumber produced from it are sometimes designated.

[6]Cypress includes types designated as Red Cypress, White Cypress, and Yellow Cypress. Red Cypress is frequently classified and sold separately from the other types.

[7]Balsam fir lumber is sometimes designated either as Eastern fir or as Balsam.

[8]When Douglas fir is specified by region, it is specified as either Coast Region Douglas fir or as Inland Region Douglas fir. If not specified, both types are allowed.

[9]The commercial requirements for Longleaf Pine lumber are that it must be produced not only from trees of the botanical species Pinus elliottii and Pinus palustris, but each piece in addition must average either on one end or the other not less than six annual rings per inch and not less than one-third summerwood. Longleaf Pine lumber is sometimes designated as Pitch Pine in the export trade.

B

Terms describing standard grades of lumber

This chapter contains the definitions of terms used in describing standard grades of lumber of the American Softwood Lumber Standard (American Lumber Standard Committee), Voluntary Product Standard PS 20-94.

B1

The commonly recognized characteristics and conditions occurring in softwood lumber are as follows:

Bark pockets	Pitch pockets
Checks	Pitch seams
Cross breaks	Pitch streaks
Decay	Pith
Gum spots, streaks, etc.	Shake
Holes	Splits
Knots	Wane
Mis-manufacture	Warp
Pitch	

B2: Metric units

ASTM Standard E 380 was used as the authoritative standard in developing the metric dimensions found in this Standard. Metric dimensions are calculated at 25.4 millimeters (mm) times the actual dimension in inches. The nearest mm is significant for dimensions greater than ⅛", and the nearest 0.1 mm is significant for dimensions equal to or less than ⅛".

The rounding rule for dimensions greater than ⅛": If the digit in the tenths of mm position (the digit after the decimal point) is less than 5, drop all fractional mm digits; if greater than 5 or it is 5 followed by at least one non-zero digit, round one mm higher; if 5 followed by only zeroes, retain the digit in the unit position (the digit before the decimal point) if it is even or increase it one mm if it is odd.

The rounding rule for dimensions equal to or less than ⅛": If the digit in the hundredths of mm position (the second digit after the decimal point) is less than 5, drop all digits to the right of the tenths position; if greater than 5 or it is 5 followed by at least one non-zero digit, round one-tenth mm higher; if 5 followed by only zeros, retain the digit in the tenths position if it is even or increase it one-tenth mm if it is odd.

In case of a dispute on size measurements, the conventional (inch) method of measurement shall take precedence.

B3: Definitions of terms used in describing standard grades of lumber

air dried Seasoned by exposure to the atmosphere, in the open or under cover, without artificial heat.

all-heart Of heartwood throughout; that is, free of sapwood.

annual ring Denotes the amount of growth for a tree in a single year.

bark pocket Patch of bark partially or wholly enclosed in the wood. Classified by size the same as pitch pockets.

blemish Anything marring the appearance of lumber.

bow *See* warp.

boxed heart With the pith enclosed in the piece.

bright Unstained.

burl A distortion of grain, usually caused by abnormal growth due to injury of the tree. The effect of burls is assessed in relation to knots.

check A separation of the wood normally occurring across or through the annual rings and usually as result of seasoning. Types of checks:

roller check—Crack in the wood structure caused by a piece of cupped lumber being flattened in passing between the machine rollers.

surface check—A separation that occurs on a face of a piece.

small check—Not over 1/32" (0.8 mm) wide or 4" (102 mm) long.

medium check—Not over 1/32" (0.8 mm) wide or 10" (254 mm) long.

large check—Over 1/32" (0.8 mm) wide or longer than 10" (254 mm) or both.

through check—A separation that extends from one surface of a piece to the opposite or adjoining surface.

chipped grain A barely perceptible irregularity in the surface of a piece caused when particles of wood are chipped or broken below the line of cut. It is too small to be classed as torn grain and is not considered unless in excess of 25% of the surface involved.

chip marks Shallow depressions or indentations on or in the surface of dressed lumber caused by shavings or chips getting embedded in the surface during dressing.

very light chip marks—Not over 1/64" (0.4 mm) deep.

light chip marks—Not over 1/32" (0.8 mm) deep.

medium chip marks—Not over 1/16" (1.6 mm) deep.

heavy chip marks—Not over 1/8" (3.2 mm) deep.

clear Free or practically free of all blemishes, characteristics, or defects.

compression wood Abnormal wood that forms on the underside of leaning and crooked coniferous trees. It is characterized, aside from its distinguishing color, by being hard and brittle and by its relatively lifeless appearance. Compression wood shall be limited in effect to other appearance or strength reducing characteristics permitted in the grade.

corner The intersection of two adjacent faces.

crook *See* warp.

cross break Separation of the wood across the width.

crosscutting Cutting with a saw across the width.

cup *See* warp.

cutting Resulting pieces after crosscutting and/or ripping.

decay (unsound wood) A disintegration of the wood substance due to action of wood-destroying fungi, and is also known as dote or rot. Types of decay:

advanced decay—An older stage of decay in which disintegration is recognized because the wood has become punky, soft, spongy, stringy, shaky, pitted, or crumbly. Decided discoloration or bleaching of the rotted wood is often apparent.

heart center decay—A localized decay developing along the pith in some species and is detected by visual inspection. Heart center decay develops in the living tree and does not progress further after the tree is cut.

honeycomb—Similar to white specks but the pockets are larger. Where permitted in the grading rules, it is so limited that it has no more effect on the intended use of the piece than other characteristics permitted in the same grade. Pieces containing honeycomb are no more subject to decay than pieces which do not contain it.

incipient decay—An early stage of decay in which disintegration of the wood fibers has not proceeded far enough to soften or otherwise change the hardness of the wood perceptibly. It is usually accompanied by a slight discoloration or bleaching of the wood.

peck—Channeled or pitted areas or pockets found in cedar and cypress. Wood tissue between pecky areas remains unaffected in appearance and strength. All further growth of the fungus causing peckiness ceases after the trees are felled.

pecky—Characterized by peck.

pocket rot—Decay which appears in the form of a hole, pocket, or area of soft rot, usually surrounded by apparently sound wood.

water soak or stain—Water-soaked area in heartwood, usually interpreted as the incipient stage of certain wood rots.

white specks—Small white or brown pits or spots in wood caused by the fungus Fomes pini. It develops in the living tree and does not develop further in wood in service. Where permitted in grading rules, it is so limited that it has no more effect on the intended use of the pieces than other characteristics permitted in the same grade. Pieces containing white speck are no more subject to decay than pieces which do not contain it.

degrades Pieces which on reinspection prove of lower quality than the grade in which they were shipped.

diagonal grain A deviation in the slope of grain caused by sawing at an angle with the bark of the tree. *See* slope of grain.

dry Lumber of less than nominal 5" thickness which has been seasoned or dried to a maximum moisture content of 19 percent. Lumber of nominal 5" or greater in thickness (timbers) is often manufactured and sold without drying. When the maximum moisture content is specified for lumber of nominal 5" or greater thickness, it shall be in accordance with the provisions of the applicable lumber grading rules certified by the Board, which for some species defines dry lumber as having a maximum moisture content higher than 19 percent.

eased edge Slightly rounded surfacing on pieces of lumber to remove sharp corners. Advisory note: Lumber nominal 4" or less in thickness is frequently shipped with eased edges unless otherwise specified.

edge Either (1) the narrow face of rectangular-shaped pieces, or (2) the corner of a piece at the intersection of two longitudinal faces, or (3) in stress grades, that part of the wide face nearest the corner of the piece.

edge grain (EG) [vertical grain (VG)] (rift grain) A piece or pieces sawn at approximately right angles to the annual rings so that the rings form an angle of 45 degrees or more with the surface of the piece.

firm red heart A stage of incipient decay characterized by a reddish color in the heartwood which does not render the wood unfit for the majority of yard purposes.

flat grain (FG) [slash grain (SG)] A piece or pieces sawn approximately parallel to the annual rings so that all or some of the rings form an angle of less than 45 degrees with the surface of the piece.

f.o.h.c. (free of heart centers) Without pith (side cut). An occasional piece, when showing pith for not more than ¼ the length on the surface, shall be accepted.

free of wane Without wane but with either eased or square edges.

grain The fibers in wood and their direction, size, arrangement, appearance, or quality.

green Lumber of less than nominal 5" thickness, which has a moisture content in excess of 19 percent. For lumber of nominal 5" or greater thickness (timbers), green shall be defined in accordance with the provisions of the applicable lumber grading rules certified by the Board.

gum pocket An opening between growth rings which contains or has contained resin, or bark, or both.

gum seam Check or shake filled with gum.

gum spot An accumulation of gumlike substance occurring as a small patch. Often occurs in conjunction with a bird-peck or other injury to the growing wood.

gum streak A well-defined accumulation of gum in more or less regular streak but classified as pitch streak.

heart center The pith or center core of the log.

heart face Face side free of sapwood.

heart shake *See* shake—pith shake.

heartwood The inner core of the tree trunk comprising the annual rings containing nonliving elements. In some species, heartwood has a prominent color different from sapwood. Heartwood and sapwood of equivalent character are compared as follows: With regard to strength, heartwood and sapwood are equal. No requirement of heartwood is made when strength alone is the governing factor. With regard to durability, heartwood is more durable than sapwood. When wood is to be exposed to decay-producing conditions without preservative treatment, it is permissible to specify the minimum percentage of heartwood to be present in all pieces of a shipment. With regard to preservatives, sapwood takes preservative treatment more readily than heartwood.

hit-and-miss A series of skips not over $\frac{1}{16}''$ (1.6 mm) deep with surfaced areas between.

hit-or-miss Lumber that is completely or partly surfaced or entirely rough with a maximum scantness of $\frac{1}{16}''$ (1.6 mm).

holes Openings that either extend partially or wholly through a piece. An alternate designation for holes which extend only partially through a piece is surface pits. Holes are classified by size as follows:

pin hole—Not over $\frac{1}{16}''$ (1.6 mm) in diameter.

medium hole—(Small hole) not over $\frac{1}{4}''$ (6 mm) in diameter.

large hole—Not over 1″ (25 mm) in diameter.

very large hole—Over 1″ (25 mm) in diameter.

kiln-dried Seasoned in a chamber by means of artificial heat.

knife marks The imprints or markings of the machine knives on the surface of dressed lumber.

very slight knife marks—Marks that are visible only from a favorable angle and are perfectly smooth to the touch.

slight knife marks—Marks that are readily visible but evidence no unevenness to the touch.

knot A portion or a branch or limb that has become incorporated in a piece of lumber. In lumber, knots are classified as to form, size, quality, and occurrence. Knot types include:

oval knot—Produced when the limb is cut at slightly more than a right angle to the long axis.

round knot—Produced when the limb is cut at approximately right angles to its long axis.

spike knot—Produced when the limb is cut either lengthwise or diagonally.

knot sizes:

pin knot—Not over $\frac{1}{2}''$ (13 mm) in diameter.

small knot—Not over $\frac{3}{4}''$ (19 mm) in diameter.

medium knot—Not over 1½" (38 mm) in diameter.

large knot—Over 1½" (38 mm) in diameter.

knot quality:

black knot—Results from a dead branch which the wood growth of the tree has surrounded.

decayed knot—Softer than the surrounding wood, and contains advanced decay.

encased knot—Not intergrown with the annual rings of the surrounding wood.

firm knot—Solid across its face but contains incipient decay.

fixed knot—Retains its place in dry lumber under ordinary conditions but is movable under pressure though not easily pushed out.

hollow knot—A sound knot containing a hole greater than ¼" (6 mm) in diameter. The through opening of a hollow knot is limited to the size of other holes permitted.

intergrown knot—A knot whose annual rings are partially or completely intergrown on one or more faces with the annual rings of the surrounding wood.

loose knot—Not firmly fixed; a knot not held tightly in place by growth, shape, or position.

pith knot—Sound in all respects except it contains a pith hole not over ¼" (6 mm) in diameter.

red knot—One that results from a live branch grown in the tree and is intergrown with the surrounding wood.

sound knot—Contains no decay.

star-checked knot—Has radial checks.

tight knot—So fixed by growth, shape, or position that it retains its place in the piece.

unsound knot—Contains decay.

water-tight knot—Has annual rings completely intergrown with those of the surrounding wood on one surface of the piece, and it is sound on that surface.

knot occurrences:

branch knots—Two or more divergent knots sawed lengthwise and tapering toward the pith at a common point.

corner knot—A knot located at the intersection of adjacent faces.

knot cluster—Two or more knots grouped together as a unit with the fibers of the wood deflected around the entire unit. A group of single knots is not a knot cluster.

single knot—A knot that occurs by itself. The fibers of the wood are deflected around it.

loosened grain A grain separation or loosening between spring-wood and summerwood without displacement. Types of loosened grain:

very light loosened grain—Not over ¼₄" (0.4 mm) separation.
light loosened grain—Not over ½₂" (0.8 mm) separation.
medium loosened grain—Not over ¹⁄₁₆" (1.6 mm) separation.
heavy loosened grain—Not over ⅛" (3.2 mm) separation.
very heavy loosened grain—Over ⅛" (3.2 mm) separation.

lumber The wood product of a sawmill and/or planing mill with all four sides sawn and/or planed.

machine bite A depressed cut of the machine knives at the end of a piece. Types of machine bites:

very light machine bite—Not over ¼₄" (0.4 mm) deep.
light machine bite—Not over ½₂" (0.8 mm) deep.
medium machine bite—Not over ¹⁄₁₆" (1.6 mm) deep.
heavy machine bite—Not over ⅛" (3.2 mm) deep.
very heavy machine bite—Over ⅛" (3.2 mm) deep.

machine burn A darkening of the wood due to overheating by machine knives or rollers when pieces are stopped in the machine.

machine gouge A groove cut by the machine below the desired line. Types of machine gouges:

very light machine gouge—Not over ¼₄" (0.4 mm) deep.
light machine gouge—Not over ½₂" (0.8 mm) deep
medium machine gouge—Not over ¹⁄₁₆" (1.6 mm) deep.
heavy machine gouge—Not over ⅛" (3.2 mm) deep.
very heavy machine gouge—Over ⅛" (3.2 mm) deep.

machine offset An abrupt dressing variation in the edge surface which usually occurs near the end of the piece without reducing the width or without changing the plane of the wide surface. Type of machine offsets:

very light machine offset—A variation not over ¼₄" (0.4 mm).
light machine offset—A variation not over ½₂" (0.8 mm).
medium machine offset—A variation not over ¹⁄₁₆" (1.6 mm).
heavy machine offset—A variation not over ⅛" (3.2 mm).
very heavy machine offset—A variation over ⅛" (3.2 mm).

metric units *See B2.*

mis-manufacture All defects or blemishes, produced in manufacturing. *See* chipped grain, hit-and-miss, hit-or-miss, loosened grain, machine burn, machine gouge, mismatched lumber, raised grain, skip, torn grain, and variation in sawing.

mismatch An uneven fit in worked lumber when adjoining pieces do not meet tightly at all points of contact or when the surfaces of adjoining pieces are not in the same plane. Type of mismatches:

slight mismatch—A barely evident trace of mismatch.

very light mismatch—Not over 1/64" (0.4 mm).

light mismatch—Not over 1/32" (0.8 mm).

medium mismatch—Not over 1/16" (1.6 mm).

heavy mismatch —Not over 1/8" (3.2 mm).

mixed grain (MG) Either vertical or flat grained pieces or both.

moisture content The weight of the water in wood expressed in percentage of the weight of oven-dry wood.

occasional pieces Not more than 10% of the pieces in a parcel or shipment.

pitch An accumulation of resinous material. Type of pitches:

light pitch—The light but evident presence of pitch.

medium pitch—A somewhat more evident presence of pitch than in the light pitch.

heavy pitch—A very evident accumulation of pitch showing by its color and consistency.

massed pitch—A clearly defined accumulation of solid pitch in a body by itself.

pitch seam A shake or check which contains pitch.

pitch streak A well-defined accumulation of pitch in the wood cells in a streak. Pitch streaks, with equivalent areas being permissible, are described as follows:

very small pitch streak—3/8" (10 mm) in width and 15" (381 mm) in length.

small pitch streak—1/12 the width and 1/6 the length of the piece.

medium pitch streak—1/6 the width and 1/3 the length of the piece.

large pitch streak—Not over 1/4 the width by 1/2 the length of the surface.

very large pitch streak—Over 1/4 the width by 1/2 the length of the surface.

pith The small soft core in the structural center of a log. Type of piths:

very small pith—Not over 1/8" (3.2 mm) wide and occupies on the face surface not over 1/4 square inch (161 square mm) [1/8" wide by 2" long (3.2 mm by 51 mm), or 1/16" by 4" (1.6 mm by 102 mm)].

small pith—Not over 3/4 square inch (484 square mm) on the face surface [1/4" by 3" (6 mm by 76 mm), 3/16" by 4" (5 mm by 102 mm), 1/8" by 6" (3.2 mm by 152 mm), or 1/16" by 12" (1.6 mm by 305 mm)].

free of pith—The prohibition of pith on or within the body of the piece.

boxed pith—Pith that is within the four faces of an end of a piece.

pocket A well-defined opening, between the rings of annual growth, which develops during the growth of the tree. It usually contains pitch or bark. Pockets are described as follows with equivalent areas being permissible:

>*very small pocket*—¹⁄₁₆" (1.6 mm) in width and 3" (76 mm) in length, or ⅛" (3.2 mm) in width and 2" (51 mm) in length.

>*small pocket*—¹⁄₁₆" (1.6 mm) in width and 6" (152 mm) in length, or ⅛" (3.2 mm) in width and 4" (102 mm) in length, or ¼" (6 mm) in width and 2" (51 mm) in length.

>*medium pocket*—¹⁄₁₆" (1.6 mm) in width and 12" (305 mm) in length, or ⅛" (3.2 mm) in width and 8" (203 mm) in length, or ⅜" (10 mm) in width and 4" (102 mm) in length.

>*large pocket*—Not over 4 square inches (2581 square mm) in area.

>*very large pocket*—Over 4 square inches (2581 square mm) in area.

>*closed pocket*—An opening on one surface only.

>*open (through) pocket*—An opening on opposite surfaces. A through opening is considered the same as a through hole of equal size.

raised grain A roughened condition of the surface of dressed lumber in which the hard summerwood is raised above the softer springwood, but not torn loose from it. Types of raised grain:

>*very light raised grain*—Not over ¹⁄₆₄" (0.4 mm).

>*light raised grain*—Not over ¹⁄₃₂" (0.8 mm).

>*medium raised grain*—Not over ¹⁄₁₆" (1.6 mm).

>*heavy raised grain*—Not over ⅛" (3.2 mm).

resawn lumber The product of sawing any thickness of lumber to develop thinner lumber.

ripped lumber The product of sawing any width of lumber to develop narrower lumber.

sapwood The outer layers of growth between the bark and heartwood that contain the sap.

>*bright sapwood*—Sapwood that shows no stain and is not limited in any grade unless specifically stated in the grade description.

>*sapwood restrictions waived*—A lifting of any restrictions in a rule on the amount of sapwood permitted in pieces graded under that rule.

>*bright sapwood no defect (BSND)*—An indication that bright sapwood is permitted in each piece in any amount.

seasoning Evaporation or extraction of moisture from green or partially dried wood.

shake A lengthwise separation of the wood which occurs between or through the annual rings. Type of shakes:

fine shake—A barely perceptible opening.

light shake—Not over ½" (0.8 mm) wide.

medium shake—Not over ⅛" (3.2 mm) wide.

open shake—Over ⅛" (3.2 mm) wide.

ring shake—Occurs between the annual rings to partially or wholly encircle the pith.

surface shake—Occurs on only one surface of a piece.

through shake—Extends from one surface of a piece to the opposite or to an adjoining surface.

pith shake (heart check or heart shake)—Extends through the annual rings from or through the pith towards the surface of a piece, and is distinguished from a seasoning check by the fact that its greatest width is nearest the pith, whereas the greatest width of a season check in a pith-centered piece is farthest from the pith.

side cut Pith is not enclosed within the four sides of the piece.

skip An area on a piece that failed to surface clean. Skips are described as follows:

very light skip—Not over ¹⁄₆₄" (0.4 mm) deep.

light skip—Not over ½" (0.8 mm) deep.

medium skip—Not over ¹⁄₁₆" (1.6 mm) deep.

heavy skip—Not over ⅛" (3.2 mm) deep.

slope of grain The deviation of the line of fibers from a straight line parallel to the sides of the piece.

softwood One of the group of trees which have needle-like or scale-like leaves. The term has no specific reference to the softness of the wood.

sound Free of decay.

spiral grain A deviation in the slope of grain caused when the fibers in a tree take a spiral course around the trunk of the tree instead of the normal vertical course.

split A separation of the wood through the piece to the opposite surface or to an adjoining surface due to the tearing apart of the wood cells. Type of splits:

very short split—Equal in length to ½ the width of the piece.

short split—Equal in length to the width of the piece and in no case exceeds ⅙ the length.

medium split—Equal in length to twice the width of the piece and in no case exceeds ⅙ the length.

long split—Longer than a medium split.

springwood The portion of the annual ring formed during the early part of the yearly growth period. It is lighter in color, less dense, and not as strong mechanically as summerwood.

square corners Without eased edges but has an allowance for wane in certain grades.

square edged Free from wane and without eased edges.

stained wood A discoloration in wood.

stained heartwood or firm red heart—Heartwood that shows a marked variation from the natural color. In grades where it is permitted, stained heartwood has no more effect on the intended use of a piece than other characteristics permitted in the grade. Advisory note: Stained heartwood ranges from pink to brown, and is not to be confused with natural red heart. Natural color is usually uniformly distributed through certain annual rings, whereas stains are usually in irregular patches.

stained sapwood Sapwood with discoloration. In grades when it is permitted, stained sapwood has no more effect on the intended use of a piece than other characteristics permitted in the grade but it does affect appearance in varying degrees.

light stained sapwood—A discoloration so slight that it does not affect natural finishes.

medium stained sapwood—A pronounced difference in coloring. Advisory note: Sometimes the usefulness for natural finishes but not for paint finishes is affected.

heavy stained sapwood—A so pronounced difference in color that the grain of the wood is obscured, but a piece containing it is acceptable for paint finishes.

stained wood resulting from exposure to the elements— Wood that is permitted in all grades of framing and sheathing lumber.

stress grades Lumber having assigned working stresses and modulus of elasticity values in accordance with accepted basic principles of strength grading, and the provisions of 6.3.2.1 and 6.3.2.2 of this Standard.

summerwood The portion of the annual ring formed during the latter part of the yearly growth. It is darker in color, more dense, and stronger mechanically than springwood.

torn grain An irregularity in the surface of a piece where wood has been torn or broken out by surfacing. Types of torn grain:

very light torn grain—Not over $\frac{1}{64}$" (0.4 mm) deep.

light torn grain—Not over $\frac{1}{32}$" (0.8 mm) deep.

medium torn grain—Not over $\frac{1}{16}$" (1.6 mm) deep.

heavy torn grain—Not over $\frac{1}{8}$" (3.2 mm) deep.

very heavy torn grain—Over ⅛" (3.2 mm deep).

trim To cross-cut a piece to a given length.

double-end trimmed (DET)—Lumber trimmed square on both ends. Tolerances are found in certified grading rules.

precision-end trimmed (PET)—Lumber trimmed square on both ends to uniform lengths with a manufacturing tolerance of ¹⁄₁₆" (1.6 mm) over or under in length in 20% of the pieces.

square-end trimmed—Lumber trimmed square and having a manufacturing tolerance of ¹⁄₆₄" (0.4 mm) for each nominal 2" of thickness or width.

unsound *See* decay.

variation in sawing A deviation from the line of cut.

slight variation—Not over ¹⁄₁₆" (1.6 mm) scant in nominal 1" lumber, ⅛" (3.2 mm) in nominal 2", ³⁄₁₆" (5 mm) in nominal 3" to 7", and ¼" (6 mm) in nominal 8" and greater thickness or width.

wane Bark or lack of wood from any cause, except eased edges, on the edge or corner of a piece of lumber. Common deviations include:

warp—Any deviation from a true or plane surface, including bow, crook, cup, twist, or any combination thereof. Warp restrictions are based on the average form of warp as it occurs normally, and any variation from this average form, such as short kinks, shall be appraised according to its equivalent effect. Pieces containing two or more forms of warp shall be appraised according to the combined effect in determining the amount permissible. In grading rules, warp is classified as very light, light, medium, and heavy, and applied to each width and length as set forth in the various grades in accordance with the following provisions.

bow—A deviation flatwise from a straight line drawn from end to end of a piece. It is measured at the point of greatest distance from the straight line.

crook—A deviation edgewise from a straight line drawn from end to end of a piece. It is measured at the point of greatest distance from the straight line.

cup—A deviation in the face of a piece from a straight line drawn from edge to edge of a piece. It is measured at the point of greatest distance from the straight line.

twist—A deviation flatwise, or a combination of flatwise and edgewise, in the form of a curl or spiral, and the amount is the distance an edge of a piece at one end is raised above a flat surface against which both edges at the opposite end are resting snugly.

wavy dressing An involvement of more uneven dressing than knife marks. Types of wavy dressing:

   very light wavy dressing—Not over ¹⁄₆₄" (0.4 mm) deep.
   light wavy dressing—Not over ¹⁄₃₂" (0.8 mm) deep.
   medium wavy dressing—Not over ¹⁄₁₆" (1.6 mm) deep.
   heavy wavy dressing—Not over ⅛" (3.2 mm) deep.
   very heavy wavy dressing—Over ⅛" (3.2 mm) deep.

C

Contributing organizations and companies

The *Builder's Guide to Decks* would not have been possible without the information, photos, and drawings provided by the organizations and companies listed here. I am grateful for their cooperation and assistance.

Please note that while the companies are listed under specific categories, they also market products associated with other categories.

Accessories

Barlow Tyrie
1263/230 Glen Avenue
Moorestown, NJ 08057

Dynamic Cooking Systems, Inc.
10850 Portal Drive
Los Alamitos, CA 90720

Alternative products

Dream Space Decks
Thermal Industries, Inc.
301 Brushton Avenue
Pittsburgh, PA 15221-2168

E-Z Deck
5436 N. Lake Drive
Whitefish Bay, WI 53217

Mobil Chemical Company
800 Connecticut Avenue
Norwalk, CT 06856

Outwater Plastics Industries, Inc.
4 Passaic Street
Wood Ridge, NJ 07075

Phoenix Recycled Plastics
228 Washington Street
Conshohocken, PA 19428

Re-Source Building Products
920 Davis Road, Suite 101
Elgin, IL 60123

Associations

American Lumber Standard Committee
P.O. Box 210
Germantown, MD 20875-0210

American Wood-Preservers' Association
P.O. Box 286
Woodstock, MD 21163-0286

American Wood Preservers Institute
1945 Old Gallows Road, Suite 150
Vienna, VA 22182

California Redwood Association
405 Enfrente Drive, Suite 200
Navato, CA 94949

Forest Products Laboratory
One Gifford Pinchot Drive
Madison, WI 53705-2398

National Deck Care Association
10101 Bacon Drive, Suite G
Beltsville, MD 20705

National Timber Piling Council, Inc.
446 Park Avenue
Rye, NY 10580

Southern Forest Products Association
P.O. Box 641700
Kenner, LA 70064-1700

Western Red Cedar Lumber Association
1200-555 Burrard
Vancouver, British Columbia
CANADA V7X 1S7

Western Wood Preservers Institute
601 Main Street, Suite 401
Vancouver, WA 98660

Western Wood Products Association
522 SW Fifth Avenue
Portland, OR 97204-2122

Awnings

Somfy System, Inc.
47 Commerce Drive
Cranbury, NJ 08512

Sunbrella
Glen Raven Mills, Inc.
Custom Fabrics Division
1831 North Park Avenue
Glen Raven, NC 27217-1100

Chemicals

Chemical Specialties, Inc.
One Woodlawn Green, Suite 250
Charlotte, NC 28217

Hickson Corporation
1955 Lake Park Drive, Suite 250
Smyrna, GA 30080

Osmose Wood Preserving, Inc.
P.O. Drawer O
Griffin, GA 30224-0249

Samuel Cabot Inc.
100 Hale Street
Newburyport, MA 01950

The Flood Company
P.O. Box 399
Hudson, OH 44236-0399

Wolman Wood Care Products
1824 Koppers Building
436 Seventh Avenue
Pittsburgh, PA 15219

Deck builders

Rick Parish Showroom
DECKS APPEAL
3131 Custer Rd., Suite 250
Plano, TX 75075

Russell C. Glickman—Design/Build
Glickman Design/Build
15746 Crabbs Branch Way
Rockville, MD 20855

George B. Sagatov, Inc.
P.O. Box 476
Oakton, VA 22124

Deck care specialist

Deckshield, Inc.
10101 Bacon Drive, Suite G
Beltsville, MD 20705

Deck plans

CaddCon Designs
4701 O'Donnell Street
Baltimore, MD 21224

Decking material

Georgia-Pacific Corporation
133 Peach Tree Street, N.E.
Atlanta, GA 30303

Louisiana-Pacific Corporation
111 S.W. Fifth Avenue
Portland, OR 97204-3601

Supreme Decking Inc.
10125 Richmond Highway
Lorton, VA 22079

Weyerhaeuser Company
P.O. Box 787
Plymouth, NC 27962

Franchise

Archadeck (U.S. Structures, Inc.)
2112 W. Laburnum Ave.
Richmond, VA 23227

Doctor Deck, Inc.
3410 Babcock Boulevard
Pittsburgh, PA 15237

Barry Klemons
Archadeck of Charlotte
9303-F Monroe Rd.
Charlotte, NC 28270-1472

Garden accessories and landscaping materials

Cal Pump
13278 Ralston Avenue
Sylmar, CA 91342

MacCourt Products, Inc.
111 S. Virginia Street
Crystal Lake, IL 60014

Lighting
Intermatic, Inc. (Intermatic Malibu)
Intermatic Plaza
Spring Grove, IL 60081

Mel-Nor
303 Gulf Bank
Houston, TX 77037

Thompson Industries, Inc.
Rt. 1, Box 142
Russellville, AR 72801

Hardware

Advanced Connector Systems
3335 E. Broadway
Phoenix, AZ 80540

Crawford Products, Inc.
301 Winter Street
West Hanover, MA 02339

Cross Industries, Inc.
3174 Marjan Drive
Atlanta, GA 30340

DeckMaster
140 S. High Street
Sebastopol, CA 95472-4365

Grabber Construction Products
205 Mason Circle
Concord, CA 94520

LouveRail
P.O. Box 507
Concordville, PA 19331

P. A. STRATTON & Co., Inc.
P.O. Box 436
Milan, OH 44846

Sanko Fastem USA, Inc.
8230 Industry Avenue
Pico Rivera, CA 90660

Simpson Strong-Tie Company, Inc.
4637 Chabot Drive, Suite 200
Pleasanton, CA 94588

W. H. Maze Company (Maze Nails)
100 Church Street
Peru, IL 61354

Landscaping material

Thompson Industries, Inc.
Rt. 1, Box 142
Russellville, AR 72801

Lighting

Intermatic, Inc. (Intermatic Malibu)
Intermatic Plaza
Spring Grove, IL 60081

Mel-Nor
303 Gulf Bank
Houston, TX 77037

Magazines

The Journal of Light Construction
RR 2, Box 146
Richmond, VT 05477

Millwork designs/brackets/gazebos

Carrousel Wood Products, Ltd.
1617 Fifth Avenue
Arnold, PA 15068

Cox Wood Preserving Co.
P.O. Box 1124
Orangeburg, SC 29116

Cumberland Woodcraft Co., Inc.
P.O. Drawer 609
Carlisle, PA 17013

Railing parts

Canadian Dekbrands
P.O. Box 1027
Cobourg, Ontario, Canada K9A 4W5

Feeney Wire Rope
2603 Union Street
Oakland, CA 94607-2420

Waddell Manufacturing Co.
3688 Wyoga Lake Road
Stow, OH 44224

Roofing systems

Bird Roofing Division
1077 Pleasant Street
Norwood, MA 02062

Gaco Western Inc.
P.O. Box 88698
Seattle, WA 98138-2698

Resource Conservation Technology, Inc.
2633 North Calvert Street
Baltimore, MD 21218

Software

Books That Work
2300 Gent Road, Bldg. 3, Suite 100
Palo Alto, CA 94303

Tools

Adjustable Clamp Company
417 North Ashland Ave.
Chicago, IL 60622-6397

Brotherwood LTD.
70 Main Street
Plaistow, NH 03865

Calculated Industries, Inc.
4840 Hytech Drive
Carson City, NV 89706

Creative Building Products
A Division of Spirit of America
10206 Lima Road
Fort Wayne, IN 46818-9515

DeWalt Industrial Tool Company, Inc.
626 Hanover Pike
Hampstead, MD 21074

Freud Inc.
218 Feld Avenue
High Point, NC 27264

Hitachi Power Tools USA, LTD
3950 Steve Reynolds Blvd.
Norcross, GA 30093

Iowa Manufacturing, Inc.
Hiway L67, Box 106
Battle Creek, IA 51006

Johnson Level & Tool
6333 West Donges Bay Road
Mequon, WI 53092-4456

Macklanburg-Duncan
4041 North Santa Fe
Oklahoma City, OK 73118

Makita U.S.A., Inc.
14930 Northam Street
LaMirada, CA 90638-5753

Milwaukee Electric Tool Corporation
13135 West Lisbon Road
Brookfield, WI 53005

Miracle Point Inc.
P.O. Box 71
Crystal Lake IL 60039-0071

Portable Products, Inc.
58 East Plato Blvd.
St. Paul, MN 55107

Power Tool Specialists, Inc.
3 Craftsman Rd.
East Windsor, CT 06088

S-B Power Tool Company
4300 West Peterson Avenue
Chicago, IL 60646

Sonin Inc.
Milltown Office Park
Suite B201, Route 22
Brewster, NY 10509

Stanley Tools
600 Myrtle Street
New Britain, CT 06053

Swanson Tool Co., Inc.
1010 Lambrecht Road
Frankfort, IL 60423

Takagi Tools Inc.
337A Figueroa Street
Wilmington, CA 90744

T. C. Manufacturing
P.O. Box 122
Fredericktown, OH 43019

Thomas Industries Inc.
1419 Illinois Avenue
Sheboygan, WI 53081

TrimTramp LTD.
151 Carlingview Drive, Unit #11
Toronto, Ontario
CANADA M9W 5S4

Trojan Manufacturing Inc.
P.O. Box 15114
Portland, OR 97215-0114

UVEX SAFETY, Inc.
10 Thurber Blvd.
Smithfield, RI 02917

Zircon Corporation
1580 Dell Avenue
Campbell, CA 95008

D

Special offer

To order the three- and four-page itemized bid sheets discussed in Chapter 5, or other helpful business forms, complete and mail the order form on the page 306. Also available are Extra Work and/or Change Order Sheets and Contract/Agreement Sheets. The Complete Contractors Helping Hands Packet contains one of each type of form.

Index

Illustrations are in **boldface**.

About the author

Photograph of the author taken by James McClintock.

Leon A. Frechette has over 20 years' experience in construction, remodeling, and related fields. He has appeared on many TV and radio talk shows, providing practical know-how to both consumers and construction professionals. Over the course of his career he has filmed demonstration and training videotapes, provided expert testimony in court cases, and designed a toy collection. He has a broad range of expertise and is a noted expert within the construction industry.

Leon's interests lie in the tool business: designing and testing new products, refining structure and technique. He has tested many hand and power tools as well as other construction-related products and submitted written evaluations for in-house company use and articles for both newsstand and industry publications. His column, "Frechette on Tools," runs monthly in *Tech Directions*, a publication for vocational educators.

Leon authored *The Helping Hands Guide to Hiring a Remodeling Contractor*, published by C.R.S., Inc., which featured his simplified business forms. He's the author of *The Pre-Development Handbook for the City of Spokane and the Spokane Housing Authority*, also published by C.R.S., Inc., a user-friendly guide for builders and developers to the many agencies overseeing construction and rehabilitation within the city. *Bathroom Remodeling*, his last book, was published by McGraw-Hill in 1994. Other book projects are currently in development.

TO ORDER FORMS:

	Product	Price (Ea.)	Quantity	Amount
Extra Work and/or Change Order Sheets	1EWCO	1.75	_____	_____
Contract/Agreement Sheets	2CA	1.75	_____	_____
Itemized Bid Sheets (3-Page Set)	3IBS	3.50	_____	_____
Itemized Bid Sheets (4-Page Set)	4IBS	4.75	_____	_____
Complete Contractors Helping Hands™ Packet	5CHHP	10.00	_____	_____
Shipping & Handling (Orders Up to 6)				3.50
SUBTOTAL				_____

TO ORDER BOOK:

	Product	Price (Ea.)	Quantity	Amount
The Helping Hands™ Guide To Hiring A Remodeling Contractor	HHG	14.00	_____	_____
Shipping & Handling (Orders Up to 2)				2.25
SUBTOTAL				_____
WA (Only) 8% Tax				_____
TOTAL				_____

Make Check or Money Order Payable To:
C.R.S., Inc.
P.O. Box 4567
Spokane, WA 99202-0567
Phone: (509) 926-1724

Name _____

Address _____

City _____ State _____ Zip _____

Phone _____

C.R.S., Inc.